The Stable Marriage Problem:
Structure and Algorithms

Foundations of Computing
Michael Garey and Albert Meyer, editors

The Stable Marriage Problem: Structure and Algorithms

Dan Gusfield and Robert W. Irving

The MIT Press
Cambridge, Massachusetts
London, England

Library of Congress Cataloging-in-Publication Data

Gusfield, Dan.
    The stable marriage problem: structure and algorithms/Dan Gusfield and Robert W. Irving.
        p. cm. — (Foundations of computing)
    Includes bibliographies and index
    ISBN 0-262-07118-5
        1. Marriage theorem. I. Irving, Robert W. II. Title.
III. Series.
QA164.G87 1989   89-32042
511'.6—dc20   CIP

To Carrie and Gwen, our marriage partners,

and to our parents

Contents

Series Foreword

Theoretical computer science has now undergone several decades of development. The "classical" topics of automata theory, formal languages, and computational complexity have become firmy established, and their importance to other theoretical work and to practice is widely recognized. Stimulated by technological advances, theoreticians have been rapidly expanding the areas under study, and the time delay between theoretical progress and its practical impact has been decreasing dramatically. Much publicity has been given recently to breakthroughs in cryptography and linear programming, and steady progress is being made on programming language semantics, computational geometry, and efficient data structures. Newer, more speculative, areas of study include relational databases, VLSI theory, and parallel and distributed computation. As this list of topics continues expanding, it is becoming more and more difficult to stay abreast of the progress that is being made and increasingly important that the most significant work be distilled and communicated in a manner that will facilitate further research and application of this work. By publishing comprehensive books and specialized monographs on the theoretical aspects of computer science, the series on Foundations of Computing provides a forum in which important research topics can be presented in their entirety and placed in perspective for researchers, students, and practitioners alike.

Michael R. Garey
Albert R. Meyer

Preface

In 1962 David Gale and Lloyd Shapley published a paper entitled "College Admissions and the Stability of Marriage", in which they introduced and solved the *Stable Marriage Problem*. Informally, a stable marriage, or matching, is a one-one pairing of a set of men to a set of women, containing no man and woman who would agree to leave their assigned partners in order to marry each other. The Gale-Shapley paper also introduced a polygamous version of the stable marriage problem, and gave an algorithm for finding a stable matching in both the polygamous and monogamous versions. They also discussed an unsolved (at the time) generalization called the *Stable Roommates Problem*. Since the publication of their paper, many additional variants of the basic problem have been introduced and studied, and these problems have proven to be of unending interest to people working in a wide range of disciplines, including computer science, mathematics, economics, game theory, management science, and operations research. There have appeared to date over one hundred technical papers, several textbook expositions, several masters and doctoral theses, and one entire book devoted to the stable marriage problem and variants; several additional papers and one book are in press, and there seems to be no end in sight to the ideas stimulated by these problems.

On the practical side, a polygamous version of the basic Gale-Shapley method has been used for many years (actually predating the Gale-Shapley paper) by several national programs, to assign "job applicants" to "job positions". The largest and best known of these programs places resident doctors in training hospitals, but similar ongoing programs are used by other professional groups and placement agencies. What is common to all these applications is that the parties being matched are not required to accept the suggested matching, so the assignment method will be used only if the matchings produced have the property that no coalition of the parties has an incentive to reject a suggested matching in favor of a better matching among themselves. As we will see in Chapter 1, a stable matching has precisely this property.

In 1976 Donald Knuth wrote a short book on the stable marriage problem, which summarized most of what was known about the problem up until that

time. Knuth's book was based on a series of lectures he gave on the analysis
of algorithms, in which he focused on the stable marriage problem. He chose
that focus partly because of an interest in the stable marriage problem itself, but also because the algorithmic aspects of the stable marriage problem
and variants provide a rich set of illustrations of the techniques of algorithm
analysis. Knuth discussed a number of unsolved problems throughout the
book, and included a final chapter listing an additional twelve open questions covering both algorithmic analysis issues and structural and algorithm
design issues in stable marriage. From the algorithmic perspective, the most
interesting open questions were to find an efficient algorithm for the stable
roommates problem and to find an efficient algorithm that produces a fairer
stable matching than does the Gale-Shapley algorithm.

Since the publication of Knuth's book, much more has been learned about
the stable marriage problem and its variants. Most of the problems posed
by Knuth that directly concern stable marriage and roommates, rather than
algorithm analysis, have now been solved. Most notably, in 1985, the stable
roommates problem was shown to be solvable in polynomial time. This
solution, and extensions of it, will be discussed in Chapter 4.

In addition to the solution of the stable roommates problem, two very
productive approaches to stable matching problems have recently been developed. One approach, pioneered principally by ourselves and our students,
has been to study the structure of the set of solutions to the stable marriage and stable roommates problems, and then to exploit this structure
to obtain fast algorithms for a number of variants of the basic problems.
These structural results will be discussed in Chapters 2 and 4, and their use
will be discussed in Chapters 3 and 4. The most valuable consequence of
this approach has been the development of efficient algorithms to find stable
matchings other than those obtained by the original Gale-Shapley method
and to give information about the set of all the stable matchings. In particular, these results lead to the solution of the "egalitarian" stable marriage
problem and extensions of it, answering Knuth's question about fair stable
matchings. These results are of practical importance, for the solution given
by the Gale-Shapley method has an extremely strong property that is often
undesirable, limiting its appropriateness and use. That solution is necessarily the "best possible" solution from the perspective of one sex, while it is
necessarily the "worst possible" solution for the members of the other sex.
This asymmetry will be described precisely in Chapter 1.

The other recent approach has been developed principally by mathematical economists and game theorists, groups to which Gale and Shapley belong.
Their involvement with stable matching is based on an interest in modeling
mechanisms that encourage mutual, but voluntary, cooperation and agree-

ment by competing parties and groups. Much of the recent research along
these lines has been motivated, as ours has been, by the asymmetry inherent in the Gale-Shapley solution. But rather than looking for other stable
matchings, this approach has studied how users of the original Gale-Shapley
algorithm can adjust to, or affect, its asymmetry through the use of deceit,
manipulation, money, side-payments, and the formation of coalitions. Many
of these results are intriguing and have importance for economics and game
theory, but from the practical and algorithmic standpoint, these results are
mostly negative, since they do not lead to acceptable ways to produce desirable stable matchings using the Gale-Shapley algorithm.

In this book we will be concerned mostly with the first of these two recent
approaches, focusing on the algorithmic and structural aspects of stable
matching problems, although we will include in Chapter 1 some of the most
notable results concerning deceit and coalitions. The structure of the book
is as follows. Chapter 1 is principally an introduction to the stable marriage
problem and some of its variants, containing results that do not depend on
the structural theory developed later in the book. Chapters 2 through 4
are principally derived from the work of ourselves and our students, Eyton
Ronn and Paul Leather, but also include some recent related contributions
by others. In Chapter 2 we develop the structure of the set of solutions
to the stable marriage problem, and we exploit this structure in Chapter
3 to obtain a variety of algorithmic and complexity results. In Chapter 4
we develop the solution to the stable roommates problem, we generalize the
structure of the stable marriage problem to the roommates problem, and we
then exploit this structure to solve analogues of some of the problems solved
in the stable marriage case. Finally, in spite of the considerable recent
progress in this field, many questions remain unanswered, so that in the
Appendix we follow Knuth's example and discuss a number of interesting
open problems.

This book has several notable goals and features. First, it presents in one
place and in one coherent exposition most of the algorithmically and structurally interesting results that are known about stable matching problems.
With this exposition we have simplified and unified many earlier proofs,
we have strengthened earlier results, and we have obtained new results and
efficient algorithms not previously published.

As a second feature, the book develops the structure of the set of stable
matchings in the stable marriage problem in a more general and algebraic
context than has been done previously. It was shown in Knuth's book that
the set of stable matchings in the stable marriage problem forms a distributive lattice under a natural relation, and although there are some very deep

theorems about distributive lattices, this fact has been almost entirely ignored in the published literature on the stable marriage problem. The importance of this viewpoint has only recently been appreciated, and some of the
technical tools developed in earlier papers can now be viewed as corollaries
of previously existing theorems, specialized to the stable marriage problem.
Hence, in this book the development of the structure of the stable marriage
problem does not follow previous published work, but rather it is heavily
influenced by the theory of distributive lattices, principally Birkhoff's representation theorem for finite distributive lattices. However, as we will explain
in the notes for Chapter 2, for algorithmic applications, Birkhoff's theorem
is not the ideal tool to develop the structure of the solutions to the stable
marriage problem. Therefore, although Birkhoff's theorem lies just beneath
the surface, we have chosen to discuss the structure of the stable matchings
in terms of rings of sets. This approach allows an algorithmic exploitation
of structural features of rings of sets, providing the critical link between
structural results and the design of efficient algorithms. This link, between
structure and algorithms, is one of the main themes of the book. In addition, the ring-of-sets approach exposes the similarities of the stable marriage
problem to (the many) other combinatorial problems whose solutions also
form a ring of sets. In this way, many of the most useful structural features
of the stable marriage problem can be seen as features of a more general set
of problems.

As a third feature, the book demonstrates, as best we understand it, the
relationship between the structure of the stable marriage problem and the
more general stable roommates problem. In developing the structure of
the stable roommates problem, we see many commonalities between it and
that of the stable marriage problem. In this way, we have tried to explain
which features of the stable marriage problem are special to it and which
features are properties of a larger class of problems. As one (incomplete)
reflection of the relationship, we show that the set of solutions to the stable
roommates problem forms a semilattice under a natural relation, while the
set of solutions to the stable marriage problem forms a distributive lattice
under a relation specializing the semilattice relation.

As a fourth feature, the results in this book provide an algorithmic response to the practical and political problems created by the asymmetry
inherent in the Gale-Shapley solutions. With the tools developed here —
which include more than the solution to the egalitarian stable marriage
problems and extensions — it is feasible to find much better compromises
between the desires of the two sexes than is provided by the Gale-Shapley
method. Agencies that use the Gale-Shapley method can no longer defend
its asymmetric solutions with the claim that there are no alternative methods.

Finally, in contrast to Knuth's book, which mainly illustrates the application of mathematics to the *analysis* of algorithms, our book illustrates the productive and almost inseparable relationship between mathematical insight and the *design* of efficient algorithms. In view of the many open questions remaining, further insight of this kind should continue to be valuable, and stable marriage should surely continue as a fruitful source of fascinating and challenging problems involving both the design of efficient algorithms, and their analysis.

The book has been written mainly with graduate-level computer scientists in mind, but it should be accessible to any interested reader with a moderate background in algorithms or combinatorics. We expect that many people working in mathematics, operations research, and economics will also find it valuable and stimulating.

Acknowledgments

There are many people whom we wish to thank for their help in making this book possible. Several of these people helped us directly in our effort to produce the book, and many more helped us in our general study of stable matchings over a longer period of time. Several of these people may even be unaware of their contribution, and we wish to thank all of them together: Dana Angluin, Tomás Feder, Sally Floyd, Zvi Galil, Mike Garey, Dan Hirschberg, David Johnson, Dick Karp, Donald Knuth, Conrad Kwok, Gene Lawler, Paul Leather, Chip Martel, Dalit Naor, Cheng Ng, Boris Pittel, Eyton Ronn, Alvin Roth, Mike Saks, David Shmoys, Ashok Subramanian, Greg Sullivan, Bob Tarjan, S.S. Tseng, David Warren, John Vande Vate, Avi Wigderson, Les Wilson. We would also like to thank the various agencies that have supported us during this extended period of research and writing: The National Science Foundation under grants MCS-81/05894 and CCR-8803740, The United States Bureau of the Census under grant JSA86-9, and The Carnegie Trust for the Universities of Scotland. Thanks are also due to whoever invented e-mail and whoever pays for it; many bits were pushed between California and Scotland, and this book would never have happened without that facility. Finally, thanks are due to Terry Ehling of MIT Press for her constant help and encouragement.

Chapter 1

Elementary Concepts and Results

1.1 Introduction

1.1.1 The Background

The subject of this book is the stable marriage problem in particular, and stable matching problems in general. Stable matching problems have held a fascination for many computer scientists, mathematicians, and economists, among others, ever since their introduction in 1962 in the seminal paper of Gale and Shapley [22]. This fascination shows no sign of diminishing, and in recent years our understanding of the problems, knowledge of how to solve them, and appreciation of their structural relationships with other combinatorial problems have all evolved rapidly.

Matchings and Stability

The term *matching* implies that the participants (elements of some underlying set or sets) are to be matched or assigned to each other in some way to meet some specified criterion. The criterion in question is that of *stability*, and it depends entirely on fixed preferences expressed by the participants; the essence of a *stable* matching is that it cannot be undermined by some unmatched pair of participants acting together or indeed by any coalition of participants.

This general scenario provides a model for a variety of problems with a practical interpretation. In the classical *stable marriage problem*, there are two equal-sized sets of participants, the men and the women, and a matching is just a one-one mapping between the two sets. In the *stable roommates problem*, there is a single (even-cardinality) set of participants, and a matching is a partition of the set into disjoint pairs (of roommates). In the problem that is variously referred to as the *hospitals/residents*, or *college admissions problem* the participants are residents (or students) and hospitals (or colleges), each of the latter having some fixed number of "places"; a matching is an assignment of residents to hospitals so that no hospital exceeds its number of available places.

In all of these problems and their variants, the particular matchings that are of interest are those with the crucial *stability* property. Each party (resident or hospital) has a rank-ordered preference list of some of the other parties. In the case of stable marriage, each person's preference list contains all of the members of the opposite sex. In the stable roommates problem, each person's list contains all of the other people. In the hospitals/residents problem, each hospital's list contains the residents, and each resident's list contains the hospitals. (In all three cases, however, one possible generalization allows preference lists to be incomplete.) A particular matching is *unstable* if there are two parties who are not matched with each other, each of whom strictly prefers the other to his/her partner in the matching (or in the case of hospitals, to one of its assigned residents). A *stable* matching is, not surprisingly, a matching that is not unstable. The significance of stability is obvious: in a system where acceptance of the matching is voluntary, an unstable matching cannot be expected to remain intact, for the destabilizing pair (or pairs) will realize that both can improve their situation by joint action, independent of the effect of that action on the others. Notice that if a matching cannot be undermined in this way by an unmatched pair (i.e., if it is a stable matching), then neither can it be undermined by any coalition; for if all members of a coalition were to improve simultaneously, then the coalition must contain at least one destabilizing pair.

The Gale-Shapley Theorem and Algorithm

Gale and Shapley's fundamental result [22], a result that is by no means obvious from the statement of the problem, is that every instance of the stable marriage problem admits at least one stable matching. Gale and Shapley proved this result by describing an algorithm that is guaranteed to find such a matching. Furthermore, Gale and Shapley showed that their algorithm finds a stable matching with a remarkable property, namely that it simultaneously gives all the men (or all the women, if the roles of the sexes are reversed) the best partner that they can have in any stable matching. The existence not only of a stable matching but of one with such a remarkable extremal property gives perhaps the first hint that the set of all stable matchings for a given stable marriage instance may have some special and useful structure.

Gale and Shapley generalized their stable marriage algorithm to deal with the hospitals/residents problem (although they used the college admissions terminology — indeed, this was the the problem that had motivated their work), and they showed that their amended algorithm finds a stable matching that is simultaneously best for all the residents. However, the stable roommates problem seemed less amenable to such methods, and Gale and Shapley's discussion of this problem was confined to the observation that, in contrast to the case of stable marriage, some roommates instances admit no stable matching.

Matchings of Residents and Hospitals

Many years later, it was discovered that what was essentially the Gale-Shapley algorithm had been in use since 1952 by the National Intern Matching Program (now called the National Resident Matching Program, NRMP) to match graduating medical students (residents) in the United States with hospitals, thus predating the Gale-Shapley paper by some ten years. One notable difference between the Gale-Shapley and NRMP algorithms is that the latter is designed to find the stable matching that is simultaneously optimal for the hospitals rather than for the residents.

The history of the labor market for residents prior to 1952 shows very clearly the importance of the stability condition in such a situation, and for this reason, and because the NRMP is the largest and the best-known application of a stable matching algorithm, it is appropriate to give a brief summary of that history.

From the inception of the position of intern around the turn of the century (residents were called interns until fairly recently), the market was characterized by intense competition among hospitals for (an inadequate supply of) interns. Each hospital would make offers of appointment to some of its applicants independently of its rivals, and one effect of this unrestrained competition was that the whole process degenerated into a race, with hospitals steadily advancing the date at which they finalized binding contracts with applicants, in an attempt to gain an advantage over their competitors. This tendency accelerated to the point where, by 1944, appointments were being made up to *two years* before the position was to be taken up, a state of affairs that was quite unsatisfactory for all the parties involved.

To combat this trend, it was eventually agreed that information about medical students would not be released by medical schools until some fixed date, so that before that date, hospitals would have no basis for offering appointments. This development had the desired effect, insofar as the date at which appointments were made was moved much closer to the actual starting date. However, the original problem was replaced by a new one. Since hospitals continued to make offers independently, and at least some applicants were likely to receive several offers, it was essential that each offer should carry with it a deadline for acceptance. An applicant receiving an offer from a hospital relatively low among his preferences would be inclined to wait until the last possible moment before accepting, in the hope that a better offer would turn up; an applicant accepting such an offer would be unhappy if a better offer was subsequently forthcoming. Also, a hospital receiving a late rejection would be unhappy if many of its preferred alternatives had, in the meantime, accepted other offers. For reasons such as these, the deadline for acceptance was gradually set closer and closer to the date of the offer — eventually within as little as twelve hours. However, compression of the waiting period clearly did not solve the basic problem, namely that a competitive system such as this was almost bound to lead to an unstable matching.

Finally, it was agreed around 1950 to switch from a competitive market to a centralized system involving voluntary cooperation between the hospitals, in which each applicant would submit to a central body a rank-ordered preference list of hospitals, and each hospital would submit a ranked list of its applicants. A matching would then be arranged centrally on the basis of these preferences. However, the algorithm that was initially proposed did not, in general, lead to a stable matching, and furthermore, it was soon recognized that in some circumstances an applicant could benefit by deliberately misrepresenting his preferences. In response to such objections, the proposed algorithm was altered, and the final NRMP algorithm, which is guaranteed to produce a stable matching, was introduced in 1952.

A measure of the success of the NRMP algorithm, as compared to previous practice, is that it has remained in use, in essentially unchanged form, until the present day. Participation in the centralized scheme is voluntary — applicants are free to attempt to arrange appointments independently with individual hospitals — and a further measure of the success of the scheme is the very high participation rate; over 95% of applicants and hospitals participated in the scheme in the early years.

Recent issues that have been of interest in the context of the NRMP algorithm include the question of whether one or more parties can benefit by misrepresenting their preferences, and the question of how to respond to the inability of the algorithm, in its original form, to cater to the increasing number of married couples, whose preferences are not independent. Indeed, the latter shortcoming has been suggested as one reason for a fall-off (to around 85%) in the participation rate in recent years. These are issues that we shall return to later in the chapter.

Beyond Gale-Shapley

As far as the stable marriage problem is concerned, the paper of Gale and Shapley, with its neat and, in a sense, conclusive result, might have been expected to mark the end of the matter. On the contrary, however, it was only the beginning. Such is the elegance of the fundamental result and of the Gale-Shapley algorithm that it has, over the years, sparked much interest in stable matching problems from a variety of viewpoints.

The appearance in 1976 of the book by Donald Knuth [59], the first book devoted to the stable marriage problem and its associated issues, provided a further stimulus to work in this area. Although one of Knuth's prime motives was to use the stable marriage problem as a vehicle to illustrate a whole range of algorithm analysis techniques, nonetheless the intrinsic interest of the problem itself is apparent throughout. A particular feature of Knuth's book is the list of open problems, a number of which have since been solved — see the *Notes and References* section in each of the chapters, and the Appendix.

Recent developments, which will be explored in detail in subsequent chapters, have led to a much deeper understanding of the rich mathematical structure that underlies instances of the stable marriage problem. This structure reveals a close relationship between the stable marriage problem and certain other combinatorial problems, and it can be exploited to obtain efficient algorithms, and to prove complexity results, for a number of associated matching problems. Furthermore, an efficient algorithm for the stable roommates problem has recently been obtained, together with at least a partial understanding of the mathematical structure that underlies this apparently more complex problem and of its relationship with the stable marriage problem. The structural results for the stable marriage problem form the subject matter of Chapter 2, their exploitation is the main theme of Chapter 3, and Chapter 4 contains a detailed study of the stable roommates problem. Finally, the Appendix discusses open problems.

In the remainder of Chapter 1, we present many of the more elementary results associated with the stable marriage problem and its "bipartite" variants and extensions (therefore excluding roommates, which is a nonbipartite extension). "Elementary" in this context does not necessarily imply "easy" but rather that these are results, many of them established in the twenty years following the publication of the Gale-Shapley paper, that do not depend on a full appreciation of the underlying algebraic structure.

In Section 1.2, we explore the basic Gale-Shapley algorithm for the stable marriage problem, together with some of its implications. Section 1.3 contains some preliminary material on the set of stable matchings, including some initial insight into its algebraic structure. Simple variants of stable marriage are considered in Section 1.4, and in Section 1.5, lower bounds are established for a number of algorithmic problems associated with stable marriage, showing in particular that the Gale-Shapley algorithm is asymptotically optimal. Section 1.6 covers in some detail the college admissions or hospitals/residents problem (which we shall refer to henceforth, for consistency, as the hospitals/residents problem). Finally, Section 1.7 considers briefly some of the issues involved if one or more of the participants attempts to influence the outcome of the Gale-Shapley algorithm, or one of its variants, by falsifying preferences — issues of deceit, strategy, and coalition that have received a good deal of attention in the literature in recent years and that are of some practical importance in the context of the NRMP algorithm.

1.1.2 Stable Marriage: Basic Terminology and Notation

An instance of *size* n of the stable marriage problem involves two disjoint sets of size n, the men and the women. Associated with each person is a *strictly* ordered *preference list* containing *all* the members of the opposite sex. Person p prefers q to r, where q and r are of the opposite sex to p, if and only if q precedes r on p's preference list.

For such an instance, a matching M is a one-one correspondence between the men and the women. If man m and woman w are matched in M, then m and w are called *partners* in M, and we write $m = p_M(w)$, $w = p_M(m)$; $p_M(m)$ is the M-partner of m, and $p_M(w)$ the M-partner of w.

A man m and a woman w are said to *block* a matching M, or to be a *blocking pair* for M, if m and w are not partners in M, but m prefers w to $p_M(m)$ and w prefers m to $p_M(w)$. A matching for which there is at least one blocking pair is called *unstable*, and is otherwise *stable*.

The basic stable marriage problem involves the determination, for a given instance, of a stable matching (which, as already mentioned in Section 1.1.1, always exists). Of course, over and above this basic question, there are many other interesting questions that can be asked about stable matchings.

Example Consider the stable marriage instance of size 4 specified by the preference lists in Figure 1.1. Here, as throughout, it is assumed that the men and women are separately and arbitrarily labeled $1, \ldots, n$, and the men's and women's preference lists are arranged horizontally in two separate arrays.

The matching $\{(1,4),(2,3),(3,2),(4,1)\}$ is stable. Here, and elsewhere in the text, a matching is specified as a set of ordered man-woman pairs. Stability may be verified by considering each man in turn as a potential member of a blocking pair. Man 1 could form a blocking pair only with woman 2, but she prefers her partner,

1	2	4	1	3		1	2	1	4	3
2	3	1	4	2		2	4	3	1	2
3	2	3	1	4		3	1	4	3	2
4	4	1	3	2		4	2	1	4	3

Men's Preferences	Women's Preferences

Figure 1.1: A first stable marriage instance of size 4

man 3, to man 1. Each of men 2 and 3 is matched with his favorite woman, so neither can be in a blocking pair. Finally, man 4 could form a blocking pair only with woman 4, but she would rather stick with her partner, man 1.

A second example of a stable matching, indeed the only other stable matching in this case, is $\{(1,4),(2,1),(3,2),(4,3)\}$, as may be verified in a similar way. On the other hand, the matching $\{(1,1),(2,3),(3,2),(4,4)\}$, for example, is unstable because of the blocking pair $(1,4)$; man 1 prefers woman 4 to his partner, woman 1, and woman 4 prefers man 1 to her partner, man 4. Some other unstable matchings may have many more blocking pairs: for example, the matching $\{(1,1),(2,2),(3,4),(4,3)\}$ has six, which the reader may care to find.

Stability Checking

It may not be immediately obvious from the problem statement that a stable matching always exists, or how stable matchings may be found, but it should be obvious, as illustrated in the example, how a given matching may be checked for stability. It suffices to consider each member of one sex, say the men, as a potential member of a blocking pair. For each man, only the women that he prefers to his partner need be checked. More precisely, Figure 1.2 contains a stability checking algorithm, and since there are n men in an instance of size n, and for each, at most $n-1$ women need be examined, it should be clear that with appropriate data structures, the algorithm has $O(n^2)$ worst-case complexity.

Note that here, as elsewhere in the book, algorithms are expressed in an informal Pascal-like language that should be self-explanatory.

Finally, we introduce some additional, fairly obvious, terminology. A man m and a woman w constitute a *stable pair* if and only if m and w are partners in some stable matching; in these circumstances, m is a *stable partner* of w, and vice versa. If some man m and woman w are partners in *all* stable matchings, then (m, w) is called a *fixed pair*.

For stylistic reasons, we use a number of phrases as synonyms for "m

```
for m := 1 to n do
    for each w such that m prefers w to p_M(m) do
        if w prefers m to p_M(w) then
        begin
            report matching unstable ;
            halt
        end ;
report matching stable
```

Figure 1.2: Simple stability-checking algorithm

prefers v to w"; these include "v is a *better* and w a *poorer* or *worse* partner for m" and "v is *more favored* and w *less favored* by m".

1.2   The Gale-Shapley Algorithm

1.2.1   The Basic Algorithm

We now develop the fundamental theorem, due to Gale and Shapley, that there always exists at least one stable matching in an instance of the stable marriage problem. To prove this theorem, we describe a version of the original Gale-Shapley algorithm. This simple algorithm always finds a stable matching, which, as mentioned earlier, turns out to be uniquely favorable to the men or to the women, depending on the respective roles of the two sexes in the algorithm. In our description of the algorithm, we will adopt the traditional approach, regarding the men as "suitors" in a "courtship" process, but analogous results may be obtained by reversing the roles of the sexes.

Informally, the algorithm may be expressed in terms of a sequence of "proposals" from men to women. At any point during the algorithm's execution, each person is either *engaged* or *free*; each man may alternate between being engaged and being free, but once a woman is engaged, she is never again free, although the identity of her fiancé may change. A man who is engaged more than once obtains fiancées who are successively less desirable to him, while each successive engagement brings a woman a more favored partner.

When a free woman receives a proposal, she will immediately accept it, becoming engaged to the proposer. When an engaged woman receives a proposal, she compares the proposer with her current fiancé and rejects the less favored of the two men; that is, if she prefers her fiancé, she rejects the new proposal, but if she prefers the proposer, she breaks her current engagement, setting her ex-fiancé free, and becomes engaged to the current proposer.

Each man proposes to the women on his preference list, in their order of appearance, until he becomes engaged. If ever that engagement is broken (by the woman), then he becomes free again, and he resumes his sequence of proposals, starting with the next woman on his list. The algorithm terminates when everyone is engaged, and we will see that this will happen before any man exhausts his preference list. Furthermore, we will show that, on termination, the engaged couples constitute a stable matching.

The basic Gale-Shapley algorithm in which the men propose — the *man-oriented* version — is summarized in Figure 1.3.

---

assign each person to be free ;
while some man m is free do
begin
    $w :=$ first woman on m's list to whom m has not yet proposed ;
    if w is free then
        assign m and w to be engaged {to each other}
    else
        if w prefers m to her fiancé m' then
            assign m and w to be engaged and m' to be free
        else
            w rejects m {and m remains free}
end ;
output the stable matching consisting of the n engaged pairs

Figure 1.3: Basic Gale-Shapley algorithm

As expressed in Figure 1.3, the Gale-Shapley algorithm involves an element of nondeterminism, since the order in which the free men propose is not specified. However, it turns out, as we will see, that this nondeterminism is of no consequence: the order in which the free men propose is immaterial to the outcome.

The fundamental nature of the Gale-Shapley algorithm is summarized in the following theorem.

Theorem 1.2.1 *For any given instance of the stable marriage problem, the Gale-Shapley algorithm terminates, and, on termination, the engaged pairs constitute a stable matching.*

Proof First, we show that no man can be rejected by all the women. A woman can reject only when she is engaged, and once she is engaged she never again becomes free. So the rejection of a man by the last woman on his list would imply that all the women were already engaged. But since there are equal numbers of men and women, and no man has two fiancées, all the men would also be engaged, which is a contradiction. Also, each iteration involves one proposal, and no man ever proposes twice to the same woman, so the total number of iterations cannot exceed n^2 (for an instance involving n men and n women). Termination is therefore established.

It is clear that, on termination, the engaged pairs specify a matching, which we denote by M. If man m prefers woman w to $p_M(m)$, then w must have rejected m at some point during the execution of the algorithm. But this rejection implies that w was, or became, engaged to a man she prefers to m, and any subsequent change of her fiancé brings her a still better partner. So w cannot prefer m to $p_M(w)$, and therefore (m, w) cannot block M. It follows that there are no blocking pairs for M, and therefore that M is a stable matching. $\square$

Example Consider the instance of size 4 defined by the preference lists in Figure 1.4.

1		4	1	2	3		1		4	1	3	2
2		2	3	1	4		2		1	3	2	4
3		2	4	3	1		3		1	2	3	4
4		3	1	4	2		4		4	1	3	2
		Men's Preferences							Women's Preferences			

Figure 1.4: A stable marriage instance of size 4

One possible execution of the algorithm results in the following sequence of proposals: man 1 to woman 4 (accepted); man 2 to woman 2 (accepted); man 3 to woman 2 (accepted, and woman 2 now rejects man 2); man 2 to woman 3 (accepted); man 4 to woman 3 (rejected, for woman 3 prefers man 2); man 4 to woman 1 (accepted). Hence the stable matching generated by the man-oriented version of the algorithm is $\{(1,4),(2,3),(3,2),(4,1)\}$.

1.2.2   Man and Woman Optimal Stable Matchings

As already mentioned, all possible executions of the Gale-Shapley algorithm (with the men as proposers) lead to the same stable matching. Furthermore, this stable matching has the remarkable property that every man achieves in it the best partner that he can possibly have in any stable matching. It is perhaps surprising that all the men, who are essentially in competition with each other for the women, can agree on a stable matching that is simultaneously optimal for all of them. This result is stated formally in the next theorem, which also establishes the insignificance of the nondeterminism in the algorithm.

Theorem 1.2.2 *All possible executions of the Gale-Shapley algorithm (with the men as proposers) yield the same stable matching, and in this stable matching, each man has the best partner that he can have in any stable matching.*

Proof Suppose that an arbitrary execution E of the algorithm yields the stable matching M, and that, in contradiction of the theorem, there is a stable matching M' and a man m such that m prefers $w' = p_{M'}(m)$ to $w = p_M(m)$. Then during E, w' must have rejected m. Suppose, without loss of generality, that this was the first occasion, during E, that a woman rejected a stable partner, and suppose that this rejection took place because of the engagement of w' to m' (so that w' prefers m' to m). Then m' can have no stable partner whom he prefers to w' (for no woman had previously rejected a stable partner). So m' prefers w' to his partner in M', and the supposed stable matching M' is blocked by (m', w'). Each man m is therefore matched in M with his favorite stable partner w, and since E was an arbitrary execution of the algorithm, it follows that all possible executions of the algorithm leads to this same stable matching. □

This is a remarkable result. It implies that if each man is independently given his best stable partner, then the result is a stable matching. Yet there seems no a priori reason why this should even be a matching.

For obvious reasons, the stable matching generated by the man-oriented version of the Gale-Shapley algorithm is called *man-optimal*. If the roles of the sexes in the algorithm are interchanged, then the resulting *woman-optimal* stable matching, obtained by the *woman-oriented* version of the Gale-Shapley algorithm, is analogously optimal for the women. It may happen that the man and woman optimal stable matchings are identical, but this will not, in general, be the case. Throughout the book, we shall denote the man-optimal stable matching by M_0 and the woman-optimal by M_z.

It is perhaps not surprising that the optimality property from the point of view of the members of one sex is gained at the expense of the members of the other sex. Specifically, in the man-optimal stable matching, each woman has the worst partner that she can have in any stable matching, so that, to coin what seems an appropriate term, man-optimal is also *woman-"pessimal"*; likewise, woman-optimal is *man-pessimal.*

Theorem 1.2.3 *In the man-optimal stable matching, each woman has the worst partner that she can have in any stable matching.*

Proof Suppose not. Let M_0 be the man-optimal stable matching, and suppose there is a stable matching M' and a woman w such that w prefers $m = p_{M_0}(w)$ to $m' = p_{M'}(w)$. But then (m, w) blocks M' unless m prefers $p_{M'}(m)$ to $w = p_{M_0}(m)$, in contradiction of the fact that m has no stable partner better than his partner in M_0. $\square$

Example The illustration in Figure 1.4 on page 10 shows that it can happen that the man-oriented and woman-oriented versions of the algorithm yield the same stable matching, in which case it is immediate, by combining the optimality and pessimality properties, that this is the unique stable matching for that instance.

The reader may verify that this is the case by executing the woman-oriented version of the algorithm.

Example The second illustration, this time of size 8, shows that different stable matchings can arise from the man-oriented and woman-oriented versions of the algorithm. The preference lists for this instance appear in Figure 1.5.

1	5	7	1	2	6	8	4	3		1	5	3	7	6	1	2	8	4
2	2	3	7	5	4	1	8	6		2	8	6	3	5	7	2	1	4
3	8	5	1	4	6	2	3	7		3	1	5	6	2	4	8	7	3
4	3	2	7	4	1	6	8	5		4	8	7	3	2	4	1	5	6
5	7	2	5	1	3	6	8	4		5	6	4	7	3	8	1	2	5
6	1	6	7	5	8	4	2	3		6	2	8	5	3	4	6	7	1
7	2	5	7	6	3	4	8	1		7	7	5	2	1	8	6	4	3
8	3	8	4	5	7	2	6	1		8	7	4	1	5	2	3	6	8

Men's Preferences   Women's Preferences

Figure 1.5: A stable marriage instance of size 8

The reader may verify, by applying the Gale-Shapley algorithm with men and then women as proposers, that the man-optimal and woman-optimal stable matchings are

$$M_0 = \{(1,5),(2,3),(3,8),(4,6),(5,7),(6,1),(7,2),(8,4)\}$$

and
$$M_z = \{(1,3),(2,6),(3,2),(4,8),(5,1),(6,5),(7,7),(8,4)\}$$
respectively.

In addition to these two extreme stable matchings, there are a number of others (8 in total), including, for example,

$$M_1 = \{(1,8),(2,3),(3,1),(4,6),(5,7),(6,5),(7,2),(8,4)\},$$
$$M_2 = \{(1,8),(2,3),(3,1),(4,6),(5,2),(6,5),(7,7),(8,4)\},$$
$$M_3 = \{(1,3),(2,6),(3,5),(4,8),(5,7),(6,1),(7,2),(8,4)\},$$

as the reader may verify.

Weak-Pareto Optimality

We observe at this point that the man-optimal and woman-optimal solutions possess a further optimality property, sometimes referred to as *weak Pareto-optimality*, as described in Theorem 1.2.4 below. This fact can be most conveniently proved by reference to the Gale-Shapley algorithm. Once again, the man-oriented version is stated, though of course, an analogous result applies for the women.

Theorem 1.2.4 *For a given stable marriage instance, there is no matching, stable or otherwise, in which every man has a partner whom he strictly prefers to his partner in the man-optimal stable matching M_0.*

Proof There can clearly be no *stable* matching with the property stated. Suppose that there is an *unstable* matching M' with this property. If w is the last woman to become engaged during a particular execution of the man-oriented Gale-Shapley algorithm, then no man is rejected by w, since the algorithm terminates when the last woman receives her first proposal. But if w's partners in M_0 and M' are m and m' respectively, then m' prefers w to his partner in M_0, so w must have rejected m', a contradiction. □

1.2.3 Implementation and Analysis

Let us assume that a stable marriage instance is described by the sets of preference lists, represented as arrays mp and wp defined by

$mp[m,i] = w \iff$ woman w is in position i in the list of man m;
$wp[w,i] = m \iff$ man m is in position i in the list of woman w.

For efficient implementation of the basic Gale-Shapley algorithm, we need to be able to determine, in constant time, whether or not woman w prefers man m to man m', for arbitrary w, m and m'. This can be achieved with the aid of a women's ranking array wr defined by

$wr[w, m] = i \iff$ man m occupies position i in the list of woman w.

An analogous men's ranking array mr, defined by

$mr[m, w] = i \iff$ woman w occupies position i in the list of man m

would be used in the woman-oriented version of the algorithm, and will be needed in some of the algorithms to be discussed later.

Clearly, for a problem instance of size n, these ranking arrays can be constructed from the preference lists in $O(n^2)$ time.

A second crucial requirement is the ability to locate a free man in constant time. This may be achieved in a number of ways, for example by maintaining a list of free men that is initialized to contain all the men. During each iteration, one man is removed from the list and at most one man (possibly the same one) is added to it. For simplicity, and in view of the irrelevance of the proposal order, the list may as well be organized as a stack, and indeed, after the initialization phase, no further man need be pushed onto the stack; whenever a rejection takes place, the rejected man can be taken as the free man in the next iteration. This is the strategy that was employed in the illustrative example on page 10.

All other aspects of the implementation are straightforward; we merely have to keep track of which women are engaged, and to whom. The total number of operations carried out during the main loop of the algorithm is bounded by a constant times the number of proposals. Since, as observed earlier, the algorithm terminates when the last woman receives her first proposal, the number of proposals cannot exceed $n(n - 1) + 1$, that is n proposals to each of $n - 1$ women and a single proposal to the nth woman. So the complexity of the algorithm is $O(n^2)$ in the worst case.

That a total of $n^2 - n + 1$ proposals may indeed be necessary can be seen by considering the family of instances in the next example.

Example In the instance specified by the preference lists in Figure 1.6, if the men begin their proposal sequences in strict numerical order, and the implementation strategy described above, involving a stack, is followed, then it may be verified that the ith proposal is from man $((i-1) \bmod n) + 1$ to woman $((i-1) \bmod (n-1)) + 1$, for $i = 1, \ldots, n^2 - n$, and the last proposal is from man 1 to woman n.

The *average-case* analysis of the Gale-Shapley algorithm is an interesting exercise in its own right. Such an analysis reveals that the average number of proposals made, taken over all possible instances involving sets of size n, is $nH_n + O((\log n)^4)$, where $H_n = 1 + 1/2 + 1/3 + \ldots + 1/n$ is the nth harmonic number, and it follows that the average-case complexity of the algorithm is $\Theta(n \log n)$. However, this result is not of central importance

1	1	2	...	n-1	n
2	2	3	...	1	n
3	3	4	...	2	n
			...		
n-1	n-1	1	...	n-2	n
n	1	2	...	n-1	n

Men's Preferences

1	2	3	...	n	1
2	3	4	...	1	2
3	4	5	...	2	3
			...		
n-1	n	1	...	n-2	n-1
n	1	2	...	n-1	n

Women's Preferences

Figure 1.6: A worst-case instance for the Gale-Shapley algorithm

for our purposes, and its derivation involves techniques that are of a quite different flavor from the rest of the material in the book.

1.2.4 An Extended Version of the Algorithm

The discussion of a number of aspects of stable marriage will be considerably simplified with the aid of an extended version of the Gale-Shapley algorithm that is designed to do more than find a single stable matching. In particular, this extended version "reduces" the preference lists by eliminating certain pairs that can readily be identified as not belonging to any stable matching. By *deleting a (man-woman) pair* (m, w), we mean deleting m from w's preference list and w from that of m.

Considering the man-oriented version of the algorithm, we observe that if woman w receives a proposal from man m, then w's partner in the man-optimal/woman-pessimal stable matching can be no worse than m; so if m' is any successor of m in w's list, the pair (m', w) cannot be a part of any stable matching. So, from the point of view of finding stable matchings, such a pair may as well be deleted from the preference lists. We can further justify such deletions by observing that no deleted pair can block any matching consisting exclusively of undeleted pairs, for each woman prefers all the surviving men on her list to those that have been deleted.

The extended algorithm (man-oriented version) can be expressed as in Figure 1.7.

```
assign each person to be free ;
while some man m is free do
begin
        w := first woman on m's list ;
        if some man p is engaged to w then
            assign p to be free ;
        assign m and w to be engaged {to each other} ;
        for each successor m' of m on w's list do
            delete the pair (m',w)
end
```

Figure 1.7: Extended Gale-Shapley algorithm

Notice that, in the extended algorithm, when a man m "proposes" to a woman w, the proposal is always accepted. For if w already held a proposal from someone she prefers to m, then the pair (m, w) would already have been deleted.

As before, the algorithm terminates when everyone is engaged — a situation that arises before any single list becomes empty. Furthermore, it is easily verified that, on termination, each man is engaged to the first woman in his (reduced) list, and each woman to the last man in hers. These engaged pairs constitute the man-optimal stable matching. Clearly, it is once again the case that the nondeterminism inherent in our description of the algorithm is of no consequence.

For a given problem instance, we will refer to the final preference lists generated by the extended Gale-Shapley algorithm, with men as proposers, as the *man-oriented Gale-Shapley lists*, or *MGS-lists* for short. Similarly, if the roles of men and women in the algorithm are reversed, we obtain the *WGS-lists*. Finally, if we take for each person the intersection of his/her MGS-list and WGS-list, we obtain the *GS-lists*. It should be clear that the GS-lists for any instance can be obtained by applying the extended algorithm with the men as proposers, and then, starting with the MGS-lists, applying the extended algorithm with the women as proposers.

The following theorem summarizes the properties of the GS-lists that we have discussed above.

Theorem 1.2.5 *For a given instance of the stable marriage problem,*
(i) all stable matchings are contained in the GS-lists;
(ii) no matching contained in the GS-lists can be blocked by a pair that is not in the GS-lists;
(iii) in the man-optimal (respectively woman-optimal) stable matching, each man is partnered by the first (respectively last) woman on his GS-list, and each woman by the last (respectively first) man on hers.

Example In the illustration of Figure 1.4 on page 10, each person's GS-list contains only his/her unique stable partner, since the man-optimal and woman-optimal stable matchings coincide in this case.

Example For the instance introduced in Figure 1.5 on page 12, it may be verified that the GS-lists are as shown in Figure 1.8.

1	5	8	3				1	5	3	6	
2	3	8	6				2	3	5	7	
3	8	5	1	6	2		3	1	2		
4	6	8					4	8			
5	7	2	1				5	6	7	3	1
6	1	5					6	2	3	4	
7	2	5	7				7	7	5		
8	4						8	4	1	2	3
	Men's Preferences							Women's Preferences			

Figure 1.8: The GS-lists for the instance of size 8

It is not hard to see that the extended algorithm can also be implemented to run in $O(n^2)$ time, with the aid of a suitably chosen data structure that maintains throughout a faithful representation of the (changing) preference lists.

1.3 The Set of Stable Matchings

1.3.1 The Lattice Structure

We have seen in Section 1.2 that, for a general stable marriage instance, the man-optimal and woman-optimal solutions are extreme stable matchings in a very precise sense, and that, in general, other stable matchings may also exist. It turns out, as we will see shortly, that the set of all stable matchings forms a distributive lattice under a natural ordering relation, and that the man-optimal and woman-optimal matchings represent the minimum and maximum elements of the lattice.

We extend the notion of preference so that it applies to matchings as well as to individuals. A person x is said to *prefer* a matching M to a matching M' if x prefers his/her partner in M to his/her partner in M'. Note that this is *strict* preference. Given two stable matchings M and M', a person x may prefer M to M', or M' to M, or may, if $p_M(x) = p_{M'}(x)$, be indifferent between them.

We now establish a preliminary theorem that is of some interest in its own right, though its prime role is to serve as a tool in our investigation of the structure of the stable matchings.

Theorem 1.3.1 *Let M and M' be stable matchings, and suppose that m and w are partners in M but not in M'. Then one of m and w prefers M to M', and the other prefers M' to M.*

Proof Let $\mathcal{X}$ and $\mathcal{Y}$ (respectively $\mathcal{X}'$ and $\mathcal{Y}'$) denote the sets of men and women who prefer M to M' (respectively M' to M).

In M there can be no pair (m, w) with $m \in \mathcal{X}$, $w \in \mathcal{Y}$, for such a pair would block M'. So every man in $\mathcal{X}$ has an M-partner in $\mathcal{Y}'$, and therefore $|\mathcal{X}| \le |\mathcal{Y}'|$.

Likewise, in M' there can be no pairs (m, w) with $m \in \mathcal{X}'$, $w \in \mathcal{Y}'$, for such a pair would block M. So every man in $\mathcal{X}'$ has an M'-partner in $\mathcal{Y}$, and therefore $|\mathcal{X}'| \le |\mathcal{Y}|$.

But $|\mathcal{X}| + |\mathcal{X}'| = |\mathcal{Y}| + |\mathcal{Y}'|$, since the left-hand side is the number of men, and the right-hand side the number of women, who have different partners in the two matchings. It follows that $|\mathcal{X}'| = |\mathcal{Y}|$ and $|\mathcal{X}| = |\mathcal{Y}'|$. Hence every man in $\mathcal{X}'$ has an M-partner in $\mathcal{Y}$, and, since every man in $\mathcal{X}$ has an M-partner in $\mathcal{Y}'$, the statement of the lemma follows. $\square$

Theorem 1.3.1 has an immediate corollary that is of some interest in its own right.

Corollary 1.3.1 *If M and M' are stable matchings for the same stable marriage instance, then the number of people who prefer M to M' is equal to the number who prefer M' to M.*

It may be worth observing at this point that an argument almost identical to that used in the proof of Theorem 1.3.1 may be used to establish another interesting property of stable matchings, namely that if M is a stable matching and M' is any matching, stable or not, then at least as many people prefer M to M' as prefer M' to M.

For a given stable marriage instance, we define the (man-oriented) dominance relation as follows: stable matching M is said to *dominate* stable matching M', written $M \preceq M'$, if every man has at least as good a partner in M as he has in M'; i.e., every man either prefers M to M' or is indifferent between them. We use the term *strictly dominates*, written $M \prec M'$, if $M \preceq M'$ and $M \neq M'$.

Throughout, we will use the symbol $\mathcal{M}$ to represent the set of all stable matchings for a stable marriage instance. It is a trivial matter to show that the set $\mathcal{M}$ is a partial order under the dominance relation; when considered as a partial order, we denote it by $(\mathcal{M}, \preceq)$.

Of course, an analogous woman-oriented dominance relation could be defined, and we have the following immediate corollary of Theorem 1.3.1.

Corollary 1.3.2 *M dominates M' from the man's point of view if and only if M' dominates M from the woman's point of view. So the woman-oriented dominance relation is the inverse, denoted $\succeq$, of the man-oriented, and gives rise to the dual partial order $(\mathcal{M}, \succeq)$.*

Example Referring back to the example given by the preference lists in Figure 1.5 on page 12, we see, of course, that the man-optimal matching M_0 dominates, and the woman-optimal matching M_z is dominated by, all the other stable matchings. Also, as far as the stable matchings M_1, M_2 and M_3 are concerned, M_1 clearly dominates M_2, but neither of these dominates, nor is dominated by, M_3.

We now show that the partial order $(\mathcal{M}, \preceq)$ is, in fact, a distributive lattice, a fact that will be of central, although somewhat disguised, importance in Chapters 2 and 3.

A *distributive lattice* is a partial order in which

i. each pair of elements a, b has a greatest lower bound, or *meet*, denoted by $a \wedge b$, so that $a \wedge b \preceq a$, $a \wedge b \preceq b$, and there is no element c such that $c \preceq a$, $c \preceq b$ and $a \wedge b \prec c$;

ii. each pair of elements a, b has a least upper bound, or *join*, denoted by $a \vee b$, so that $a \preceq a \vee b$, $b \preceq a \vee b$, and there is no element c such that $a \preceq c$, $b \preceq c$ and $c \prec a \vee b$;

iii. the *distributive laws* hold, namely $a \vee (b \wedge c) = (a \vee b) \wedge (a \vee c)$ and $a \wedge (b \vee c) = (a \wedge b) \vee (a \wedge c)$.

We begin the demonstration that $(\mathcal{M}, \preceq)$ is a distributive lattice by presenting two lemmas that lead to the interpretation of meet and join in $\mathcal{M}$.

Lemma 1.3.1 *For a given stable marriage instance, let M and M' be two (distinct) stable matchings. If each man is given the better of his partners in M and M', then the result is a stable matching.*

    Proof We first show that a matching results, and then that it is stable.

    If men m and m' receive the same partner w, say because (m, w) is a pair in M and (m', w) is a pair in M', then m prefers M to M' and m' prefers M' to M. Then Theorem 1.3.1 applied to the pair (m, w) implies that w prefers m' to m, and applied to the pair (m', w) implies that w prefers m to m', giving a contradiction. Hence a matching does result.

    Now suppose that the matching is blocked by the pair (m, w). Then m strictly prefers w to both $p_M(m)$ and $p_{M'}(m)$, and w strictly prefers m to her partner in the new matching. If w has $p_M(w)$ as her partner in this matching, then the pair (m, w) blocks M, while if w has $p_{M'}(w)$ as her partner then (m, w) blocks M'. But these are the only two possibilities for w's partner, so in either case there is a contradiction. $\square$

It follows from Lemma 1.3.1 that if each man is given the best of his partners in any fixed set of stable matchings, then the result is a stable matching. From the case where the fixed set consists of all the stable matchings, we obtain independent confirmation of the existence of a stable matching that dominates all of the others — the man optimal — as proved in Theorem 1.2.2.

    In anticipation of the lattice property, we denote by $M \wedge M'$ the stable matching in which each man obtains the better of his partners in M and M', and by $\bigwedge_{M \in S} M$, or $\bigwedge S$ for brevity, the stable matching in which each man is given the best of his partners in all the stable matchings in the set S. The following corollary is an immediate consequence of Theorem 1.3.1.

Corollary 1.3.3 *In $M \wedge M'$, each woman obtains the poorer of her partners in M and M'.*

It is an easy consequence of this corollary that the man-optimal stable matching is also the woman-pessimal, as was shown earlier in Theorem 1.2.3.

    The next lemma is essentially the dual of Lemma 1.3.1.

Lemma 1.3.2 *For a given stable marriage instance, let M and M' be two (distinct) stable matchings. If each man is given the poorer of his partners in M and M', then the result is a stable matching.*

Proof If each man is given the poorer of his partners in M and M', then by Theorem 1.3.1, each woman receives the better of her partners in M and M'. Hence the present lemma is really just a restatement of Lemma 1.3.1 with the roles of men and women interchanged. $\square$

As with Lemma 1.3.1, the result of Lemma 1.3.2 can be extended to apply to any fixed set of stable matchings, and again leads to independent confirmation of the existence of a stable matching that is dominated by all others — the man-pessimal (and woman-optimal).

Again anticipating the lattice property, we denote by $M \vee M'$ the stable matching in which each man receives the poorer of his partners in M and M' (and, by Theorem 1.3.1, each woman the better of hers). As before, the notation is extended to $\bigvee_{M \in S} M$, or $\bigvee S$ for brevity, for the stable matching in which each man is given the worst of his partners in all the stable matchings in the set S.

These lemmas describe results that are really quite striking: there seems no a priori reason why assigning each man to the better, or the worse, of his partners in two arbitrary stable matchings should even yield a matching, far less a stable matching, and this is perhaps one of the first indications we have seen of the rich structure underlying stable marriage instances.

It is now a simple matter to observe that $M \wedge M'$ is the greatest lower bound for M and M' under the dominance relation, and $M \vee M'$ the least upper bound, thereby establishing that the partial order $(\mathcal{M}, \preceq)$ is in fact a lattice. We state this as a theorem, incorporating also the distributive property.

Theorem 1.3.2 *For a given instance of the stable marriage problem, the partial order $(\mathcal{M}, \preceq)$ forms a distributive lattice, with $M \wedge M'$ representing the meet of M and M', and $M \vee M'$ the join.*

Proof It is immediate that $M \wedge M' \preceq M$, $M \wedge M' \preceq M'$. Further, if M^* is any stable matching satisfying $M^* \preceq M$, $M^* \preceq M'$, then each man must have a partner in M^* at least as good as his partner in each of M and M', so that $M^* \preceq M \wedge M'$. So $M \wedge M'$ is the greatest lower bound for M and M', as the notation already suggests. The proof that $M \vee M'$ is the least upper bound is similar, and this establishes that $(\mathcal{M}, \preceq)$ is a lattice.

For the first distributive property, let X, Y, and Z be stable matchings. If $p_Y(m) = p_Z(m) = w$, then it is immediate that in both $U = X \wedge (Y \vee Z)$ and $V = (X \wedge Y) \vee (X \wedge Z)$, m is partnered by whichever of $p_X(m)$ and w he most prefers. Otherwise, it is easy to verify that, in both U and V, m is partnered by $p_Z(m)$ if m prefers Y to Z to X, by $p_Y(m)$ if m prefers Z to Y to X, and in all other cases by $p_X(m)$. Hence every man has the same partner in U as he has in V, and therefore $U = V$.

The second distributive law may be established in a similar way. $\square$

Example   Consider the example of size 4 described by the preference lists in Figure 1.9.

1	1	2	3	4		1	4	3	2	1
2	2	1	4	3		2	3	4	1	2
3	3	4	1	2		3	2	1	4	3
4	4	3	2	1		4	1	2	3	4

Men's Preferences   Women's Preferences

Figure 1.9: A particular stable marriage instance of size 4

This instance admits a total of ten stable matchings. The lattice structure is illustrated in Figure 1.10, which contains its so-called *Hasse diagram*. This is a directed graph with a node for each element of the lattice (i.e., each stable matching), and a directed edge from node x to node y if $x \prec y$ and there is no z such that $x \prec z \prec y$. In other words, all precedences implied by transitivity are suppressed in the diagram. (Note that, following convention, all edges in this digraph are assumed to be directed downward.)

The label $w_1 w_2 w_3 w_4$ on a node indicates that it represents the stable matching in which man i is matched with woman w_i ($1 \leq i \leq 4$).

In Chapter 2 we will examine more closely the structure of the set $\mathcal{M}$ of stable matchings, and will derive several simple compact representations of $\mathcal{M}$.

1.3.2   Numbers of Stable Matchings

We have seen that the man-optimal and woman-optimal solutions may coincide, in which case the instance in question admits just one stable matching. However, in general, stable marriage instances may admit many stable matchings, and it is our main purpose in this subsection to show that the number of stable matchings can grow exponentially with the size of the instance.

As a consequence of this result, any algorithm that generates all of the stable matchings may require exponentially many steps to do so. Furthermore, if we are seeking a stable matching with a particular property, say optimality relative to some chosen criterion, then a brute force algorithm that examines every stable matching is doomed to be of exponential time complexity in the worst case.

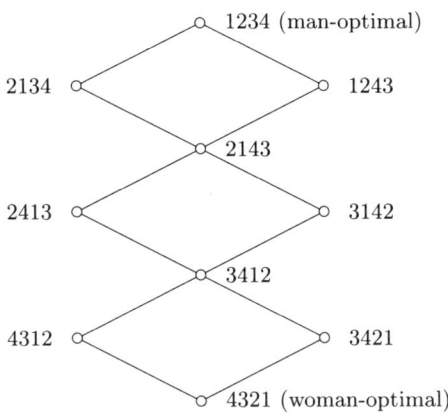

1234 (man-optimal)

2134   1243

2143

2413   3142

3412

4312   3421

4321 (woman-optimal)

Figure 1.10: Lattice structure for the current instance

It is an open problem to determine, for stable marriage instances of a given size n, the largest possible number $f(n)$ of stable matchings and the structure of the maximizing preference lists. However, we will give below a construction that at least provides a reasonable lower bound for $f(n)$.

On the other hand, the *average* number $g(n)$ of stable matchings, taken over all instances of given size n, grows much more slowly than the maximum number; it is known that $g(n)$ is asymptotic to $e^{-1}n \ln n$. We omit the proof of this fact, which involves some highly technical probability arguments.

The exponential growth rate of the function $f(n)$ can be established using the following lemma.

Lemma 1.3.3 *Given stable marriage instances of sizes m and n with x and y stable matchings respectively, there is an instance of size mn with at least $\max(xy^m, yx^n)$ stable matchings.*

Proof Suppose that the men and women in the given instances are labeled $a_1, \ldots, a_m$, $c_1, \ldots, c_m$ and $b_1, \ldots, b_n$, $d_1, \ldots, d_n$ respectively. Consider the instance of size mn in which

   i. the men are labeled (a_i, b_j), $i = 1, \ldots, m$, $j = 1, \ldots, n$;

   ii. the women are labeled (c_i, d_j), $i = 1, \ldots, m$, $j = 1, \ldots, n$;

   iii. man (a_i, b_j) prefers (c_k, d_l) to $(c_{k'}, d_{l'})$ if b_j prefers d_l to $d_{l'}$, or if $l = l'$ and a_i prefers c_k to $c_{k'}$;

   iv. woman (c_i, d_j) prefers (a_k, b_l) to $(a_{k'}, b_{l'})$ if d_j prefers b_l to $b_{l'}$, or if $l = l'$ and c_i prefers a_k to $a_{k'}$.

Let $M_1, \ldots, M_n$ be any sequence of (not necessarily distinct) stable matchings in the instance of size m, and let M be any stable matching in the instance of size n. The total number of choices available for $M_1, \ldots, M_n$ and M is clearly yx^n. Then we claim that the mapping

$$(a_i, b_j) \longrightarrow (p_{M_j}(a_i), p_M(b_j))$$

is a stable matching in the composite instance.

It is immediately clear that this mapping is actually a matching, since both M_j and M are matchings. So suppose that this matching is blocked by the pair $((a, b), (c, d))$. Then, of the following conditions, we must have either (i) or (ii) together with either (iii) or (iv).

   i. b prefers d to $p_M(b)$;

   ii. $d = p_M(b)$ and a prefers c to $p_{M_j}(a)$;

   iii. d prefers b to $p_M(d)$;

   iv. $b = p_M(d)$ and c prefers a to $p_{M_j}(c)$.

Of the four possibilities, the combination of (i) with (iii) is precluded by the stability of M, (ii) with (iv) by the stability of M_j, and the others by simple incompatibility.

Hence our claim is justified, and we have demonstrated an instance with at least yx^n stable matchings. Likewise, by interchanging the roles of the original two instances, we establish the corresponding result for xy^m. $\square$

Theorem 1.3.3 *For each $n \geq 0$, n a power of 2, there is a stable marriage instance of size n with at least 2^{n-1} stable matchings.*

Proof The proof is by induction. For $n = 2^0$, the trivial instance of size 1 admits a single stable matching. Assuming the result true for $n = 2^k$, we apply Lemma 1.3.3, with $m = 2$ and the instance of size 2 shown in Figure 1.11 below. For this instance, both possible matchings are stable, so that $x = 2$ and, by the inductive hypothesis, $y = 2^{2^k - 1}$. Hence, by Lemma 1.3.3, there exists an instance of size $2 \cdot 2^k = 2^{k+1}$ with at least $\max(2 \cdot (2^{2^k - 1})^2, 2^{2^k - 1} \cdot 2^{2^k}) = 2^{2^{k+1} - 1}$ stable matchings, as required. $\square$

1	1	2	1	2	1
2	2	1	2	1	2

Men's Preferences   Women's Preferences

Figure 1.11: An example instance of size 2

It turns out that Theorem 1.3.3 gives a rather low estimate of the number of stable matchings for the family of instances generated. For example, the generated instance of size 4 is shown in Figure 1.9 on page 22, and, as we have seen, this has 10 stable matchings rather than 8. In fact, it can be shown that if x_n represents the number of stable matchings in the instance of size n so generated, then

$$x_n = 3x_{n/2}^2 - 2x_{n/4}^4$$

for $n \geq 4$. This recurrence relation leads to the table of values shown in Figure 1.12, where the values are compared to the bound 2^{n-1} given by Theorem 1.3.3.

k	$n = 2^k$	2^{n-1}	x_n
1	2	2	2
2	4	8	10
3	8	128	268
4	16	32768	195472
5	32	2147483648	104310534400

Figure 1.12: Lower bounds for the maximum number of stable matchings

1.4 Some Simple Extensions of Stable Marriage

In this section, we consider three extensions of the basic stable marriage problem. In Section 1.4.1, we investigate the implications if the sets of men and women in a stable marriage instance are of unequal size. In Section 1.4.2, we allow for the possibility that preference lists may be incomplete, in other words, that a person may declare one or more of the members of the opposite sex as unacceptable. Then, in Section 1.4.3, we study the effect of indifference between potential partners, resulting in the occurrence of "ties" in the preference lists.

1.4.1 Sets of Unequal Size

Throughout Sections 1.2 and 1.3, we assumed that the sets of men and women were of equal size. However, most of the results of these sections apply, in slightly amended form, to the case of unequal sized sets.

Let $\mathcal{X}$ and $\mathcal{Y}$ be the sets of men and women, respectively, and suppose that $|\mathcal{X}| = n_x < n_y = |\mathcal{Y}|$. To extend the notion of stability in a natural way, we say that a matching M is unstable if there is a man m and a woman w such that

i. m and w are not partners in M;

ii. m is either unmatched in M, or prefers w to his partner in M;

iii. w is either unmatched in M, or prefers m to her partner in M.

Note that this definition of stability is based on the assumption that a person prefers to be married rather than to remain single. It follows at once that any stable matching consists of n_x ordered pairs, with $n_y - n_x$ of the women unmatched.

If we apply the man-oriented version of the Gale-Shapley algorithm, then it terminates with each man engaged, and the resulting matching is stable; it is again man-optimal and woman-pessimal in the usual sense, but of course $n_y - n_x$ of the women have no partner.

If we apply the woman-oriented version of the *extended* algorithm, then it again terminates with each man engaged, and the resulting matching — the woman-optimal/man-pessimal — is stable. However, the WGS-lists of all the unmatched women will be empty, so that, by an analogue of Theorem 1.2.5(i), none of these women can be matched in any stable matching. So we have the following theorem.

Theorem 1.4.1 *In a stable marriage instance in which the sets of men and women are of unequal size, there is at least one stable matching in which all the members of the smaller set are matched. Furthermore, all the members of the smaller set are matched in all stable matchings, and the larger set is partitioned into two subsets, the members of one subset being matched in all stable matchings and the members of the other in none.*

It follows from an analogue of Theorem 1.2.5(ii) that if a problem instance with unequal-sized sets has the same GS-lists as a standard problem instance, then the sets of stable matchings in the two instances are the same. Further, given the GS-lists L of an instance with unequal-sized sets, a standard instance with the same GS-lists can be generated from L by discarding all unmatched members of the larger set and appending all missing entries to the end of each list. It follows from this correspondence that all results concerning lattice structure, etc., carry over to this case.

1.4.2 Unacceptable Partners

Suppose that a person may declare one or more of the members of the opposite sex to be an unacceptable partner, so that the preference list of such a person contains a proper subset of the members of the opposite sex. Then a man and a woman can be matched only if they are acceptable to each other.

First of all, we note that, in this setting, stable matchings may be partial, in the sense that not all of the members of either sex need be matched. In these circumstances, it is natural to regard a matching M as unstable if there is a man m and a woman w such that

    i. m and w are not partners in M, but each is acceptable to the other;

    ii. m is either unmatched in M, or prefers w to his partner in M;

    iii. w is either unmatched in M, or prefers m to her partner in M.

It is also natural to extend the notion of preference between matchings so that a person prefers a matching in which he/she has an acceptable partner to one in which he/she has no partner. Furthermore, if person q is absent from person p's list, then p may as well be deleted from the list of q, for p and q cannot form a stable pair; nor can they block any matching.

With these extended notions of stability and preference, it is easy to show that Theorem 1.3.1 remains true, namely that if m and w are partners in the stable matching M but not in the stable matching M', then one of m, w prefers M to M' and the other prefers M' to M.

We can use this to establish the fundamental result in the case of unacceptable partners.

Theorem 1.4.2 *In a stable marriage instance that allows unacceptable partners, the men and the women are each partitioned into two sets — those that have partners in all stable matchings and those that have partners in none.*

Proof Given distinct stable matchings M and M', we define a directed graph $G = G(M, M')$ with one node for each person. For each man m who has a partner in M there is a directed edge from m to $p_M(m)$, and for each woman w who has a partner in M' there is a directed edge from w to $p_{M'}(w)$. So every node in G has in-degree at most one, and out-degree at most one.

Now suppose, for a contradiction, that man m is matched in M, say with woman w, but is unmatched in M'. There is a unique directed path in G starting at node m, and since every node has in-degree at most one, and m has in-degree zero, it follows that this path cannot cycle. Hence the path must end either with a man who is matched in M' but not in M (and so who prefers M' to M), or with a woman w who is matched in M but not in M' (and so who prefers M to M').

But, since m prefers M to M', it follows from Theorem 1.3.1 that w prefers M' to M, and by successive applications of that Theorem along the path, it follows that each man on the path prefers M to M' and each woman on the path prefers M' to M. So either of the two ways in which the path can terminate leads to a contradiction. $\square$

In view of Theorem 1.4.2, application of the Gale-Shapley algorithm, modified to handle unacceptable partners, will reveal precisely those men and women who have stable partners. Once again, by an analogue of Theorem 1.2.5(ii), we can conclude that the set of stable matchings for such an instance is identical to that for a standard instance with the same GS-lists (with unmatchable men and women discarded). So all results concerning lattice structure, etc., carry over to this case also.

A natural question that arises in this context concerns the size of the stable matchings for any instance (by Theorem 1.4.2 they all have the same size) and how this may be related to the total number of unacceptable pairings. In fact, relatively few unacceptable pairings can greatly reduce the size of the resulting stable matching. Referring to the instance of Figure 1.6 on page 15 in which the only stable matching is $\{(1,n), (2,1), (3,2), \ldots, (n,n-1)\}$, it can be seen that if woman n is unacceptable to man 1, then the maximum size of a stable matching is $n-1$, and if for any i $(2 \leq i \leq n)$ woman n and woman $i-1$ are unacceptable to man i, then there is no stable matching in which man i has a partner. So as few as $2k-1$ unacceptable pairs can reduce the size of the stable matching by k.

A further interesting, though perhaps not surprising fact, in the context of unacceptable partners, is contained in Theorem 1.4.3.

Theorem 1.4.3 *If, in a stable marriage instance, some man m appends a previously unacceptable woman w to the end of his list, then in both the man and woman-optimal stable matchings for the extended instance, no woman is worse off and no man, except possibly man m himself, is better off.*

Proof If man m has a stable partner in the original instance, then the man-oriented algorithm for the extended instance will be identical to that for the original instance, terminating before m reaches w in his list. So the man-optimal stable matching is unchanged. Otherwise, the algorithm may proceed exactly as before, only where it would have terminated with the same man-optimal matching, m may instead propose to w. This, and any subsequent proposal that may follow, can only lead to an improvement for some woman, and possibly a deterioration for some man.

If, in the woman-optimal matching, woman w has a partner whom she prefers to m, then the woman-oriented algorithm for the extended instance will proceed exactly as for the original instance, since w will not reach m in her proposal sequence, and the same stable matching will result. Otherwise, woman w will, at some point, propose to man m. Although this proposal itself may be rejected, it cannot cause any other immediate or subsequent rejections, because w is last in m's list. So no other rejections will take place that would not have happened in the woman-oriented algorithm for the original instance. It follows that, on termination of the woman-oriented algorithm for the extended instance, no woman can have gone further along her list than in the original instance, so no woman is worse off in the woman-optimal matching, and no man, with the possible exception of m, can be better off. $\square$

1.4.3 Indifference

If we relax the requirement that each person has a preference list that is strictly ordered, so that tied entries in the preference lists become possible, then we must first of all establish a suitable extension of the notion of stability. We will consider three possible notions of stability in this context.

As a first notion of stability, suppose that we regard a matching as unstable if there is a man and a woman who are not partners, each of whom likes the other at least as well as his/her partner in the matching. Let us call a matching that is stable under this criterion *super-stable*. Then it is easy to find instances for which no super-stable matching exists — as a trivial example, in a situation of complete indifference, in which no strict preference is expressed by anyone, there can be no super-stable matching.

A second, more relaxed, notion of stability would have us regard a matching as unstable if there exists a man and woman who are not partners, such that one strictly prefers the other to his/her partner and the other is at least indifferent. We will call a matching that is stable in this sense *strongly stable*. Once again, there are instances for which no matching is strongly stable. Consider the instance of size 2 described by the preference lists in

Figure 1.13, in which all preferences are strict except those of man 2 (indicated by the parentheses in the preference list of man 2). The matching $\{(1,1), (2,2)\}$ is blocked by the pair $(2,1)$, while the matching $\{(1,2), (2,1)\}$ is blocked by the pair $(2,2)$.

1		1	2			1		2	1
2	(	1	2	)		2		2	1

Men's Preferences	Women's Preferences

Figure 1.13: An instance of size 2 with ties

It turns out that the (extended) Gale-Shapley algorithm can be suitably exploited to determine the existence of a super-stable or strongly stable matching for any given stable marriage instance that allows indifference. We describe the amended form of the algorithm in outline only, leaving details of verification to the reader.

The proposal sequence in the man-oriented extended Gale-Shapley algorithm proceeds in the usual way, except that a free man who has two or more women tied at the head of his current list proposes to all of them simultaneously. If a woman receives a proposal, all men strictly inferior to the proposer are deleted from her list, and she from theirs, but she may hold more than one proposal if the men in question are tied in her list. The proposal sequence may terminate with one or more of the men's lists empty, in which case no super-stable or strongly stable matching exists. Otherwise, each man is engaged to one or more women, and if to more than one, then they must be tied in his list.

In the case of super-stability, no woman who is multiply engaged can have a stable partner from among any of her fiancés, nor from among any men who are tied with them in her list. So any such pairs must be deleted, and the proposal sequence re-activated. The whole process is repeated until it produces a one-one engagement relation, which will be a super-stable matching, or until some man's list becomes empty, indicating that no super-stable matching is possible.

In the case of strong stability, if the bipartite graph defined by the engaged pairs contains a perfect matching, then this will be a strongly stable matching. Otherwise, it is well known that there must be a set of m men who are collectively engaged to fewer than m women, for some m. Such a set is called *deficient*. If we choose a minimal deficient set $\mathcal{X}$, that is, a deficient set containing no smaller deficient set, then any woman who is engaged to more than one of the men in $\mathcal{X}$ cannot have any of these men, nor any man who is tied with them in her list, as a stable partner. Hence all such pairs must be deleted, and the proposal sequence re-activated. The whole process is continued until a perfect matching exists in the bipartite graph of engaged pairs, which will be a strongly stable matching, or until some man's list becomes empty, indicating the absence of any strongly stable matching.

The problems of finding a perfect matching in a bipartite graph, and of finding a minimal deficient set of vertices if no perfect matching exists, have been widely studied, and polynomial-time algorithms for these problems, using a network-flow approach, for example, are well-known.

Hence one can determine in polynomial-time whether a super-stable or a strongly-stable matching exists.

A third, and perhaps the most reasonable notion of stability when indifference is allowed, is as follows: a matching is unstable if there is a man and a woman who are not partners, each of whom *strictly* prefers the other to his/her given partner. In this case, it is immediate that if an instance with strict preferences is created by breaking all ties arbitrarily, then any matching that is stable in that standard instance will also be stable in the original instance with ties.

It follows that, for this weaker notion of stability, a stable matching can always be found by breaking ties arbitrarily and applying the Gale-Shapley algorithm. It may well happen, of course, that different ways of breaking ties may lead the algorithm to generate different stable matchings. The problem of characterizing the structure of the set of all stable matchings in this case remains open.

1.5 Lower Bounds for Stable Marriage

1.5.1 Introduction

We have seen two fundamental problems in stable marriage that can be solved in $O(n^2)$ time, where n is the size of the instance, namely that of checking a matching for stability (see Section 1.1.2), and that of finding a stable matching (by the Gale-Shapley algorithm — see Section 1.2.3). Furthermore, in Chapter 3 we will meet $O(n^2)$ algorithms for some other problems in stable marriage, including that of identifying all the stable pairs, and, by implication, that of testing a given pair for stability.

In this section we examine the question of whether any of these problems can be solved by algorithms that run in $o(n^2)$ time, that is, significantly faster than the presently known methods. Of course, in one sense, it is

immediate that no improvement on these $O(n^2)$ bounds is possible, since
the number of data items required merely to specify a problem instance is
$\Omega(n^2)$. So any algorithm designed to solve one of these problems requires
$\Omega(n^2)$ time just for input operations and to set up the preference and/or
ranking arrays. But if we choose to discount these input and initialization
operations, the question as to whether any of the problems mentioned can
be solved in $o(n^2)$ time, under this revised model of computation, has no
such obvious answer. Nonetheless, we shall see that no improvement on
the $O(n^2)$ worst-case performance is possible for any of the problems listed
above, so that the known $O(n^2)$ algorithms are asymptotically optimal in
each case.

We first show that, given the preference lists alone (without the ranking
arrays), every algorithm that solves any of the four above-mentioned problems must, in the worst case, query the preference lists at least $n(n-1)/2$
times. We then show that even if the ranking arrays are also provided, each
of these problems still requires, in the worst case, $\Omega(n^2)$ time. The proofs
that we present involve so-called *adversary arguments*, and, although the details of the arguments differ in the two cases, they share certain properties
that we will discuss before presenting the particular arguments.

In both of the cases, the women's preference lists are fixed and are particularly simple — every woman has the same preference list, in which the men
are ranked in numerical order; for arbitrary w, woman w prefers man m to
man m' if and only if $m < m'$. These lists are referred to as the *canonical
women's preferences*. Further, in both cases, we will allow the algorithm to
query the women's lists for free; the lower bounds are based on counting the
number of necessary queries of the men's data.

In the first argument, the algorithm gets information about the preferences
of the men by successively specifying a cell in one of the men's lists and being
told (by the adversary) which woman is in that cell. That is, if the algorithm
asks about the jth cell in the list of man m, it is told which woman is the jth
choice of man m. In the second argument, the algorithm can query either
the preference lists or the ranking arrays.

We state a preliminary lemma that gives us information about any stable
marriage instance that involves the canonical women's preferences.

Lemma 1.5.1 *A stable marriage instance in which all the women have the
same preference list admits exactly one stable matching.*

Proof Suppose there is a stable matching $M \neq M_0$ for this instance.
Since M_0 is woman-pessimal, there is a nonempty set W of women such
that every woman in W has a strictly better partner in M than in M_0,
but the women not in W have the same partner in the two matchings. Let

$w \in W$ be the (unique) woman whose partner in M_0 has the highest index. Then in M, no woman can be paired with $p_{M_0}(w)$, since the preference lists of all the women are identical. Hence M cannot even be a matching, let alone a stable matching. $\square$

The next lemma identifies a simple but important property of the unique stable matching for any instance that involves the canonical women's preferences.

Lemma 1.5.2 *In the unique stable matching M for a stable marriage instance involving the canonical women's preferences, for each i $(1 \leq i \leq n)$, man i is partnered by his favorite woman among those women not matched with any of men $1, \ldots, i-1$.*

Proof If man i prefers woman j to his partner in M, and if woman j is not partnered by any of men $1, \ldots, i-1$, then woman j prefers man i to her partner in M, and the pair (i, j) blocks M — a contradiction of M's stability. $\square$

In both of the adversary arguments, the matching $\{(1,1), \ldots, (n,n)\}$, called the *identity matching*, will play a central role. The adversary will respond to queries in such a way that, until at least the claimed number of queries are made, it will be possible for the adversary to fill in the remaining list entries either to make the identity matching or a nonidentity matching the unique stable matching. Further, in the nonidentity matching, (n, n) will not be a matched pair. Hence, until at least the claimed number of queries are made, no algorithm can correctly find the stable matching for the instance, or determine whether the identity matching is stable, or whether the pair (n, n) is stable.

1.5.2   The Case of Preferences Only

Theorem 1.5.1 *Given only the preference lists, any algorithm that finds a stable matching, or determines if a specified matching is stable, or determines if a specified pair is stable, must, in the worst case, query the men's preference lists at least $n(n-1)/2$ times.*

Proof For any row i and any $k \leq i-1$, the adversary answers the kth query into row i by replying that woman k is in the cell being queried. That is, for any row i, the adversary answers with women 1 through $i-1$ for the first $i-1$ queries into row i, no matter where those queries are in row i. After the algorithm has made $i-1$ queries in row i, the adversary notes the leftmost unqueried cell in row i and "reserves" that cell for woman i. If that

cell is later queried, then the adversary replies with woman i; if any other
cell in row i is queried, it replies with any woman other than i who has not
yet been placed in row i. In this way, the adversary can fill in the men's
lists so that for any row i, the numbers to the left of i are smaller than i;
hence by Lemma 1.5.2, the identity matching is the unique stable matching
for the problem instance completed in this way.

However, if in any row i, where $i < n$, the algorithm does not query at
least i cells, then there is an unqueried cell on or before the diagonal, and
by the adversary strategy, there is a number $z > i$ that has not been placed
in row i. If the adversary puts z in the leftmost unqueried cell, then no
matter how the rest of the lists are filled in, man i will not match woman
i in the resulting unique stable matching. Hence, if there is a row $i < n$
in which fewer than i queries are made, the adversary can fill in the table
to make the unique stable matching either the identity matching or some
other matching. So any algorithm must make at least $n(n-1)/2$ queries to
determine the unique stable matching, and hence to determine whether a
specified matching is stable.

For the question of whether the pair (n, n) is stable, notice that the adversary never reveals the position of woman n in any row $i < n$ until after
at least i queries have been made in that row. So if fewer than i queries
have been made in row $i < n$, the adversary can fill in the lists either to
force (n, n) to be in the resulting unique stable matching, or to exclude it.
Hence the lower bound of $n(n-1)/2$ queries again applies. $\square$

1.5.3 The Case of Both Preferences and Rankings

Theorem 1.5.1 shows that the Gale-Shapley algorithm is asymptotically optimal, given the natural input to the problem, the preference lists (and this
applies also to other $O(n^2)$ algorithms that we will see later). However,
every efficient algorithm we know of for stable marriage problems makes
use of the ranking arrays as well as the preference lists. To construct the
ranking arrays from the preference lists requires $2n(n-1)$ queries of the
preference lists, and hence Theorem 1.5.1 leaves open the possibility that
once the ranking arrays are available, the tasks of finding a stable matching
or testing a matching or a pair for stability, can be carried out in $o(n^2)$ time.
No such fast methods are presently known, and we will now show that such
methods are not possible.

The adversary in this case is more passive than in the previous case. The
adversary constructs ahead of time canonical men's preference lists, in addition to the canonical women's lists we have already seen. The adversary
answers all queries of the men's data according to the canonical men's prefer-

ences. However, if the algorithm halts before the claimed number of queries are made, the adversary can fill in the remaining data to make the output of the algorithm false.

We begin by describing the *canonical men's preferences* for this case:
(i) for man i ($1 \leq i \leq \lfloor \frac{n}{2} \rfloor$), the first entry in his list is woman i, and the remaining entries are fixed but arbitrary;

(ii) for man $\lfloor \frac{n}{2} \rfloor + i$ ($1 \leq i \leq \lfloor \frac{n-1}{2} \rfloor$), the first i entries in his list are women $1, \ldots, i$, followed by woman $\lfloor \frac{n}{2} \rfloor + i$, followed by woman n, and then the other women in fixed but arbitrary order;

(iii) the list of man n is fixed but completely arbitrary.

Example Figure 1.14 shows the canonical men's preferences in the case $n = 11$. In each list, ... means all remaining women in fixed but arbitrary order.

1	1	...						
2	2	...						
3	3	...						
4	4	...						
5	5	...						
6	1	6	11	...				
7	1	2	7	11	...			
8	1	2	3	8	11	...		
9	1	2	3	4	9	11	...	
10	1	2	3	4	5	10	11	...
11	...							

Figure 1.14: Canonical men's preferences for the case $n = 11$

Henceforth, we denote by $\mathcal{C}$ a canonical stable marriage instance specified by the canonical women's preferences and a chosen fixed set of canonical men's preferences.

Lemma 1.5.3 *The identity matching is the unique stable matching for the canonical instance $\mathcal{C}$.*

Proof This is an easy induction argument based on Lemma 1.5.2 and the structure of the canonical men's preferences. $\square$

"Near-Canonical" Instances

We now describe the family $\mathcal{F}(\mathcal{C})$ of instances, each member of which is similar to the canonical instance but has a unique stable matching different from the identity matching. Any member of the family $\mathcal{F}(\mathcal{C})$ will be denoted by $\mathcal{C}'$.

An instance of $\mathcal{F}(\mathcal{C})$ is obtained from $\mathcal{C}$ by choosing a man $m = \lfloor \frac{n}{2} \rfloor + i$ for some i ($1 \leq i \leq \lfloor \frac{n-3}{2} \rfloor$) and two women j and k ($1 \leq j \leq i$, $m+1 \leq k \leq n-1$), and interchanging the positions of women j and k in the list of man m. All other lists remain unchanged.

Lemma 1.5.4 *For any instance $\mathcal{C}'$ in $\mathcal{F}(\mathcal{C})$, the pair (n, n) is not stable, and therefore the matching $\{(1, 1), \ldots, (n, n)\}$ is not stable.*

Proof Suppose that in the list of man $m = \lfloor \frac{n}{2} \rfloor + i$ ($1 \leq i \leq \lfloor \frac{n-3}{2} \rfloor$) the positions of women j ($1 \leq j \leq i$) and k ($m+1 \leq k \leq n-1$) are interchanged. Because the women's lists are unchanged, we conclude from Lemma 1.5.1 that $\mathcal{C}'$ has exactly one stable matching, and Lemma 1.5.2 continues to hold. Clearly, in that stable matching, men $1, \ldots, m-1$ are partnered, as in $\mathcal{C}$'s stable matching, by women $1, \ldots, m-1$ respectively.

However, by Lemma 1.5.2, man $m+1$ will now be partnered by woman k, who occupies position j in his list. For woman k cannot be a partner of any of men $1, \ldots, m-1$, since $k \geq m+1$, whereas each of the women preceding her in the list of man m *is* the partner of one of these men.

Now, none of men $m+1, \ldots, k-1$ has his stable partner altered by the change from $\mathcal{C}$ to $\mathcal{C}'$, but man k can no longer have woman k as his stable partner. Furthermore, it is an immediate consequence of the definition of the men's canonical preferences that the only other women whom man k prefers to woman n are women numbered $\leq \lfloor \frac{n}{2} \rfloor$, i.e., women partnered by men numbered $\leq \lfloor \frac{n}{2} \rfloor$. So, by Lemma 1.5.2, the stable partner of man k in $\mathcal{C}'$ is woman n, and the uniqueness of the stable matching for $\mathcal{C}'$ implies that (n, n) is not a stable pair in $\mathcal{C}'$. $\square$

It follows from Lemmas 1.5.1 and 1.5.4 that any algorithm to check the stability of the matching $\{(1, 1), \ldots, (n, n)\}$, or to find a stable matching, or to check the stability of the pair (n, n), must be able to distinguish between the canonical instance $\mathcal{C}$ and any of the instances $\mathcal{C}'$.

Lemma 1.5.5 *The number of queries needed to distinguish $\mathcal{C}$ from a $\mathcal{C}'$ is at least $(n-4)^2/16$. More precisely, it is at least k^2, if $n = 4k+1$ or $4k+2$, and at least $k(k+1)$ if $n = 4k+3$ or $4k+4$.*

Proof We establish the result for $n = 4k+1$, the other cases being similar. In order to distinguish $\mathcal{C}$ from a $\mathcal{C}'$, in the list of man $\lfloor \frac{n}{2} \rfloor + i$ ($1 \leq i \leq \lfloor \frac{n-3}{2} \rfloor$), the algorithm must at least query either all of the positions occupied by women $1, \ldots, i$, or all of the positions occupied by women $\lfloor \frac{n}{2} \rfloor + i + 1, \ldots, n-1$. There are i of the former and $4k - (2k + i) = 2k - i$ of the latter, so that at least $\min(i, 2k - i)$ queries are needed. So, in total, the number of queries is at least $\sum_{i=1}^{2k-1} \min(i, 2k - i) = \sum_{i=1}^{k} i + \sum_{i=k+1}^{2k-1} (2k - i) = k^2$, as claimed. $\square$

We now state the main result of this section, which follows immediately from Lemma 1.5.5.

Theorem 1.5.2 *Any algorithm to find a stable matching or to check if a given matching is stable or to determine whether a given pair is stable requires $\Omega(n^2)$ time in the worst case, even when both the preference lists and ranking arrays are given as input.*

Note that Theorem 1.5.2 implies $\Omega(n^2)$ lower bounds for the three problems in the case that only the preference lists are given. However, we proved those results separately in order to obtain a larger constant in the lower bounds.

1.6 The Hospitals/Residents Problem

1.6.1 Introduction

The Hospitals/Residents problem introduced in Section 1.1.1 involves an asymmetric extension of the standard model in which each member of one set (the hospitals) has one *or more* places to fill. Each hospital therefore seeks to be matched, under the appropriate stability criterion, with a number of residents not exceeding its number of available places.

We shall describe our "standard" version of the problem so that the ideas introduced in sections 1.4.1 and 1.4.2 are incorporated from the outset; in other words, the total number of places does not necessarily equal the total number of residents, and we allow any particular member of either set to declare one or more members of the other set as unacceptable. We shall see that, even in this more general setting, results analogous to most of those obtained in Sections 1.2 and 1.3 can be established. (We do not, however, consider indifference in this context.)

In this setting, a *matching* is a (partial) mapping from the set of residents to the set of hospitals in which the number of residents mapped (or assigned) to a particular hospital does not exceed the number of places at that hospital. A matching is unstable if there is a resident r and hospital h such that all of the following hold:

    i. h is acceptable to r and r to h;

    ii. either r is unmatched, or r prefers h to his assigned hospital;

    iii. either h does not have all its places filled in the matching, or h prefers r to at least one of its assigned residents.

It is convenient to use similar terminology and notation to that used in the stable marriage context. For example, a pair (h, r) is stable, and h and r are stable partners, if resident r is assigned to hospital h in some stable matching; if M is a stable matching, $p_M(r)$ denotes the hospital to which r is assigned in M, and $p_M(h)$ denotes the *set* of residents assigned to h in M.

Instances of this many-one matching problem may be transformed to the one-one case by a standard device: each hospital h, say with q places, is replaced by q separate identical hospitals $h_1, \ldots, h_q$, each with just one place, and each with a preference list identical to that of h. In turn, each occurrence of h in the preference list of a resident is replaced by the sequence $h_1, \ldots, h_q$. It may then be shown that the stable matchings in the derived stable marriage instance are in one-one correspondence with the stable matchings in the original instance. Furthermore, the Gale-Shapley algorithm may be applied to the derived instance, and thereby stable matchings that are in some sense extreme for the original hospitals/residents instance may be obtained. This notion of extreme solutions in the hospitals/residents problem will be made more precise later.

Here we take a slightly different approach that separates more clearly the roles of the hospitals and residents and that allows us to provide neat proofs of some structural results for this problem. These include the so-called "rural-hospitals" theorem of Section 1.6.4 and the result of Section 1.6.5, asserting that hospitals have unambiguous strict preferences over stable matchings.

It is apparent that we do not have the same symmetry with respect to residents and hospitals as applies with respect to men and women in the stable marriage problem, so that we shall consider separately the hospital-oriented and resident-oriented versions of our amended Gale-Shapley algorithm. In both cases, our algorithms generalize the extended Gale-Shapley algorithm of Section 1.2.4.

1.6.2   The Hospital-Oriented Algorithm

In the hospital-oriented version of the algorithm, which is essentially the version operated by the NRMP (see Section 1.1.1), each hospital offers a place to residents, in preference order, until all of its available places are (provisionally) filled or there are no more acceptable residents on its list. Each resident behaves exactly like a woman in the man-oriented version of the Gale-Shapley algorithm, rejecting all offers except the best received to date. To describe the extended version of this algorithm that reduces the preference lists, we introduce some suitable terminology.

We first of all assume that if a hospital h is not acceptable to a resident r then r is deleted from h's list, and vice versa, so that the lists are consistent from the outset. Clearly, no such pair (h, r) can block a matching. We use the term *provisional assignment* rather than engagement in the context of residents and hospitals. A resident who is not provisionally assigned is *free*, and a hospital having fewer residents provisionally assigned than it has places available is *undersubscribed*. The hospital-oriented algorithm is as shown in Figure 1.15.

```
assign each resident to be free ;
assign each hospital to be totally unsubscribed ;
while (some hospital h is undersubscribed) and
      (h's list contains a resident r not provisionally assigned to h) do
begin
    r := first such resident on h's list ;
    if r is already assigned, say to h', then
        break the provisional assignment of r to h' ;
    provisionally assign r to h ;
    for each successor h' of h on r's list do
        remove h' and r from each other's lists
end
```

Figure 1.15: Hospital-oriented algorithm

On termination of the hospital-oriented algorithm, each undersubscribed hospital has assigned to it all of the residents in its (reduced) list, for otherwise that hospital would have prevented termination of the loop. Further, a fully subscribed hospital with q places has assigned to it the first q residents in its (reduced) list. Note that, as in the case of the extended Gale-Shapley algorithm for the stable marriage problem, the pair removals have the effect that no offers are immediately rejected.

Also, as with the earlier Gale-Shapley algorithm (both the original and extended versions), the nondeterministic aspect of this algorithm is of no consequence, so that the provisional assignment of residents to hospitals on termination is uniquely defined for any hospitals/residents instance. Furthermore, it turns out that the matching defined by this provisional assignment is stable and, among all stable matchings, simultaneously optimal for all the hospitals. These facts are summarized in the following lemmas and theorem.

Lemma 1.6.1 *For a given instance of the hospitals/residents problem, all possible executions of the hospital-oriented extended Gale-Shapley algorithm terminate with the same preference lists.*

Proof Let E and E' be two different executions of the algorithm, and suppose that the pair (h, r) is deleted during E' but not during E. Suppose further that (h, r) is the first such pair deleted during E'.

The deletion of (h, r) must occur because r receives an offer from a better hospital h'. Therefore, during E, h' does not offer a place to r, and so h' must be fully subscribed with residents that it prefers to r. Therefore, during E', one of these residents, say r', must be deleted from the list of h' before h' makes an offer to r, contradicting our assumption. $\square$

We use the terminology *HGS-lists*, analogous to that introduced in Section 1.2.4 for the stable marriage problem, for the reduced preference lists generated by the hospital-oriented algorithm.

Lemma 1.6.2 *If the pair (h, r) is absent from the HGS-lists, then*
(i) (h, r) cannot be a stable pair;
(ii) r prefers all the hospitals in his HGS-list to h;
(iii) (h, r) cannot block any matching that is contained in the HGS-lists.

Proof (i) Suppose that (h, r) was the first stable pair deleted during a particular execution of the algorithm, and that it was deleted when hospital h' offered a place to r, so that r must prefer h' to h. So if $q(h')$ denotes the number of places available at hospital h', then the number of stable pairs (h', r') such that h' strictly prefers r' to r must be less than $q(h')$. For otherwise, one of these residents r' would have to have been deleted from the list of h' before h' offered a place to r, contradicting our assumption that (h, r) was the first stable pair deleted. Therefore, in any stable matching, h' is either undersubscribed or is assigned a resident who is inferior to r. It follows then that any supposed stable matching in which r is assigned to h is blocked by the pair (h', r).

(ii) This is immediate, because a hospital h is removed from r's list only when r becomes provisionally assigned to a hospital that he prefers to h.

(iii) This is an immediate consequence of (ii). □

Theorem 1.6.1 *(i) The matching specified by the provisional assignments after the execution of the hospital-oriented algorithm is stable.*
(ii) In this matching, a hospital h with q available places is assigned either its best q stable partners, or a set of fewer than q residents; in the latter case no other resident is assigned to h in any stable matching.
(iii) Each resident is assigned in this matching to his worst stable partner.

Proof (i) By part (iii) of the previous lemma, the matching in question cannot be blocked by any pair that is absent from the HGS-lists. Nor can it be blocked by any pair that is present in the HGS-lists, since the residents assigned to any hospital are at the head of that hospital's HGS-list.

(ii) If h's HGS-list contains at least q residents, then, after execution of the hospital-oriented algorithm, h is matched with the first q of these. Because no stable pair is absent from the HGS-lists, it follows that these are the q best stable partners for h.

On the other hand, if h's HGS-list contains fewer than q residents, then all of these are assigned to h in the matching, and, again because no stable pairs are absent, h has no other stable partners.

(iii) This follows also from Lemma 1.6.2, together with the fact that each resident is assigned to the last hospital in his HGS-list. □

In view of this theorem, we are justified in referring to the matching generated by the hospital-oriented algorithm as the *hospital-optimal* and *resident-pessimal* stable matching.

1.6.3   The Resident-Oriented Algorithm

We now set out analogous results for the resident-oriented version of the algorithm, which we express in terms of "proposals" from residents to hospitals. In this case, each resident proposes in sequence to the hospitals on his list, pausing whenever a provisional acceptance is received but continuing after any subsequent rejection, unless his list becomes empty. Each hospital, with, say, q available places, issues provisional acceptances to the best q residents who propose to it, and subsequently rejects the poorest of these if a better proposal comes along.

For the extended version of the algorithm that reduces the preference lists, we observe that deletions take place only when a particular hospital becomes fully subscribed, at which point all successors of its least favored provisionally assigned resident are removed from that hospital's list. The resident-oriented version of the algorithm is shown in Figure 1.16.

---

assign all residents to be free ;
assign all hospitals to be totally unsubscribed ;
while (some resident r is free) and (r has a nonempty list) do
begin
    $h :=$ first hospital on r's list ; $\{r$ "proposes" to $h\}$
    if h is fully subscribed then
        begin
            $r' :=$ worst resident provisionally assigned to h ;
            assign r' to be free
        end ;
    provisionally assign r to h ;
    if h is fully subscribed then
        begin
            $s :=$ worst resident provisionally assigned to h ;
            for each successor s' of s on h's list do
                remove s' and h from each other's lists
        end
end

Figure 1.16: Resident-oriented algorithm

It should be clear that, on termination of the resident-oriented algorithm, each assigned resident is provisionally assigned to the first hospital on his (reduced) list, and any unassigned resident has an empty list. We use the term *RGS-lists* for the reduced preference lists obtained by application of the resident-oriented algorithm.

The proofs of the following analogues of Lemmas 1.6.1, 1.6.2 and Theorem 1.6.1 are left as an exercise for the reader.

Lemma 1.6.3 *For a given instance of the hospitals/residents problem, all possible executions of the resident-oriented extended Gale-Shapley algorithm terminate with the same preference lists.*

Lemma 1.6.4 *If the pair (h, r) is absent from the RGS-lists then*
(i) (h, r) is not a stable pair;
(ii) h prefers all the residents in his RGS-list to r;
(iii) (h, r) cannot block any matching that is contained in the RGS-lists.

Theorem 1.6.2 *(i) The matching specified by the provisional assignments after the execution of the resident-oriented algorithm is stable.*
(ii) In this matching, each assigned resident is assigned to his best stable partner; each unassigned resident is unassigned in all stable matchings.

As a result of this theorem, we are justified in referring to the matching generated by the resident-oriented algorithm as the *resident-optimal* stable matching. However, we are not yet in a position to make a definitive statement about the "pessimality" of this matching from the point of view of the hospitals. It is certainly not true, for example, that a fully subscribed hospital with q places need be assigned its q worst stable partners in this matching. We shall resolve this matter fully in Section 1.6.5.

1.6.4   The "Rural Hospitals" Theorem

We are now in a position to state a theorem that gives us perhaps unexpected information concerning the stable matchings for a general instance of the hospitals/residents problem. The historical significance of this result, and its name, arose from the apparent uncertainty surrounding the operation of the NRMP algorithm when it was first introduced. Certain hospitals, mainly in rural areas, tended to be unpopular, and were declared to be unacceptable by a large number of residents. As a result, application of the NRMP algorithm (i.e., the hospital-oriented algorithm) resulted in such hospitals being significantly undersubscribed, and the question was posed as to whether some alternative algorithm for finding a stable matching might affect, either favorably or otherwise, the allocations made to such hospitals.

In fact, as we have seen in Theorem 1.6.1, no hospital can achieve a better allocation than in the hospital-optimal matching, and this is the matching derived by the NRMP algorithm. We will now show, in addition, that the number of residents assigned to any particular hospital is actually independent of the particular stable matching chosen, and that each undersubscribed hospital is allocated *exactly the same set* of residents in every stable matching. So, no matter what algorithm were used to find a stable matching, the "rural" hospitals would be neither better nor worse off than under the NRMP scheme.

In order to establish these results we state a preliminary lemma.

Lemma 1.6.5 *For a given instance of the hospitals/residents problem, let M be the resident-optimal matching and let M' be any stable matching. If a hospital h does not fill its quota in M', then every resident assigned to h in M is also assigned to h in M'.*

Proof If resident r were assigned to h in M but not in M', then (h, r) would block M', since h is undersubscribed in M' and r prefers h to any other of his stable partners. $\square$

Theorem 1.6.3 *For a given hospitals/residents instance,*
(i) each hospital is assigned the same number of residents in all stable matchings;
(ii) exactly the same residents are unassigned in all stable matchings;
(iii) any hospital that is undersubscribed in one stable matching is matched with precisely the same set of residents in all stable matchings.

Proof (i) Let M be the resident-optimal matching and let M' be any other stable matching. We first observe that any resident unassigned in M must be unassigned in every stable matching, by Lemma 1.6.4(i), since his RGS-list is empty. Therefore, the number of residents assigned to hospitals in M' cannot exceed the number assigned in M.

By Lemma 1.6.5, any hospital that fills all of its places in M also does so in M'. Also by Lemma 1.6.5, any hospital that has unfilled places in M must fill at least as many places in M'. So *every* hospital fills at least as many places in M' as in M. However, as already observed, the total number of residents assigned in M' cannot exceed the total number assigned in M, so in fact each hospital that is undersubscribed in M has exactly the same number of assigned residents in M'.

(ii) This follows from (i) and from the fact that no resident who is unassigned in M can be assigned in M'.

(iii) This follows immediately from (i) and Lemma 1.6.5. $\square$

In addition to its intrinsic interest, the Rural Hospitals Theorem implies that when we are interested in studying the structure of the set of stable matchings in the hospitals/residents problem, or in solving any of those variants of the basic matching problem that we will consider in Chapter 3, we may reduce the problem to one where the number of places is exactly equal to the number of residents. We outline the reasons for this.

Consider the GS-lists, formed by intersecting the HGS-list and the RGS-list for each hospital and resident. As was the case in the stable marriage context, no pair that is absent from the GS-lists can be stable, nor can it block any matching embedded in those lists. If we take the GS-lists for just the fully subscribed hospitals and the residents assigned to these hospitals, then it follows from the Rural Hospitals theorem that none of the *other* hospitals or residents is present in any of these lists, and so none of them can be part of a blocking pair for any embedded matching. We can regard these lists as defining a new hospitals/residents instance for which

the number of places is equal to the number of residents. It follows that the
stable matchings for the new instance, augmented by the fixed matching
involving the undersubscribed hospitals, are precisely the stable matchings
for the original instance.

1.6.5   Dominance in Hospitals/Residents Matchings

It is natural to regard a resident r as preferring a matching M to a matching
M' if r is assigned to a better hospital in M than in M'. This is the same
extended notion of preference as was used in the stable marriage problem
in section 1.3.1. A (resident-oriented) dominance relation can therefore be
defined on the set of stable matchings in a manner exactly analogous to the
(man-oriented) dominance relation of Section 1.3.1, namely, a matching M
dominates a matching M' if and only if every resident either prefers M to
M' or is indifferent in choosing between them.

On the other hand, it is not immediately apparent that every two stable
matchings M and M' are directly comparable from the point of view of a
particular hospital. Nor is it clear what is the precise implication for the
hospitals if M dominates M' from the point of view of the residents.

However, we shall see in this section that any hospital does indeed have an
unambiguous strict preference between any two stable matchings in which
it is not assigned identical sets of residents. As a consequence, the inverse
of the resident-oriented dominance relation has a natural and unambiguous
interpretation as hospital-oriented dominance.

The next lemma is somewhat analogous to Theorem 1.3.1, and it provides
the basis of the proof of unambiguous hospital preferences between stable
matchings.

Lemma 1.6.6 *Let M and M' be stable matchings for a hospitals/residents
instance, and suppose that resident r is assigned to hospital h in M, but
not in M'. If r prefers M to M' then h prefers the least-favored resident in
$p_{M'}(h) \setminus p_M(h)$ to the least-favored resident in $p_M(h) \setminus p_{M'}(h)$. Likewise, if r
prefers M' to M then h prefers the least-favored resident in $p_M(h) \setminus p_{M'}(h)$
to the least-favored resident in $p_{M'}(h) \setminus p_M(h)$.*

Proof   Let $\mathcal{R}$ and $\mathcal{R}'$ denote the sets of residents who (strictly) prefer
M to M' and M' to M, respectively. Let $\mathcal{H}$ denote the set of hospitals h
that prefer the least-favored resident in $p_M(h) \setminus p_{M'}(h)$ to the least-favored
resident in $p_{M'}(h) \setminus p_M(h)$. Let $\mathcal{H}'$ denote the set of hospitals h that prefer
the least-favored resident in $p_{M'}(h) \setminus p_M(h)$ to the least-favored resident
in $p_M(h) \setminus p_{M'}(h)$. Note that $\mathcal{R} \cap \mathcal{R}' = \emptyset$, and that every resident that
is assigned to different hospitals in M and M' is in either $\mathcal{R}$ or $\mathcal{R}'$. Note

also that $\mathcal{H} \cap \mathcal{H}' = \emptyset$, and that every hospital that has nonidentical sets of residents in M and M' is in either $\mathcal{H}$ or $\mathcal{H}'$. In order to prove the lemma, it will suffice to establish that (i) $r \in \mathcal{R} \Longrightarrow p_M(r) \in \mathcal{H}'$, and (ii) $r \in \mathcal{R}' \Longrightarrow p_M(r) \in \mathcal{H}$.

In M, no resident in $\mathcal{R}$ can be assigned to a hospital in $\mathcal{H}$, for that resident and hospital would block M'. So every resident in $\mathcal{R}$ is assigned in M to a hospital in $\mathcal{H}'$. So we have established the first of our requirements, and it also follows that

$$|\mathcal{R}| \le \sum_{h \in H'} n(h), \qquad (1.6.1)$$

where $n(h)$ denotes the number of residents who are assigned to h in M but not in M'.

Similarly, in M', no resident in $\mathcal{R}'$ can be assigned to a hospital in $\mathcal{H}'$, for that resident and hospital would block M. So every resident in $\mathcal{R}'$ is assigned in M' to a hospital in $\mathcal{H}$, and therefore

$$|\mathcal{R}'| \le \sum_{h \in H} n'(h), \qquad (1.6.2)$$

where $n'(h)$ denotes the number of residents who are assigned to h in M' but not in M.

Further,

$$|\mathcal{R}| + |\mathcal{R}'| = \sum_{h \in H'} n(h) + \sum_{h \in H} n'(h), \qquad (1.6.3)$$

since each side represents the number of residents assigned to different hospitals in M and M'. This is obvious for the left-hand side and is also true for the right-hand side, because, as already observed, every hospital that is assigned nonidentical sets of residents in M and M' is in $\mathcal{H}$ or $\mathcal{H}'$, but not both.

Hence, 1.6.1, 1.6.2 and 1.6.3 together imply that 1.6.1 is satisfied with equality (as indeed is 1.6.2). Therefore, in M, every resident in $\mathcal{R}'$ must be assigned to a hospital in $\mathcal{H}$, and this completes the proof. $\square$

We can now establish the result referred to above that any particular hospital h does indeed have an unambiguous strict preference between any two stable matchings in which its sets of assigned residents are not identical.

Theorem 1.6.4 *Suppose that M and M' are two stable matchings for a hospitals/residents instance, and that hospital h is assigned nonidentical sets of residents in M and M'. If h prefers the least favored resident in $p_M(h) \setminus p_{M'}(h)$ to the least favored resident in $p_{M'}(h) \setminus p_M(h)$, then h prefers all residents in $p_M(h)$ to all residents in $p_{M'}(h) \setminus p_M(h)$.*

Proof Let r be an arbitrary member of $p_M(h)$ and r' be an arbitrary member of $p_{M'}(h) \setminus p_M(h)$. In the notation of the proof of Lemma 1.6.6, h is a member of the set $\mathcal{H}$, and so r' must be a member of the set $\mathcal{R}'$. So r' prefers h (his assigned hospital in $\mathcal{M}'$) to his assigned hospital in M. If h were to prefer r' to r, then the pair (r', h) would block M, so that h must prefer r to r'. Since r and r' were chosen arbitrarily from their sets, the claimed result follows. $\square$

So we have established that any hospital either prefers all its M-partners to any of its M'-partners who are not also M-partners, or prefers all its M'-partners to any of its M-partners who are not also M'-partners. In the former case, it is natural to say that the hospital prefers M to M', and in the latter, that it prefers M' to M.

The hospital-oriented dominance relation may now be defined in the obvious way on the set of stable matchings for a hospitals/residents instance, and it is an immediate consequence of Lemma 1.6.6 that this is the inverse of the resident-oriented dominance relation defined earlier. It can be shown in a manner quite similar to the argument of Section 1.3, that the set of stable matchings forms a distributive lattice under this dominance relation. The only difference of substance concerns the precise meaning of $M \wedge M'$ and $M \vee M'$, with respect to hospitals. It follows from Lemma 1.6.6 and Theorem 1.6.4 that if $M \wedge M'$ is defined as the usual mapping from residents to hospitals, in which each resident is assigned to the better of his partners in M and M', then the result is a stable matching; in $M \wedge M'$ each hospital is assigned the entire set of residents that it was assigned in whichever of M and M' it likes least. Note that this is not necessarily the same thing as assigning to each hospital the worst residents that it is assigned in either M or M'.

If $M \vee M'$ is defined as the usual mapping from residents to hospitals, in which each resident is assigned to the poorer of his partners in M and M', then again the result is a stable matching; in $M \vee M'$, each hospital is assigned the entire set of residents that it was assigned in whichever of M, M' it prefers. In this case, because of Theorem 1.6.4, this *is* the same as saying that each hospital is assigned to the best residents that it is assigned in either M or M'.

We can also use Theorem 1.6.4 to describe precisely the sense in which the resident-optimal stable matching is also the hospital-pessimal. It is not necessarily true, as the example below will illustrate, that in the resident-optimal matching, a hospital that fills all of its q places is assigned its q worst stable partners. (Of course, this *is* true, in a trivial way, by the Rural Hospitals theorem, if the hospital does not fill all of its places.) However, if R is the resident-optimal and R' any other stable matching, then every hospital prefers all the residents assigned to it in R' to all of those assigned to it in R but not in R'.

We conclude this subsection with an example to illustrate the various aspects of the hospitals/residents problem that we have discussed.

Example Consider the instance involving 5 hospitals $h_1, \ldots, h_5$ and 11 residents $r_1, \ldots, r_{11}$ with the preference lists given in Figure 1.17

r_1	h_3	h_1	h_5	h_4	
r_2	h_1	h_3	h_4	h_2	h_5
r_3	h_4	h_5	h_3	h_1	h_2
r_4	h_3	h_4	h_1	h_5	
r_5	h_1	h_4	h_2		
r_6	h_4	h_3	h_2	h_1	h_5
r_7	h_2	h_5	h_1	h_3	
r_8	h_1	h_3	h_2	h_5	h_4
r_9	h_4	h_1	h_5		
r_{10}	h_3	h_1	h_5	h_2	h_4
r_{11}	h_5	h_4	h_1	h_3	h_2

Residents' Preferences

(4)	h_1	r_3	r_7	r_9	r_{11}	r_5	r_4	r_{10}	r_8	r_6	r_1	r_2
(3)	h_2	r_5	r_7	r_{10}	r_6	r_8	r_2	r_3	r_{11}			
(3)	h_3	r_{11}	r_6	r_8	r_3	r_2	r_4	r_7	r_1	r_{10}		
(2)	h_4	r_{10}	r_1	r_2	r_{11}	r_4	r_9	r_5	r_3	r_6	r_8	
(1)	h_5	r_2	r_4	r_{10}	r_7	r_6	r_1	r_8	r_3	r_{11}	r_9	

Places   Hospitals' Preferences

Figure 1.17: A particular hospitals/residents instance

The hospital-oriented algorithm may proceed as follows, where "$h \to r$" means that hospital h "offers a place" to resident r, causing r to become provisionally assigned to h, and "(r, h) deleted" means that resident r and hospital h are removed from each other's lists:

- $h_1 \to r_3$; (r_3, h_2) deleted;

- $h_1 \to r_7$; (r_7, h_3) deleted;

- $h_1 \to r_9$;

- $h_1 \rightarrow r_{11}$; (r_{11}, h_3), (r_{11}, h_2) deleted; h_1 now fully subscribed;

- $h_2 \rightarrow r_5$;

- $h_2 \rightarrow r_7$; (r_7, h_5), (r_7, h_1) deleted; r_7 no longer assigned to h_1, so h_1 undersubscribed;

- $h_1 \rightarrow r_5$; (r_5, h_4), (r_5, h_2) deleted; r_5 no longer assigned to h_2; h_1 again fully subscribed;

- $h_2 \rightarrow r_{10}$; (r_{10}, h_4) deleted;

- $h_2 \rightarrow r_6$; (r_6, h_1), (r_6, h_5) deleted; h_2 now fully subscribed;

- $h_3 \rightarrow r_6$; (r_6, h_2) deleted; r_6 no longer assigned to h_2, so h_2 undersubscribed;

- $h_2 \rightarrow r_8$; (r_8, h_5) deleted; h_2 again fully subscribed;

- $h_3 \rightarrow r_8$; (r_8, h_2) deleted; r_8 no longer assigned to h_2, so h_2 undersubscribed;

- $h_2 \rightarrow r_2$; h_2 again fully subscribed;

- $h_3 \rightarrow r_3$; (r_3, h_1) deleted; r_3 no longer assigned to h_1, so h_1 undersubscribed; h_3 now fully subscribed;

- $h_1 \rightarrow r_4$; (r_4, h_5) deleted; h_1 again fully subscribed;

- $h_4 \rightarrow r_1$;

- $h_4 \rightarrow r_2$; (r_2, h_2), (r_2, h_5) deleted; r_2 no longer assigned to h_2, so h_2 undersubscribed; h_4 now fully subscribed; h_2 has exhausted its list;

- $h_5 \rightarrow r_{10}$; (r_{10}, h_2) deleted; r_{10} no longer assigned to h_2.

All residents are now assigned, so the hospital-optimal stable matching is: $\{(h_1, \{r_9, r_{11}, r_4, r_5\}), (h_2, \{r_7\}), (h_3, \{r_6, r_8, r_3\}), (h_4, \{r_1, r_2\}), (h_5, \{r_{10}\})\}$.

The resident-oriented algorithm may proceed as follows, where $r \rightarrow h$ means that resident r "proposes" to hospital h, causing r to become provisionally assigned to h, and "(h, r) deleted" means that hospital h and resident r are removed from each other's lists.

- $r_1 \rightarrow h_3$;

- $r_2 \rightarrow h_1$;

- $r_3 \rightarrow h_4$;

- $r_4 \rightarrow h_3$;

- $r_5 \rightarrow h_1$;

- $r_6 \rightarrow h_4$; (h_4, r_8) deleted, since h_4 now fully subscribed;

- $r_7 \rightarrow h_2$;

- $r_8 \rightarrow h_1$;

- $r_9 \rightarrow h_4$; h_4, r_6) deleted; r_6 no longer assigned to h_4, so r_6 is free again;

- $r_6 \rightarrow h_3$; (h_3, r_{10}) deleted, since h_3 now fully subscribed;

- $r_{10} \rightarrow h_1$; h_1 now fully subscribed, but no consequent deletions;

- $r_{11} \rightarrow h_5$; (h_5, r_9) deleted, since h_5 now fully subscribed.

All residents are now assigned, so the resident-optimal stable matching is: $\{(r_1, h_3),\ (r_2, h_1),\ (r_3, h_4),\ (r_4, h_3),\ (r_5, h_1),\ (r_6, h_3),\ (r_7, h_2),\ (r_8, h_1),\ (r_9, h_4),\ (r_{10}, h_1),\ (r_{11}, h_5)\}$.

The GS-lists (obtained by intersecting the HGS-lists and RGS-lists) are shown in Figure 1.18.

r_1	h_3	h_1	h_5	h_4
r_2	h_1	h_3	h_4	
r_3	h_4	h_5	h_3	
r_4	h_3	h_4	h_1	
r_5	h_1			
r_6	h_3			
r_7	h_2			
r_8	h_1	h_3		
r_9	h_4	h_1		
r_{10}	h_1	h_5		
r_{11}	h_5	h_4	h_1	

Residents' Preferences

(4)	h_1	r_9	r_{11}	r_5	r_4	r_{10}	r_8	r_1	r_2
(3)	h_2	r_7							
(3)	h_3	r_6	r_8	r_3	r_2	r_4	r_1		
(2)	h_4	r_1	r_2	r_{11}	r_4	r_9	r_3		
(1)	h_5	r_{10}	r_1	r_3	r_{11}				

Places   Hospitals' Preferences

Figure 1.18: The GS-lists

In fact, there are a total of 7 stable matchings for this particular problem instance, and these are listed in Figure 1.19; M_1 is the resident-optimal and M_7 the hospital-optimal matching already seen.

Matching	r_1	r_2	r_3	r_4	r_5	r_6	r_7	r_8	r_9	r_{10}	r_{11}
M_1	h_3	h_1	h_4	h_3	h_1	h_3	h_2	h_1	h_4	h_1	h_5
M_2	h_1	h_3	h_4	h_3	h_1	h_3	h_2	h_1	h_4	h_1	h_5
M_3	h_3	h_1	h_5	h_3	h_1	h_3	h_2	h_1	h_4	h_1	h_4
M_4	h_1	h_3	h_5	h_3	h_1	h_3	h_2	h_1	h_4	h_1	h_4
M_5	h_5	h_3	h_3	h_4	h_1	h_3	h_2	h_1	h_1	h_1	h_4
M_6	h_5	h_4	h_3	h_1	h_1	h_3	h_2	h_3	h_1	h_1	h_4
M_7	h_4	h_4	h_3	h_1	h_1	h_3	h_2	h_3	h_1	h_5	h_1

Figure 1.19: The stable matchings

The lattice structure under the resident-dominance relation is shown in Figure 1.20.

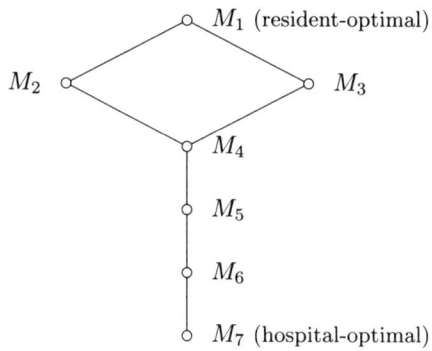

Figure 1.20: Lattice structure for the hospitals/residents instance

As an illustration of Theorem 1.6.4 on unambiguous preferences, Figure 1.21 indicates the residents assigned to hospital h_1 in the various stable matchings. It is easy to verify that h_1 has an unambiguous preference between all pairs of stable matchings (excluding those pairs in which it is assigned identical sets of residents).

Finally, we observe that this example illustrates that one of the results proved in the context of stable marriage does not have a direct analogue in the hospitals/residents case, namely the weak Pareto optimality property described in Section 1.2.2. It is true that there is no matching, stable or otherwise, that is preferred

Matching	r_3	r_7	r_9	r_{11}	r_5	r_4	r_{10}	r_8	r_6	r_1	r_2
M_1					*		*	*			*
M_2					*		*	*		*	
M_3					*		*	*			*
M_4					*		*	*		*	
M_5			*		*		*	*			
M_6			*		*	*	*				
M_7			*	*	*	*					

Figure 1.21: Residents assigned to hospital h_1

by all the residents to the resident optimal, and this may be proved by an argument similar to Theorem 1.2.4. However, with the natural assumption that a hospital prefers a matching M to a matching M' if it prefers all the residents assigned to it in M but not in M' to all of those assigned to it in M' but not in M, there is no corresponding result for the hospital optimal matching. In the present case, the matching $\{(h_1, \{r_3, r_7, r_9, r_4\}), (h_2, \{r_5\}), (h_3, \{r_{11}, r_6, r_8\}), (h_4, \{r_{10}, r_1\}), (h_5, \{r_2\})\}$. (which is, of course, unstable) is preferred to the hospital-optimal by all of the hospitals.

1.6.6   The Hospitals/Residents Problem with Couples

An extension of the hospitals/residents problem that is of considerable practical interest involves treating certain pairs of residents as couples, and allowing each such couple to submit a joint preference list consisting of ordered pairs of hospitals. This allows for the possibility that certain pairs of residents may be married, and may wish to avoid enforced separation. Indeed, in recent years, attempts have been made to cater for couples in the NRMP algorithm in precisely this way, in response to the observation that an increasing number of couples were choosing not to enter the centralized matching process (presumably because it failed to properly take account of their joint preferences). However, as we shall see in the example below, there is a fundamental problem involved in attempting to extend the algorithm to cope with couples' joint preferences, namely that in this more general setting, stable matchings may not exist, and even if they do, it may be hard to find them.

More precisely, in an instance of the hospitals/residents problem with couples,

   i. each hospital provides a preference list of acceptable residents, and has a fixed number of places to fill, as before;

ii. each *single* resident (i.e., one who is not a member of a couple) submits a preference list of acceptable hospitals, as before;

iii. each couple (r, s) provides a joint preference list, each entry of which is an ordered pair (h, k) of (not necessarily distinct) hospitals representing the assignment of r to h and s to k; of course, no resident can be a member of more than one couple.

In this situation, a matching M is unstable if at least one of the following conditions holds:

(a) the matching is blocked by a hospital h and a single resident r; i.e., h and r are mutually acceptable, r prefers h to $p_M(r)$, and h is either undersubscribed or prefers r to at least one of its assigned residents in M.

(b) the matching is blocked by a hospital h and a resident r who is coupled, say with s; that is, r is acceptable to h, (r, s) prefers $(h, p_M(s))$ to $(p_M(r), p_M(s))$, and h is either undersubscribed in M or prefers r to at least one of its assigned residents in M.

(c) the matching is blocked by a couple (r_1, r_2) and (not necessarily distinct) hospitals $h_1 \neq p_M(r_1)$, $h_2 \neq p_M(r_2)$; that is, r_1 is acceptable to h_1 and r_2 to h_2, (r_1, r_2) prefers the joint assignment (h_1, h_2) to $(p_M(r_1), p_M(r_2))$, and, for $i = 1, 2$, h_i is either undersubscribed in M or prefers r_i to at least one of its assigned residents in M.

Example Consider an example involving 4 residents r, s, t and u, with r and s forming a couple, and 2 hospitals h and k each with 2 available places. To illustrate the 3 ways in which a matching may be blocked, suppose that the preference lists are as shown in Figure 1.22.

h	r	t	s	u
k	s	r	t	u

Hospitals' Preferences

(r,s)	(h,h)	(k,k)	(k,h)	(h,k)
t	h	k		
u	k	h		

Residents' Preferences

Figure 1.22: A hospitals/residents instance with couples

Then, for example, the matching in which r and s are assigned to h, and t and u to k is blocked by h and t, since h prefers t to s and t prefers h to k. The matching in which r and t are assigned to h, and s and u to k is blocked by k and r, since k

prefers r to u and (r, s) prefers (k, k) to (h, k). The matching in which t and u are assigned to h, and r and s to k is blocked by the couple (r, s) and the hospital pair (indistinct in this case) (h, h), since h prefers r to t and s to u, and (r, s) prefers (h, h) to (k, k).

In fact, none of the possible matchings for this particular problem instance is stable; Figure 1.23 lists all the possible matchings, with a blocking pair for each.

Assignment		Blocked by
h	k	
r,s	t,u	h and t
r,t	s,u	k and r
r,u	s,t	h and t
s,t	r,u	h and r
s,u	r,t	h and t
t,u	r,s	(h,h) and (r,s)

Figure 1.23: Blocking pairs for all the matchings

This example illustrates the crucial difference between the standard version of the hospitals/residents problem and the version that allows couples, namely that there are instances of the latter that admit no stable matchings. So, the problem arises of finding an efficient algorithm that will determine, for a given instance of the problem with couples, whether a stable matching exists, and if so, will determine such a matching. However, not only is there no known polynomial-time algorithm for this problem but the problem has been shown to be NP-complete, so that it is not likely that such an algorithm will be found. This fact, the proof of which we omit, may be established by a reduction rather similar to that used in Section 4.5.3 to prove the NP-completeness of the version of the stable roommates problem that allows indifference.

1.6.7 Many-Many Matchings

A natural extension of many-one stable matching problems is to the many-many case, in which each member of both sets has one or more "places" to fill. In this case, a matching is a set of pairs, each pair containing one member of each set, and each element appearing in a number of pairs that does not exceed its number of places. A matching is unstable if there is an x in one set and a y in the other, acceptable to each other but not forming a pair, such that both of the following conditions hold:

    i. either x has unfilled places, or x prefers y to at least one of its partners, and

    ii. either y has unfilled places, or y prefers x to at least one of its partners.

It turns out that relevant aspects of the hospital and resident oriented versions of the Gale-Shapley algorithm can be combined to produce a version appropriate for this more general situation, and the resulting algorithm finds stable matchings that are optimal for one or other of the sets. So once again, the existence of a stable matching in all cases is guaranteed. Furthermore, the full lattice structure is again present, and a preference result analogous to that of Theorem 1.6.4 can be proved for the members of both sets. The details are left as an exercise for the reader.

1.7 Deceit, Coalitions, and Strategy

In this section we consider, in the context of both the stable marriage and hospitals/residents problems, questions about what can be achieved if a party (a person, hospital, or coalition) is deceitful and does not report its true preferences. There are several ways to model such a possibility, but the simplest way, which we will follow, is to assume that the deceitful party knows the true preferences of all the other parties, and that those preferences will be truthfully reported to the algorithm. Knowing those preferences, knowing the matching algorithm, and having infinite computational power, the problem for the deceitful party is to decide how it should falsify its preferences in order to optimize (with respect to its true preferences) the partner(s) it gets.

1.7.1 Machiavelli Meets Gale-Shapley

Here we discuss the most notable results about deceit and strategy in the case of the stable marriage problem. We will show that in some cases honesty is the best policy, but in general, lying cannot be totally discouraged in the stable marriage problem. We first need the following valuable lemma.

Lemma 1.7.1 *Suppose M is a matching and that the set $\mathcal{X}$ of men who strictly prefer their partners in M to their partners in M_0 (the man-optimal matching) is nonempty. Then there is a man $m \notin \mathcal{X}$ and a woman w such that (m, w) blocks M.*

Proof Matching M is clearly unstable, since there are men who strictly prefer it to M_0, so some pair must block M. We want to show that some man not in $\mathcal{X}$ is part of a blocking pair. Define $\mathcal{Y}$ to be the set of women who are partners of the men in $\mathcal{X}$ in matching M_0. The proof is divided into two cases.

In the first case, suppose there is some man m' in $\mathcal{X}$ who is matched in M to a woman w not in $\mathcal{Y}$. Since m' strictly prefers w to his partner in M_0, the stability of M_0 implies that w strictly prefers $p_{M_0}(w)$, say m, to m'. But $w \notin \mathcal{Y}$ implies $m \notin \mathcal{X}$, and $p_M(m) \neq w$, so m strictly prefers w to his $p_M(m)$. Therefore, in the first case, (m, w) blocks M, and $m \notin \mathcal{X}$, as desired.

In the second case, suppose that every man in $\mathcal{X}$ is matched in M with a woman in $\mathcal{Y}$, although, of course, the actual matching of the men in $\mathcal{X}$ with the women in $\mathcal{Y}$ is different in M and M_0. Because of the stability of M_0, every woman in $\mathcal{Y}$ prefers her partner in M_0 to her partner in M, and so during any execution of the Gale-Shapley algorithm, each such woman rejects her M-partner. Suppose that during a particular, arbitrary, execution of the Gale-Shapley algorithm, m' is the last man in $\mathcal{X}$ who makes a proposal; let w be the woman to whom this last proposal is made. Clearly, $w = p_{M_0}(m')$, so w is in $\mathcal{Y}$. Since w rejected $p_M(w)$ during the execution, w must be engaged, to m say, when m' proposes to her. So m is rejected in favor of m', and since m goes on to make a proposal, m is not in $\mathcal{X}$. Then, by definition of $\mathcal{X}$, m does not prefer his partner in M to his partner in M_0, and so m strictly prefers w to $p_M(m)$.

Similarly, since $m \notin \mathcal{X}$ is the last man rejected by w during the execution producing M_0, and $w \in \mathcal{Y}$ rejected $p_M(w) \in \mathcal{X}$ during this execution, w strictly prefers m to $p_M(w)$. Therefore, (m, w) blocks M and $m \notin \mathcal{X}$, as desired. $\square$

We now consider the question of whether a man, or a coalition of men, might gain by falsifying preferences. We let P designate the true preference lists, let $\mathcal{L}$ be the set of men who falsify their true preferences, and let P' be the preference lists incorporating the falsified preferences.

Theorem 1.7.1 *There is no stable matching, with respect to P', in which every man in $\mathcal{L}$ gets a partner he strictly prefers (with respect to P) to his partner in M_0.*

Proof Let M be a matching in which some set of men $\mathcal{L}' \supseteq \mathcal{L}$ get partners they prefer (with respect to P) to their partners in M_0. By Lemma 1.7.1 there is a pair (m, w) that blocks M (with respect to P) such that m is not in $\mathcal{L}'$. But then, m is not in $\mathcal{L}$, so P' contains the truthful preferences of both m and w, and therefore (m, w) must also block M with respect to P'.

So there is no stable matching in which every man in $\mathcal{L}$ improves over his partner in M_0. $\square$

Note that when the coalition consists of a single man, Theorem 1.7.1 says that no man can improve over his M_0-partner by lying. Note also that Theorem 1.7.1 does not rule out the possibility that *some* of the liars are better off than in M_0, while none of them obtains a worse partner than in M_0. In fact, this can happen, as we will see later. Hence, it might only take a small inducement to persuade the men who remain with their M_0-partners to cooperate with the men who improve partners, making lying an appealing strategy. However, if we insist that the only inducement that motivates a person to lie is strict improvement of that person's assigned partner, then we can in fact strengthen Theorem 1.7.1 to rule out lying by multi-gender coalitions.

Theorem 1.7.2 *Even if women, as well as men, are involved in a coalition, it is not possible for the members of the coalition to collectively falsify their preferences so that every one of them obtains a better partner than in M_0.*

Proof First note that woman w in the blocking pair (m, w) from the proof of Lemma 1.7.1 prefers her M_0-partner to her M-partner, as does man m of that pair. Hence, if $\mathcal{L}$ is now a set of men and women who falsify their true preferences P, and M is a matching in which some set of people $\mathcal{L}' \supset \mathcal{L}$ get improved partners compared to their M_0-partners, then neither m nor w is in $\mathcal{L}'$, and so neither is in $\mathcal{L}$. Therefore, P' contains the true preferences of m and w, and so (m, w) blocks M with respect to P', as well as with respect to P. $\square$

Note that Lemma 1.7.1 and Theorems 1.7.1 and 1.7.2 apply to the stable marriage problem with either unequal numbers of men and women or incomplete preference lists. In these cases, the resulting matching may be a partial matching.

Theorem 1.7.1 says that when the man-oriented Gale-Shapley algorithm is used, no man has an incentive to lie, but it also answers another more Machiavellian issue. Suppose it is possible to use some stable matching method that produces a stable matching other than the Gale-Shapley method — one that does not always produce the man-optimal matching. Clearly, the men would normally be expected to oppose the use of any such method. However, it is conceivable that some other method would be more manipulable than the Gale-Shapley method, so that some men might support its use, believing that by lying to it they could achieve better results than by honestly using the Gale-Shapley algorithm. Theorem 1.7.1 says that any such belief is an illusion, since it says that in *no* stable matching can all the liars improve. The best strategy for the men is to insist that the man-oriented Gale-Shapley algorithm be used. However, Theorem 1.7.1 should not be interpreted as saying that the men can never benefit by lying, no matter what stable matching method is used, for, as we will show next, lying may be beneficial to the men when the woman-oriented Gale-Shapley method is used.

1.7.2   Optimal Lying by Men

Let M_0 refer throughout this subsection to the man-optimal matching with respect to the true preferences P.

Theorem 1.7.3 *Even when the woman-oriented Gale-Shapley algorithm is used, producing the woman-optimal matching, the men can force the algorithm to produce the man-optimal matching (with respect to P) by submitting false preferences.*

Proof   Each man m falsifies his preference list, creating preferences P', by declaring as unacceptable any woman inferior to $p_{M_0}(m)$ on his true preference list. Clearly, by the way P' is constructed, if the man-oriented Gale-Shapley algorithm is applied to P', it again gives M_0, the man- optimal matching for P. Further, since in M_0 every man has his worst possible partner in P', M_0 is the only stable matching for P'. Therefore, M_0 is the stable matching produced by the woman-oriented Gale-Shapley algorithm applied to P'. $\square$

The above lying strategy has a stability property that encourages the men to carry through with the lies that they have agreed upon. Suppose the men agree among themselves to lie in the way specified above, but before their P' lists are reported, some subset of men form a coalition to consider double-crossing the rest of the men. These double-crossers assume that the other men will carry through with their agreed upon lies, and that the women will all submit their true preferences. Then the problem facing the double-crossers is to find preference lists to report, which optimize (with respect to P) the partners they obtain. Even if no such double-cross occurs, each man might worry that it is happening, and therefore reconsider his participation in the lie. The next theorem says that no coalition should waste its time looking for a better way to cheat, and so no man should worry that such double-dealing is occurring.

Theorem 1.7.4 *Let $\mathcal{L}$ be a subset of men, and let M be any matching in which each man in $\mathcal{L}$ prefers his M-partner to his M_0-partner. Assuming* *that each man not in $\mathcal{L}$ reports his P' list, and all women report their P lists, there is no set of lists that $\mathcal{L}$ can report such that M is stable with respect to the reported lists.*

Proof Suppose some subset $\mathcal{L}$ of the men falsify their agreed upon lists, creating preferences $P_{\mathcal{L}}$ rather than the agreed upon preference lists P'. Now M_0 is the only stable matching in P', so it is clearly the man-optimal matching in P' as well as in P. Therefore, if the men in $\mathcal{L}$ all strictly improve (with respect to P) as a result of double-dealing, then they must all receive better partners than they get in the man optimal matching in P'. But Theorem 1.7.1 says that it is impossible for all men in $\mathcal{L}$ to strictly improve their partners in P' by lying. $\square$

It may seem unsatisfactory that the optimal lying strategy for the men requires the declaration of some women as unacceptable, as this may not always be permitted by the matching system. Apparently, however, little is known about what can be achieved by lies that merely permute the original order of the women on a man's list; we will return to this issue in Section 1.8.

1.7.3 Machiavellian Hospitals

We observe at this point that Theorem 1.7.1 does not generalize to the case of the hospitals/residents problem. It follows from Theorem 1.7.1 that no coalition of *residents* has any incentive to falsify preferences if the resident-oriented algorithm is used. However, when the hospital-oriented algorithm is used, it is not true that the hospitals never have an incentive to lie, as illustrated in the following example.

Example Consider the instance specified by the preference lists in Figure 1.24, in which hospital 1 has 2 positions and hospitals 2 and 3 each have 1. The only stable matching is $(1, \{3, 4\}), (2, \{2\}), (3, \{1\})$. Now consider what happens if hospital 1 lies, reporting a preference order of 2,4,1,3, and all other parties report their preferences honestly. Then the matching $(1, \{2, 4\}), (2, \{1\}), (3, \{3\})$ is stable and hospital-optimal (with respect to the reported preferences), because it fills the positions of each of the hospitals with its most preferred residents. Further, hospital 1 has improved the set of residents that it receives, compared to what it gets when it reports its preferences honestly.

If one did not know otherwise, it might be tempting to believe that Theorem 1.7.1 would apply to the hospitals/residents problem and could be proved via the reduction of the hospitals/residents problem to the stable

1		1	2	3	4	1		3	1	2
2		1	2	3	4	2		2	1	3
3		3	1	2	4	3		1	3	2
						4		1	2	3

Hospitals' Preferences   Residents' Preferences

Figure 1.24: Hospital lying helps

marriage problem discussed in Section 1.6.1. It is worth taking some time
to consider why the reduction does not imply the suggested theorem.

When the hospitals/residents problem is reduced, via cloning of hospitals,
to an instance of the stable marriage problem (making each clone a man),
and the man-oriented Gale-Shapley algorithm is used, Theorem 1.7.1 correctly implies that none of the newly created men has an incentive to lie, for
no coalition of men can *all* improve their lot by lying. Hence no matter how
the hospitals lie, it is not possible for all the associated men (cloned hospitals) to simultaneously improve as a result. But a hospital receives a *set* of
residents, and so even if it cannot improve every entry in that set by lying,
it certainly would prefer a set where some of the entries improve and the
others remain the same, and it might even prefer a set where a loss in some
entries is more than compensated for by large improvements in other entries.
Theorem 1.7.1 does not exclude the possibility of obtaining these improved
sets by lying. And, this is precisely what the example of this section shows
can happen. A similar explanation holds for why Theorem 1.2.4, concerning
weak Pareto optimality in the stable marriage problem, does not generalize
to the hospitals/residents problem (see the remark in the example on page
51). Also, when the hospitals in that example have been cloned into men,
the resulting preference lists provide an example where lying by some men
can give some of the liars improved partners, while leaving the partners of
the other liars unchanged.

To end this section, we consider a more Machiavellian way to use a good
lie. Suppose hospital h lies and receives as a result a better set of residents
than it would otherwise have received. That matching must be unstable
with respect to the true preferences. But where is the blocking pair? The
matching is stable with respect to the publicly reported (distorted) preferences, and so none of the truth-telling hospitals can be part of a blocking
pair, for their true preferences and those of the residents were used in finding

the matching. So it is one of the lying hospitals that is in a blocking pair. Therefore, after the matching is determined, a lying hospital h not only has a better set of residents than it would have had without lying, but there is at least one resident r who prefers h to his assigned hospital, and is preferred by h to one of its assigned residents r'. Since we assume that no one is required to accept their given assignment, as is the case in NRMP, h can now drop r' and pick up r, further improving its set of residents. In our illustrative example, hospital 1 can drop resident 4 in favor of resident 1. Of course, this may set off another wave of proposals, negotiations, etc., and a system would be unlikely to remain intact in the face of such post-assignment jockeying. Further, the truthful hospitals might (correctly) conclude that the hospitals initiating the new round of proposals had been dishonest in the first place. So in the long run it would not be in the interests of the lying hospitals, even if they really had the information needed to lie successfully in the first place, to get involved with this form of post-assignment greed.

1.8   Notes and References

The seminal paper in the study of stable matching problems is by Gale and Shapley [22], who introduced the stable marriage problem, the stable roommates problem, and the college admissions problem, which we have referred to as the hospitals/residents problem. (We chose to use this terminology because most of the literature concerns applications in the hospital context, and the NRMP is the largest and the best-known application.)

The history of the labor market for residents and the origins and operation of the NRMP algorithm are described in detail by Roth [99, 96], who was the first to study systematically an actual labor market from the perspective of these matching models. The description given in Section 1.1 is based on the presentation given in [99].

The early history of hospitals/residents matching, as described in [99], is strikingly similar to the situation today in a different, but often compared, profession. The following excerpts are from an article in the New York Times, March 17, 1989 by David Margolick.[1]

Annual race for clerks becomes a mad dash,
with judicial decorum left in the dust

The once-decorous process by which Federal judges select their law clerks has degenerated into a free-for-all in which some of the nation's most eminent judges scramble for the top law school students.

---

[1]Copyright ©1989 by the New York Times Company. Reprinted by permission.

Since last fall, the students and Federal appeals court judges have engaged in a frenzied mating ritual, pairing off for prestigious one-year apprenticeships that are keys to the best jobs ... Both partners agree that this year the process has reached a new low despite efforts over the last several years to restore order.

In their eagerness to capture the best clerks, the judges have steadily pushed up the hiring process; instead of looking for students in their third year of law school as custom once required, judges surreptitiously began recruiting second-year students in fall and offered some jobs as early as February, disrupting studies and making decisions on the basis of fewer grades and flimsier evidence.

"It was positively surreal, the most ludicrous thing I've ever been through," said one Stanford student who recently endured the process.

"Here are these brilliant, respected people — they're Federal judges, for God's sake — and they're behaving like 6-year olds".

The judges agree that the process is one in which the law of jungle reigns and badmouthing, spying and even poaching among judges is rife. "When it comes to hiring law clerks, there is no collegiality," one judge lamented. "Perfectly honorable people will stop at nothing."

Concerned about the disruptive effects on students, the Association of American Law Schools suggested that judges agree not to hire students before Sept. 15 of the third year. That effort proved fruitless.

Other attempts by the judges have proved equally fruitless. In 1985 Judge Stephen Breyer of the First Circuit in Boston convinced most of his colleagues nationwide to say they would withold all job offers until April 1. But cheating was rampant and last year he threw in the towel....

The first to move was judge Wald. Last month her clerk called the Harvard Law Review for the names of all freshly minted editors, then promptly invited them to Washington for interviews. That set off a mad dash among Harvard students that enriched resumé services, copying centers and Federal Express....

Convincing clerkship candidates to accept offers requires a carrot and a stick. Exploiting those prone to panic, some extend offers for only a few hours, a practice known in the clerkship vernacular as a "short fuse" or a "hold up". Two years ago, for instance, Judge Winter offered a Yale student a clerkship at 11:35 and gave her until noon to accept. At 11:55, as she was trying to reach a California judge to whom she had also applied, he withdrew his offer.

It is great fun to watch history repeating itself. It is a little like watching a movie thriller when you have already read the book; you know how it should end, but you won't know for sure until it does. Will the lawyers repeat the full residents/hospitals history? Perhaps the future will see the establishment of a centralized National Clerkship Matching Program (NCMP). Will the first efforts fail to ensure stability? And if they are wise enough to insist on stable matchings, will they be clerk-optimal or judge-optimal matchings, or one of the compromises discussed in Chapter 3? Whichever method they may use, a profession dealing so intimately with issues of truth and honesty will surely avoid the problems discussed in Section 1.7.

The version of the Gale-Shapley algorithm described in [22] differs slightly from that of Section 1.2.1. The algorithm was expressed as a sequence of "stages"; at each stage *every* free man would propose (simultaneously) to the next free woman in his list, and each woman would reject all but her best proposal to date. An alternative (recursive) formulation of the algorithm, in which the men initiate their proposal sequences in a fixed order and every rejection causes the rejected man to make his next proposal immediately, was given by McVitie and Wilson [71], together with an ALGOL implementation [72]. (Curiously, these early papers contained no explicit observation that the order in which the free men propose is immaterial.) An implementation of the Gale-Shapley algorithm in terms of co-routines appears in [1].

The man-optimality property was established by Gale and Shapley [22], and the fact that man-optimal implies woman-pessimal was first observed by McVitie and Wilson [71]. The result of Section 1.2.2 on weak Pareto-optimality first appears in [98] with a proof attributed to Gale, and an alternative proof was given by Gale and Sotomayor [24].

Gale and Shapley observed that their algorithm involved at most $n^2 - 2n + 2$ stages, but the $O(n^2)$ bound is first properly established in Knuth's book [59], where it is attributed to Bulnes and Valdes [6]. A worst case example was given by Knuth [59], and further discussion of the worst case appears in [52] and [57]. Wilson [124] proved that the algorithm has $O(n \log n)$ average-case complexity, and Knuth [59] gave a detailed analysis of its average-case performance, including the derivation of the $\theta(n \log n)$ result.

The observation that the set of stable matchings forms a distributive lattice under the dominance relation first appears in [59], and is attributed to John Conway. Also in [59], Knuth proved Theorem 1.3.1 (though with a different proof to the one given here).

Knuth was also the first to point out that the number of stable matchings can grow exponentially with problem size; he gave an illustration to show that, for each n, there is a stable marriage instance of size n with $2^{n/2}$ stable matchings. The stronger bound of Theorem 1.3.3, the associated family of instances, and the recurrence relation leading to the table of Figure 1.12 are due to Irving and Leather [48], but Lemma 1.3.3 is new. A less general version of that theorem was given by Hwang [42].

The fact that the average number of stable matchings, taken over all instances of size n, is asymptotic to $e^{-1} n \ln n$ is due to Pittel [84]. A related result, that each person has between $(\frac{1}{2} - \epsilon) \ln n$ and $(1 + \epsilon) \ln n$ stable partners, with probability tending to 1 as $n \to \infty$, where ϵ is any positive constant, has recently been established by Knuth, Motwani, and Pittel [60].

McVitie and Wilson [70] investigated the stable marriage problem for sets of unequal size, and essentially proved Theorem 1.4.1. Theorem 1.4.2 on unacceptable partners is really just a special case of parts (i) and (ii) of the Rural Hospitals theorem, and these results were first established by Gale and Sotomayor [24], who also proved Theorem 1.4.3 in the context of the hospitals/residents problem. Some aspects of indifference were studied by Gardenfors [26]; these included the observations that strongly stable matchings need not exist and that ties may be broken arbitrarily if we consider only the weakest notion of stability discussed in Section 1.4.3. The algorithms of that section for super-stable and strongly-stable matchings are new, and details of the network-flow approach to finding bipartite matchings and deficient sets may be found, for example, in [65]. Further extensions of the stable marriage problem, to the situation where new persons arrive in an already stably-matched community, and to a probabilistic setting, may be found in [50] and [51].

Theorem 1.5.2, establishing the $\Omega(n^2)$ lower bound on matching problems when both preference and ranking lists are used, is due to Ng and Hirschberg [80], and it resolves one of Knuth's twelve open questions from [59]. The canonical instance used here is a modification of the canonical instance in [80]; their construction gives a constant of $\frac{1}{6}$ in the lower bound, rather than the $\frac{1}{16}$ shown here. It is shown in [35] that the stability of a matching in an instance of size n (n men and n women) can be checked with $n(n-1)/2+2n$ (rather than the obvious $n(n-1)$) accesses of the preference and ranking arrays. Theorem 1.5.1 is new.

Gale and Shapley [22] gave informal versions of the resident-oriented and hospital-oriented algorithms (in the context of the college admissions problem), and proved the resident-optimal property of the matching generated by the former. Dubins and Freedman [11] presented a neat description of the resident-oriented algorithm, which included some discussion of nondeterminism. The hospital-optimal and resident-pessimal properties of the hospital-oriented algorithm appear explicitly in Roth [99], and the fact that the NRMP algorithm generates a stable matching, and that this matching is the hospital-optimal matching — in other words, that the NRMP algorithm is essentially the hospital-oriented algorithm — is also due to Roth [99]. Some of the issues involved in the application of these algorithms to university admissions are explored in [69] and [17].

Parts (i) and (ii) of Theorem 1.6.3 were proved by Gale and Sotomayor [24]. Proofs of these results are also given by Roth [99], and Roth [102] also established part (iii) (the essential Rural Hospitals result). However the proof of this latter result given here is quite different. The fact that hospitals have strict preferences between stable matchings was first established by Roth and Sotomayor [106], but again, the proof given here is quite different. The observation that the hospital-optimal matching does not necessarily have the weak Pareto-optimal property is due to Roth [95].

The hospitals/residents problem with couples was first discussed in the literature by Roth [99], where the various ways in which the NRMP has sought to accommodate couples are described. In the same paper, Roth points out that stable matchings need not exist in this case. The NP-completeness result is due to Ronn [94], and a simpler version of his proof appears in [93].

Theorem 1.7.1 was first proved by Dubins and Freedman [11], and a special case, for just a single man, was independently proved by Roth [98]. The proof of Lemma 1.7.1 and of Theorem 1.7.1 given here follows Gale and Sotomayor [24], and they credit Lemma 1.7.1 to an unpublished comment by J.S. Hwang. Theorem 1.7.2 was proved by Demange, Gale, and Sotomayor [10], and theorems 1.7.3 and 1.7.4 are from Gale and Sotomayor [23].

By Theorem 1.7.3, the men can always obtain the man-optimal matching even when the woman-optimal matching is computed, by declaring some of the women to be unacceptable. We know of no analogous general results when the men are permitted only to permute their true preferences. However, Josh Benaloh found the example of Figure 1.25 showing that lying by permuting is sometimes sufficient. The woman-optimal matching is {(1,1) (2,2) (3,3)}, in which both men 1 and 2 receive their second choice. Now suppose man 1 changes his list to 2 3 1. The woman-optimal matching now is {(1,2) (2,1) (3,3)}, which is man-optimal for the true preferences, and in which men 1 and 2 receive their true first choices.

1		2	1	3		1		1	2	3
2		1	2	3		2		2	1	3
3		1	2	3		3		1	2	3
		Men's Preferences						Women's Preferences		

Figure 1.25: Lying by permuting sometimes helps

Roth first observed that Theorem 1.7.1 does not generalize to the hospitals/residents problem, and the example of Section 1.7.3 is taken from his paper [95]. Earlier papers by Roth, by Gale and Sotomayor, and by Dubins and Freedman had claimed that the theorem did generalize via the reduction of the hospital problem to the marriage problem. Additional results and discussions concerning deceit, coalitions, and strategy can be found in the papers cited above, and in [62], [98], [99], [103], [101], [97], [96], [105], and [126].

The discussion of coalitions and deceit suggests a nontrivial connection between the stable marriage problem and game theory. In fact, game theoretic aspects of the stable marriage problem have been studied extensively by game theorists and mathematical economists. In that approach, the basic marriage problem has also been generalized to allow the introduction of money and prices, a topic that we will not discuss in this book. A good but dated introduction to the game theoretic view of stable marriage and the introduction of money appears in Shubik [112], while a comprehensive discussion of this field will shortly appear in Roth and Sotomayor [108]. The following original papers contain most of what has been published in this general area: [5], [7], [9], [21], [53], [54], [55], [56], [76], [88], [89], [90], [91], [92], [100], [104], [107], [110], [111], and [113]. A related notion of reciprocal matching is studied in [63].

The books by Knuth [59] and by Roth and Sotomayor [108] are devoted to the stable marriage problem and related issues. Among other textbook that give expositions of aspects of the stable marriage problem are those by Lawler [64], Wirth [125], Sedgewick [109], Shubik [112], Polyá, Tarjan, and Woods [85], and Korsh and Garrett [61].

Chapter 2

The Structure and Representation of All Stable Matchings

2.1 Introduction

In this chapter we return to the basic stable marriage problem — monogamous matchings of equal numbers of men and women, where each person's list contains all the people of the opposite sex, and all preferences are strict. For this basic problem, we will develop a very revealing and algorithmically powerful representation of the set of all stable matchings and of the marriage lattice $\mathcal{M}$ for any problem instance. We will show that although the number of stable matchings can grow exponentially with n, for any instance of size n there is a partial order $\Pi(\mathcal{M})$ with $O(n^2)$ elements which represents all the stable matchings. To be precise, there is a one-one correspondence between the set of stable matchings in $\mathcal{M}$ and the set of closed subsets (defined in Section 2.2 below) of $\Pi(\mathcal{M})$. Further, the relation of set containment on the closed subsets of $\Pi(\mathcal{M})$ is the dominance relation on the corresponding stable matchings. We will also see in this chapter and the next, that $\Pi(\mathcal{M})$ can be efficiently constructed from the preference lists alone, that is, without first knowing $\mathcal{M}$.

Having an efficiently computable and compact representation of the set of all stable matchings will be the key to efficient algorithms for a range of problems concerning stable marriage, to be discussed in Chapter 3. The partial order $\Pi(\mathcal{M})$ will also be used in Chapter 3 to establish complexity results through problem reductions and to show the relationship of the stable marriage problem to several other well-known problems in combinatorial optimization.

We begin this chapter by showing the existence of a compact representation $I(\mathcal{M})$ of $\mathcal{M}$ and its construction in polynomial time. This representation $I(\mathcal{M})$ is simple to describe and prove correct, and it is closely related to our desired, but conceptually more complex, partial order $\Pi(\mathcal{M})$. However, $\Pi(\mathcal{M})$ will be faster to construct and more valuable for algorithmic purposes than is $I(\mathcal{M})$.

2.2 A Simple Compact Representation

2.2.1 Irreducible Stable Matchings

For a given pair (m, w), any matching containing (m, w) is called an *(m,w)-matching*, and we use $\mathcal{M}(m, w)$ to denote the set of all (m, w)-matchings in $\mathcal{M}$. Clearly, $\mathcal{M}(m, w)$ could be empty, but if M and M' are matchings in $\mathcal{M}(m, w)$ then so are $M \vee M'$ and $M \wedge M'$. So $\mathcal{M}(m, w)$ is a sublattice of $\mathcal{M}$, and it follows that $\mathcal{M}(m, w)$ contains its own "man-optimal" matching, i.e., one that dominates all (m, w)-matchings. We will use $M(m, w)$ to denote the unique (m, w)-matching that dominates all matchings in $\mathcal{M}(m, w)$, and a stable matching M will be called *irreducible* if M is $M(m, w)$ for some m and w. That is, M is irreducible if (and only if) for some stable pair (m, w), M is the most dominant stable matching in which m and w are a matched pair. We will use $I(\mathcal{M})$ to denote the set of all irreducible stable matchings, and we will view $(I(\mathcal{M}), \preceq)$ as the partial order on $I(\mathcal{M})$ under the dominance relation $\preceq$ inherited from $\mathcal{M}$. Generally, we will refer to the partial order $(I(\mathcal{M}), \preceq)$ as $I(\mathcal{M})$, and let the context indicate whether $I(\mathcal{M})$ is being considered as a set or as a partial order.

The term "irreducible" is inherited from standard terminology for distributive lattices, but Corollary 2.2.2 below shows that the term is appropriate in the context of stable marriage alone.

Example Consider the example of size eight introduced in Section 1.2.2. For convenience, we reproduce the preference lists in Figure 2.1. Figure 2.2 shows the lattice of 8 stable matchings for this instance. Each stable matching M is described by a vector of length eight, where the number in position i of the vector indicates the M-partner of man i. Below each stable matching M is a vector indicating the the ranking of the M-partner of each man; that is, the number in position i gives the position of the M-partner of man i in his preference list. The labels on the edges should be ignored for now; they will be used in a later example. The table in Figure 2.3 displays the stable pairs for this example, and for each stable pair (m, w), it indicates the associated irreducible matching $M(m, w)$. Note that there are six irreducible matchings out of a total of eight stable matchings; neither M_4 nor M_6 is irreducible. The partial order $I(\mathcal{M})$ for this example is shown in Figure 2.4.

If $(R, \preceq)$ is a partial order, then a subset S of R is said to be *closed* in R if there is no element in $R \setminus S$ that precedes an element in S; that is every element in R that precedes any element in S is also in S. Hence a

1	5	7	1	2	6	8	4	3
2	2	3	7	5	4	1	8	6
3	8	5	1	4	6	2	3	7
4	3	2	7	4	1	6	8	5
5	7	2	5	1	3	6	8	4
6	1	6	7	5	8	4	2	3
7	2	5	7	6	3	4	8	1
8	3	8	4	5	7	2	6	1

1	5	3	7	6	1	2	8	4
2	8	6	3	5	7	2	1	4
3	1	5	6	2	4	8	7	3
4	8	7	3	2	4	1	5	6
5	6	4	7	3	8	1	2	5
6	2	8	5	3	4	6	7	1
7	7	5	2	1	8	6	4	3
8	7	4	1	5	2	3	6	8

Men's Preferences   Women's Preferences

Figure 2.1: The stable marriage instance of size 8

subset of matchings $S \subseteq \mathcal{M}$ is closed in $\mathcal{M}$ if there is no matching in $\mathcal{M} \setminus S$ that dominates a matching in S. For example, in the partial order $I(\mathcal{M})$ of Figure 2.4, $\{M_0, M_1, M_2, M_3\}$ is a closed subset, while $\{M_0, M_2, M_3\}$ is not closed.

Clearly, if S is a subset of matchings in $I(\mathcal{M})$, then $\bigvee S$ is also a stable matching in $\mathcal{M}$ (recall from Section 1.3.1 that $\bigvee S$ is the stable matching $\bigvee_{M \in S} M$). Hence, every nonempty closed subset of $I(\mathcal{M})$ generates a stable matching in this way, and this defines a mapping from the nonempty closed subsets of $I(\mathcal{M})$ to $\mathcal{M}$. Our main goal in this section is to show that this mapping is one-one.

For an arbitrary stable matching M, we define the *irreducible support* $U(M)$ of M to be $\{M(m, w) : (m, w) \in M\}$. For example, in the stable matchings of Figure 2.2, the irreducible support of matching $M_3 = \{(1, 8), (2, 3), (3, 1), (4, 6), (5, 7), (6, 5), (7, 2), (8, 4)\}$ is $\{M_0, M_1, M_3\}$, which can be verified from Figure 2.3 by finding $M(m, w)$ for each pair $(m, w) \in M_3$. As another example, the irreducible support of M_6 is $\{M_0, M_2, M_3, M_5\}$.

Lemma 2.2.1 *For any stable matching M, $M = \bigvee U(M)$. That is, any stable matching M can be obtained by assigning each man to his least preferred partner among his partners in the matchings in $U(M)$.*

Proof Suppose (m_1, w_1) is in M but not in $\bigvee U(M)$. Since (m_1, w_1) is in $M(m_1, w_1) \in U(M)$, there must be a pair (m_2, w_2) in M such that, in $M(m_2, w_2)$, man m_1 marries a woman strictly below w_1 in his list. Now $M(m_2, w_2)$ dominates all the stable matchings in which m_2 marries w_2, and in particular M. But this is a contradiction, because m_1 prefers w_1, his partner in M, to his partner in $M(m_2, w_2)$. Hence $M = \bigvee U(M)$. $\square$

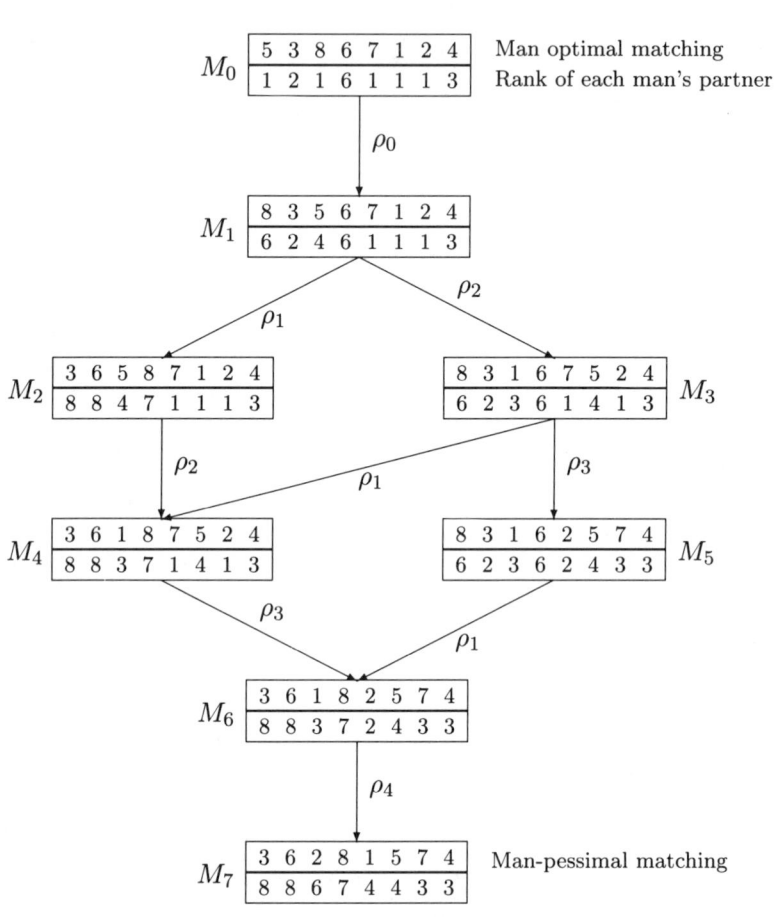

Figure 2.2: The lattice of stable matchings

(1,5)	(1,8)	(1,3)	(2,3)	(2,6)	(3,8)	(3,5)	(3,1)	(3,2)	(4,6)
M_0	M_1	M_2	M_0	M_2	M_0	M_1	M_3	M_7	M_0

(4,8)	(5,7)	(5,2)	(5,1)	(6,1)	(6,5)	(7,2)	(7,7)	(8,4)
M_2	M_0	M_5	M_7	M_0	M_3	M_0	M_5	M_0

Figure 2.3: The stable pairs, and associated irreducible matchings

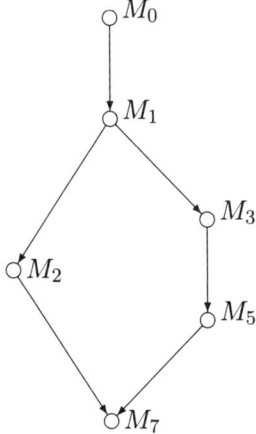

Figure 2.4: The partial order $I(\mathcal{M})$ for the irreducible stable matchings

For example, woman 3 is the worst partner for man 1 among his partners in the matchings $\{M_0, M_2, M_3, M_5\} = U(M_6)$; woman 3 is in fact the partner of man 1 in M_6. The reader should check that cases of the other men.

Corollary 2.2.1 *Let $\hat{U}(M)$ be the set of all irreducible matchings that dominate some matching in $U(M)$, i.e., $\hat{U}(M)$ is the closure of $U(M)$ in $I(\mathcal{M})$. Then $M = \bigvee \hat{U}(M)$.*

Proof If a stable matching M_1 dominates stable matching M_2 then $M_1 \vee M_2 = M_2$, so $\bigvee \hat{U}(M) = \bigvee U(M)$, since each matching in $\hat{U}(M)$ dominates some matching in $U(M)$. □

It is not difficult to see that $\hat{U}(M)$ is the set of all irreducible matchings that dominate M. We leave the proof to the reader, and it will be implied by the more general result in Lemma 2.3.2. As an example, $\hat{U}(M_6) = \{M_0, M_1, M_2, M_3, M_5\}$. Note that $\hat{U}(M_6) \neq U(M_6)$.

The following corollary of Lemma 2.2.1 justifies calling an element of $I(\mathcal{M})$ irreducible.

Corollary 2.2.2 *A stable matching M is $\bigvee S$ for a set S of stable matchings that excludes M, if and only if M is not in $I(\mathcal{M})$.*

Proof The "if" part of the corollary follows at once from Lemma 2.2.1. To prove the converse, first note that if $M = \bigvee S$, then every matching in S dominates M. So if $M \notin S$, then for any pair (m, w) in M there is a matching M' in S that contains (m, w) and that strictly dominates M. So $M \neq M(m, w)$, and this is true for all pairs (m, w) in M, so that M cannot be in $I(\mathcal{M})$. □

We now complete the demonstration that the mapping from the nonempty closed subsets of $I(\mathcal{M})$ to $\mathcal{M}$ is one-one.

Lemma 2.2.2 *If S and T are distinct closed subsets of $I(\mathcal{M})$, then $\bigvee S \neq \bigvee T$.*

Proof Clearly, no maximal matching (with respect to dominance) of $S \cup T$ can dominate any other matching in $S \cup T$. Further, since $S \neq T$ and both subsets are closed in $I(\mathcal{M})$, one of the maximal matchings of $S \cup T$ cannot be in $S \cap T$. So one of the subsets, say S, contains a matching M that does not dominate any matching in the other subset, T. Now $M = M(m, w)$ for some m and w, so that m has a partner no better than w in $\bigvee S$. On the other hand, we claim that m has a better partner than w in *every* matching in T, so $\bigvee S$ cannot be $\bigvee T$. To see this claim, suppose that m does have a partner no better than w in some matching M' in T. Then $M(m,w) \wedge M'$ dominates M', and is itself dominated by $M(m,w)$ since $M(m,w) \wedge M'$ contains the pair (m,w). But then $M(m,w)$ dominates M', contradicting the fact that $M(m,w)$ (which is in S) dominates no matching in T. $\square$

Corollary 2.2.3 *If S is a closed subset of $I(\mathcal{M})$ and $M = \bigvee S$, then $S = \hat{U}(M)$.*

In summary, we have

Theorem 2.2.1 *i) There is a one-one correspondence between the nonempty closed subsets of $I(\mathcal{M})$ and the stable matchings of $\mathcal{M}$. This correspondence associates each stable matching M with the irreducible stable matchings that dominate M.*
ii) If S is the closed subset of $I(\mathcal{M})$ corresponding to stable matching M, then $M = \bigvee S$.
iii) If closed subsets S and S' of $I(\mathcal{M})$ correspond to matchings M and M', respectively, then M dominates M' if and only if $S \subseteq S'$.

2.2.2 Constructing the Representation

We now show that $I(\mathcal{M})$ can be constructed in time polynomial in n, the size of the problem instance. First, for any man-woman pair (m,w), it is easy to test if there is a stable matching containing (m,w), and if so, to find $M(m,w)$. Simply modify the Gale-Shapley algorithm so that w rejects all proposals from anyone other than m, and such that no woman other than w accepts a proposal from m. If the algorithm produces a matching, it will be $M(m,w)$, and if the algorithm fails to find a matching, then there is no stable matching containing (m,w). It is easy to see that this method is correct, and that it runs in $O(n^2)$ time for each (m,w). Hence the set $I(\mathcal{M})$ can be found in $O(n^4)$ time.

To determine the precedence relation on partial order $I(\mathcal{M})$, simply examine each pair of matchings in $I(\mathcal{M})$ and test whether one dominates the other. Each such test takes $O(n)$ time, using the ranking array representation of the preference lists, so the partial order $(I(\mathcal{M}), \preceq)$ can be constructed from the preference lists in $O(n^5)$ time. Hence although the size of $\mathcal{M}$ can grow exponentially in n, there is a compact representation of $\mathcal{M}$ that can be constructed in polynomial time. We will see later that such a compact representation is the key to the efficient solution of a range of problems and to the derivation of complexity results concerned with stable marriage.

It is not difficult to reduce the time to find the irreducible matchings to $O(n^3)$, but that is not of central interest, since we will later develop a compact representation of $\mathcal{M}$ that can be constructed in $O(n^2)$ time.

2.3   Generalization to a Ring of Sets

Although the partial order of irreducible matchings $I(\mathcal{M})$ can be constructed in $O(n^5)$ time, and it can be used to construct polynomial time algorithms for a number of problems concerned with stable marriage, the algorithms that result are not the most efficient ones known for these problems. To improve efficiency, we will develop a different, very closely related structure, $\Pi(\mathcal{M})$, which can be "constructed" from the preference lists in $O(n^2)$ time, and which has a number of algorithmically valuable properties that $I(\mathcal{M})$ lacks. We will see that $\Pi(\mathcal{M})$ is isomorphic to the partial order obtained from $I(\mathcal{M})$ by removing the minimal element, M_0, from $I(\mathcal{M})$. Further, there is a one-one correspondence between the closed subsets of $\Pi(\mathcal{M})$ and the stable matchings of $\mathcal{M}$, similar to the situation with $I(\mathcal{M})$. Hence the major difference between $I(\mathcal{M})$ and $\Pi(\mathcal{M})$ will be in the definition of the elements of $\Pi(\mathcal{M})$, and in the interpretation of the precedence relation defined on them.

In order to develop the structure $\Pi(\mathcal{M})$ and to discuss how to construct it efficiently, we first consider the more general problem of how to compactly represent any ring of sets (to be defined below). We will develop a representation that generalizes $I(\mathcal{M})$ and then modify it to obtain a related representation. That representation will then be specialized to the case of stable marriage, yielding $\Pi(\mathcal{M})$. In addition to its application in deriving and understanding $\Pi(\mathcal{M})$, this general approach will prove valuable later when we discuss, in Chapter 3, how the stable marriage problem relates to a large class of combinatorial optimization problems.

2.3.1   Rings of Sets

Given a set B, the *base set*, a family $\mathcal{F} = \{F_0, \ldots, F_k\}$ of subsets of B is a *ring of sets* over B if $\mathcal{F}$ is closed under set union and intersection. That is, when F_i and F_j are any two subsets of B in $\mathcal{F}$, then both $F_i \cup F_j$ and $F_i \cap F_j$ are also in $\mathcal{F}$. Note that since the elements of $\mathcal{F}$ are themselves subsets of B, if S is a subset of $\mathcal{F}$, then $\bigcup\{F_i : F_i \in S\}$ is itself a set of elements of B, and therefore is an element of $\mathcal{F}$. We will sometimes write $\bigcup S$ in place of $\bigcup\{F_i : F_i \in S\}$.

Since a ring of sets is closed under union and intersection, there are unique minimal and maximal elements of $\mathcal{F}$ (with respect to set containment); that is, the minimal element is a subset, and the maximal element is a superset, of every other element of $\mathcal{F}$. It is also easy to see then that a ring of sets is a distributive lattice where the lattice relation is set containment, but this fact will not be explicitly used.

2.3.2 The Stable Matchings Form a Ring of Sets

The set of stable matchings $\mathcal{M}$ for a given problem instance can be viewed as a ring of sets. To see this, we introduce a slightly different way to describe a stable matching.

For a stable matching M, we define the *P-set* of M to be the set of all pairs (m, w), where w is either $p_M(m)$ (m's partner in M) or a woman whom m prefers to $p_M(m)$. We use the notation $P(M)$ to refer to the P-set of M, and use $P(\mathcal{M})$ to refer to the family of P-sets corresponding to the stable matchings of $\mathcal{M}$. Note that a subset P of the n^2 man-woman pairs is a P-set if and *only if* $P = P(M)$ for some stable matching M. Note also that if P is a P-set corresponding to an unknown stable matching M, then M can be explicitly obtained from P by pairing each man m with the woman w he least prefers from among the pairs (m, w) in P. For example, the stable matching M_0 from Figure 2.2 can be described as the P-set $\{(1,5), (2,2), (2,3), (3,8), (4,3), (4,2), (4,7), (4,4), (4,1), (4,6), (5,7), (6,1),$ $(7,2), (8,3), (8,8), (8,4)\}$, and the P-set for stable matching M_3 contains these pairs plus the pairs $\{(1,7), (1,1), (1,2), (1,6), (1,8), (3,5), (3,1), (6,6),$ $(6,7), (6,5)\}$. Given the above definitions, the following is now immediate.

Lemma 2.3.1 *If M and M' are two stable matchings, then $P(M \vee M') = P(M) \cup P(M')$ and $P(M \wedge M') = P(M) \cap P(M')$. Further, M dominates M' if and only if $P(M) \subseteq P(M')$.*

Lemma 2.3.1 shows that $P(\mathcal{M})$ is a ring of sets for a marriage lattice $\mathcal{M}$. For a problem instance of size n, the base set of the ring is the set of all n^2 man-woman pairs, and the family of P-sets, $P(\mathcal{M})$, is closed under set union and intersection because, by Theorem 1.3.2 (page 21), stable matchings are closed under $\vee$ and $\wedge$. This view of the set of all stable matchings as a ring of sets will be central throughout the later sections of this chapter.

Note that in $P(\mathcal{M})$ the man-optimal matching corresponds to the minimal P-set, and the woman-optimal matching corresponds to the maximal P-set. Mathematically there is no problem with this, but the reader may have to make a psychological transformation to avoid subconsciously identifying (male) dominance with maximality.

2.3.3 A Compact Representation of a Ring of Sets

In this section we show how the representation $I(\mathcal{M})$ of the marriage lattice $\mathcal{M}$ generalizes to a representation $I(\mathcal{F})$ of any ring of sets $\mathcal{F}$. The definitions and proofs in this section closely parallel those for $I(\mathcal{M})$, although there are some subtle differences, and it is valuable to present some of the proofs in full detail, if only to establish the terminology and to prepare for the newer results of the next section.

For any element $a \in B$, we let $\mathcal{F}(a)$ denote the set of all elements of $\mathcal{F}$ that contain a. It may happen that $\mathcal{F}(a)$ is empty, but if F_i and F_j belong to $\mathcal{F}(a)$, then so also do $F_i \cup F_j$ and $F_i \cap F_j$. So $\mathcal{F}(a)$ itself forms a ring of sets over B, and there is therefore a unique minimal and a unique maximal element of $\mathcal{F}(a)$; we define $F(a)$ to be the unique minimal element of $\mathcal{F}(a)$. That is, $F(a) = \bigcap \{F : F \in \mathcal{F}(a)\}$. Then, an element F of $\mathcal{F}$ that is $F(a)$ for some a will be called *irreducible*, and we use $I(\mathcal{F})$ to denote the set of all irreducible elements of $\mathcal{F}$. We also view $(I(\mathcal{F}), \preceq)$ as a partial order under the relation $\preceq$ of set containment: if F and F' are elements of $\mathcal{F}$, then F precedes F' in $(I(\mathcal{F}), \preceq)$ if and only if $F \subseteq F'$. We will usually use $I(\mathcal{F})$ to refer to both the set and the partial order, and let the context resolve any ambiguity.

Example Consider the ring of sets $\mathcal{F}$ displayed by the Hasse diagram of $\mathcal{F}$ in Figure 2.5. The base of this ring is the set $\{a, b, c, d, e, f, g, h, i\}$, and there is an edge from a set F to a set F' if and only if F is an immediate predecessor of F', i.e., $F \subset F'$, and there is no set F'' such that $F \subset F'' \subset F'$. The irreducible elements of the ring are $\{F_0, F_1, F_2, F_3, F_5, F_{11}\}$, and each such F is $F(x)$ for every underlined element x in F, i.e., F is the minimal element of $\mathcal{F}$ containing $x \in B$. The elements drawn on the edges of $\mathcal{F}$ should be ignored for now; they will be used later. The partial order $I(\mathcal{F})$ is shown in Figure 2.6.

Let S be any nonempty subset of $I(\mathcal{F})$. Since $\mathcal{F}$ is closed under union, $\bigcup \{F : F \in S\}$ is a subset of B that is in $\mathcal{F}$. Hence each nonempty closed subset of $I(\mathcal{F})$ generates an element of $\mathcal{F}$ in this way. Our immediate objective is to show that this correspondence between nonempty closed subsets of $I(\mathcal{F})$ and elements of $\mathcal{F}$ is one-one.

For an arbitrary element F of $\mathcal{F}$, we define the *irreducible support* $U(F)$ of F to be $\{F(a) : a \in F\}$.

Lemma 2.3.2 *For any element F of $\mathcal{F}$, the irreducible support of F is closed in $I(\mathcal{F})$. Equivalently, $U(F)$ is the set of all irreducible elements of $\mathcal{F}$ that precede F in $\mathcal{F}$, i.e., that are subsets of F.*

Proof Let $F_1 \subset F_2$ be two distinct irreducible elements of $\mathcal{F}$, and let F_2 be in $U(F)$. We will show that F_1 is in $U(F)$. Since F_1 is irreducible, $F_1 = F(b)$ for some $b \in B$. Similarly, $F_2 = F(a)$ for some $a \in F$, so b must be in $F(a)$. Now $a \in F$ implies that $F(a) \subseteq F$, so it follows that b is in F, and hence $F(b)$, which is F_1, is in $U(F)$. $\square$

As an example, $U(F_9) = \{F_0, F_2, F_3, F_5\}$, which is indeed closed in $I(\mathcal{F})$, and is the set of all irreducible elements of $\mathcal{F}$ that precede F_9 in $\mathcal{F}$. Note

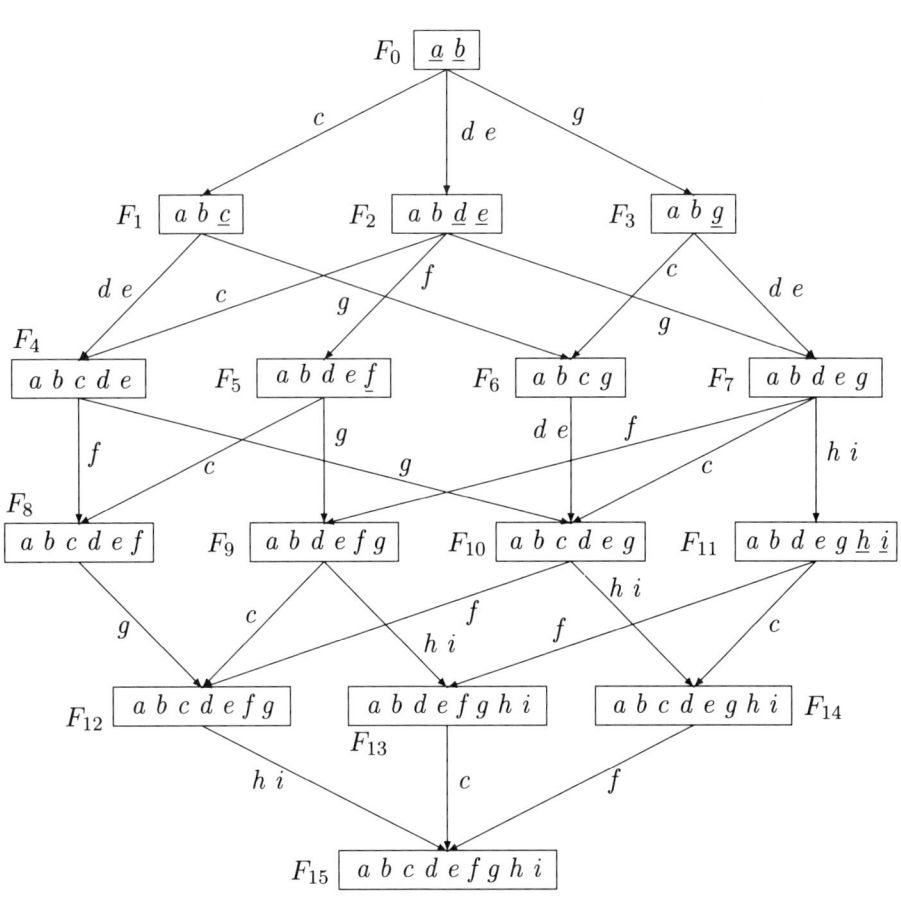

Figure 2.5: A ring of sets with $B = \{a, b, c, d, e, f, g, h, i\}$

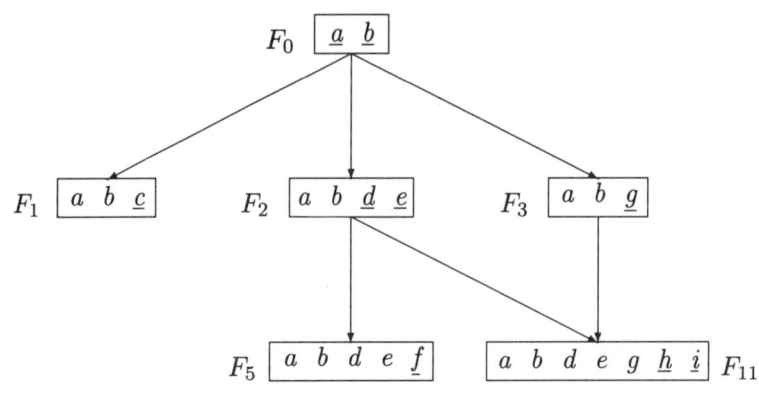

Figure 2.6: The partial order $I(\mathcal{F})$ of the irreducible elements of $\mathcal{F}$

that we have not defined any object similar to $\hat{U}$, the closure of U, which was defined in the discussion of $I(\mathcal{M})$. The reason is that, unlike $U(F)$, which is closed in $\mathcal{F}$, $U(M)$ is not always closed for any $M \in \mathcal{M}$.

Lemma 2.3.3 *For any element F of $\mathcal{F}$, $F = \bigcup U(F)$. That is, F can be expressed as the union of its irreducible support.*

Proof For any element $a \in F$, a is in $F(a)$, which is in $U(F)$, so a is in $\bigcup U(F)$, hence $F \subseteq \bigcup U(F)$. Conversely, every element of $U(F)$ is a subset of F, so $\bigcup U(F) \subseteq F$. □

Analogous to Corollary 2.2.2, we have the following lemma, whose proof is left to the reader.

Lemma 2.3.4 *F is irreducible if and only if F cannot be written as the union of members of $\mathcal{F}$ excluding F itself.*

The following lemma is an analogue of Lemma 2.2.2. Notice that the set notation permits a more direct proof than that of Lemma 2.2.2.

Lemma 2.3.5 *If S and T are distinct closed subsets of $I(\mathcal{F})$, then $\bigcup S \neq \bigcup T$.*

Proof If S and T are different closed subsets of $I(\mathcal{F})$, then one of them, say S, contains an element $F = F(a)$ that is not contained in the other set,

T. But $F(a)$ is contained in all members of $\mathcal{F}$ that contain a, so no such member of $\mathcal{F}$ is in T. Hence $a \in \bigcup S$, $a \notin \bigcup T$, and therefore $\bigcup S \neq \bigcup T$. □

In summary, we have

Theorem 2.3.1 *i) There is a one-one correspondence between the elements of $\mathcal{F}$ and the nonempty closed subsets of $I(\mathcal{F})$. In particular, an element F of $\mathcal{F}$ corresponds to $U(F)$, which is a closed subset in $I(\mathcal{F})$.*
ii) Each nonempty closed subset of $I(\mathcal{F})$ generates (by unioning) an element of $\mathcal{F}$, and each element of $\mathcal{F}$ is generated in this way by exactly one nonempty closed subset of $I(\mathcal{F})$.
iii) If S and S' are closed subsets of $I(\mathcal{F})$ that generate F and F' respectively, then $F \subseteq F'$ if and only if $S \subseteq S'$.

Example There are sixteen nonempty closed subsets of $I(\mathcal{F})$ (Figure 2.5); each generates a distinct element of $\mathcal{F}$, and each is the irreducible support of that element. Figure 2.7 shows the elements of $\mathcal{F}$, and for each one, the unique nonempty closed subset of $I(\mathcal{F})$ that generates it.

F_0:	F_0				
F_1:	F_0	F_1			
F_2:	F_0	F_2			
F_3:	F_0	F_3			
F_4:	F_0	F_1	F_2		
F_5:	F_0	F_2	F_5		
F_6:	F_0	F_1	F_3		
F_7:	F_0	F_2	F_3		
F_8:	F_0	F_1	F_2	F_5	
F_9:	F_0	F_2	F_3	F_5	
F_{10}:	F_0	F_1	F_2	F_3	
F_{11}:	F_0	F_2	F_3	F_{11}	
F_{12}:	F_0	F_1	F_2	F_3	F_5
F_{13}:	F_0	F_2	F_3	F_5	F_{11}
F_{14}:	F_0	F_1	F_2	F_3	F_{11}
F_{15}:	F_0	F_1	F_2	F_3	F_5 F_{11}

Elements of $\mathcal{F}$ Closed subsets of $I(\mathcal{F})$

Figure 2.7: The elements of $\mathcal{F}$ and their associated closed subsets of $I(\mathcal{F})$

$I(\mathcal{F})$ reduces to $I(\mathcal{M})$

When $\mathcal{F}$ is $P(\mathcal{M})$, the ring of P-sets corresponding to the stable matchings in $\mathcal{M}$, then the partial order $I(\mathcal{F})$ specializes to the partial order $I(\mathcal{M})$ defined in the previous section. Note however that not all of the ring definitions specialize directly to matching definitions. In particular, if $a = (m, w)$, then $\mathcal{F}(a)$ is the set of all P-sets containing the pair (m, w), i.e., $\mathcal{F}(a)$ is the set of all stable matchings where m marries w or a woman below w in his list. Hence $\mathcal{F}(a)$ is not $\mathcal{M}(m, w)$, since $\mathcal{M}(m, w)$ is the set of stable matchings in which m marries w. Similarly, $U(P(M))$ contains the P-sets of all the matchings of $\hat{U}(M)$, rather than just those of $U(M)$. However, $F(a)$ is equal to $M(m, w)$, and this is enough to imply that when $\mathcal{F}$ is $P(\mathcal{M})$, the partial order $I(\mathcal{F})$ specializes to the partial order $I(\mathcal{M})$ defined for $\mathcal{M}$.

2.4 Representing a Ring of Sets by Set Differences

In this section we continue our examination of a general ring of sets $\mathcal{F}$, focusing on the set differences between elements of $\mathcal{F}$. We will then use certain set differences to define a new representation of $\mathcal{F}$, $D(\mathcal{F})$, that will be more useful than $I(\mathcal{F})$ for algorithmic purposes, and in the case of the stable marriage problem, can be more efficiently constructed than $I(\mathcal{M})$.

2.4.1 The Centers of a Ring of Sets

The unique minimal element of a ring of sets $\mathcal{F}$ will be called the *zero* of $\mathcal{F}$, and will be denoted by F_0. For an irreducible element F of $\mathcal{F}$, the *center* of F, written $K(F)$, is the set $\{a \in B : F(a) = F\}$. Note that the center of an element F is defined only if F is irreducible. Note also that $K(F_0) = F_0$, but for any other irreducible element F, $K(F) \subset F$, since $F_0 \subset F$. In each irreducible element F of $\mathcal{F}$, shown in Figures 2.5 and 2.6, the elements of B in the center of F are underlined. So, for example, the center of F_2 is $\{d, e\}$.

The following lemma is trivial, but will be used repeatedly.

Lemma 2.4.1 *Every element of B is a member of at most one center of $\mathcal{F}$.*

Proof If $a \in K(F_i) \cap K(F_j)$, then $F_i = F(a) = F_j$. $\square$

The centers represent a ring of sets

Just as every element $F \in \mathcal{F}$ can be expressed as the union of the *irreducible elements* that precede it in $\mathcal{F}$, F can also be expressed as the union of the *centers of the irreducible elements* that precede F in $\mathcal{F}$. This provides a more revealing and economical expression for F, since distinct centers never intersect. This is stated precisely in the next lemma.

Lemma 2.4.2 *For any element F in $\mathcal{F}$, $F = \bigcup \{K(F_i) : F_i \in U(F)\}$. Further, this is the only way to express F as the union of a set of centers of $\mathcal{F}$.*

Proof By definition of $U(f)$, $F(a)$ is in $U(F)$ for every a in F. Also, a must be in $K(F(a))$, which is a subset of $F(a)$. It follows then that $F \subseteq \bigcup \{K(F_i) : F_i \in U(F)\}$. Conversely, for every $F(a) \in U(F)$, $F(a)$ is a subset of F, so $K(F(a))$ is a subset of F, and hence $\bigcup \{K(F_i) : F_i \in U(F)\} \subseteq F$. The uniqueness of the expression follows from the fact that no distinct centers intersect. $\square$

Illustrations of Lemma 2.4.2 are easy to find by looking at Figure 2.5 together with Figure 2.7.

We now define $D(\mathcal{F})$ to be the set of all centers of $\mathcal{F}$ other than F_0. The set $D(\mathcal{F})$ will allow us to focus on and characterize the minimal differences between elements of $\mathcal{F}$. These differences will serve as building blocks to construct and represent $\mathcal{F}$. We begin to make this precise with the following immediate corollaries of Lemma 2.4.2.

Corollary 2.4.1 *For any distinct elements F_i and F_j in $\mathcal{F}$, the symmetric difference of F_i and F_j, $(F_i \setminus F_j) \cup (F_j \setminus F_i)$, is the union of a set of centers in $D(\mathcal{F})$. Further, there is only one set of centers whose union is the symmetric difference of F_i and F_j.*

As an example, the symmetric difference of F_8 and F_{11} shown in Figure 2.5 is $\{c, f, g, h, i\}$, which is the union of $\{K(F_1), K(F_3), K(F_5), K(F_{11})\}$, as may easily be verified.

Corollary 2.4.2 *If F_0 and F_z are respectively the minimal and maximal elements of $\mathcal{F}$, then $F_z \setminus F_0$ is the union of all the centers in $D(\mathcal{F})$. i.e., $F_z \setminus F_0 = \bigcup \{K(F_i) : F_i \in I(\mathcal{F}) \setminus F_0\}$.*

The following Lemma is a partial converse to Corollary 2.4.1.

Lemma 2.4.3 *Every center $K(F)$ in $D(\mathcal{F})$ is the symmetric difference of a pair of elements of $\mathcal{F}$. In fact, $K(F) = F \setminus \hat{F}$, where $\hat{F} \subset F$ is an element of $\mathcal{F}$.*

Proof Let F be any nonzero element of $I(\mathcal{F})$, and let $\hat{F}$ be the union of all elements of $\mathcal{F}$ that strictly precede F. Clearly, $\hat{F}$ is an element of $\mathcal{F}$, and $\hat{F} \subset F$, so $F \setminus \hat{F}$ is a symmetric difference of a pair of elements of $\mathcal{F}$. Further, it follows easily from the definition of $K(F)$ that $F \setminus \hat{F} \subseteq K(F)$, and $K(F) \subseteq F \setminus \hat{F}$, so $F \setminus \hat{F} = K(F)$. $\square$

The minimal differences of $\mathcal{F}$

Lemma 2.4.3 and Corollary 2.4.1 establish that the elements of $D(\mathcal{F})$ are precisely the *minimal* elements, with respect to set containment, of the set of all symmetric differences of distinct elements in $\mathcal{F}$. That is, every symmetric difference of a pair of elements in $\mathcal{F}$ is the union of a set of centers in $D(\mathcal{F})$, and every element in $D(\mathcal{F})$ is the symmetric difference of a pair of elements of $\mathcal{F}$. This view of $D(\mathcal{F})$ will be essential, and in order to emphasize the connection of $D(\mathcal{F})$ to set differences, we will hereafter refer to a center of $F \in D(\mathcal{F})$ as a *minimal difference* of F and use the notation $D(F)$ in place of $K(F)$. The set $D(\mathcal{F})$ will be called the set of minimal differences of $\mathcal{F}$.

2.4.2   The Partial Order of Minimal Differences

Given the close connection between the sets $D(\mathcal{F})$ and $I(\mathcal{F})$, and the fact that the nonempty closed subsets of $I(\mathcal{F})$ represent $\mathcal{F}$, it should not be surprising that the closed subsets of $D(\mathcal{F})$ can also be used to represent $\mathcal{F}$ as we now show.

We define $(D(\mathcal{F}), \preceq)$ to be the partial order on the set $D(\mathcal{F})$ obtained by removing F_0 from the partial order $I(\mathcal{F})$ and then replacing each remaining element $F \in I(\mathcal{F})$ by its associated minimal difference $D(F)$. The precedence relation $\preceq$ on $D(\mathcal{F})$ is inherited from the precedence relation on $I(\mathcal{F})$ (and hence from $\mathcal{F}$): $D(F)$ precedes $D(F')$ in $(D(\mathcal{F}) \preceq)$ if and only if F precedes F' in $I(\mathcal{F})$, i.e., $F \subseteq F'$. In other words, the partial order $D(\mathcal{F})$ is isomorphic to the partial order $I(\mathcal{F})$ after the removal of the unique minimal element from $I(\mathcal{F})$. Figure 2.8 shows the representation $D(\mathcal{F})$ obtained from $I(\mathcal{F})$ of Figure 2.6.

Now each minimal difference is associated with exactly one element of $I(\mathcal{F})$, and the precedence relation on $D(\mathcal{F})$ agrees with the relation on $I(\mathcal{F})$, so there is a one-one correspondence between the *nonempty* closed subsets of $I(\mathcal{F})$ and the closed subsets (including the empty subset) of $D(\mathcal{F})$; the closed subset of $I(\mathcal{F})$ consisting of F_0 corresponds to the empty subset of $D(\mathcal{F})$. Given the one-one correspondence between the elements of $\mathcal{F}$ and the nonempty closed subsets of $I(\mathcal{F})$ (Theorem 2.3.1, page 79), the following is immediate.

Theorem 2.4.1 *There is a one-one correspondence between the elements of $\mathcal{F}$ and the closed subsets of $D(\mathcal{F})$. Further, if F_i and F_j are elements in $\mathcal{F}$ corresponding to closed subsets D_i and D_j of $D(\mathcal{F})$, then $F_i \subset F_j$ if and only if $D_i \subset D_j$.*

Note that, given a closed subset S of $D(\mathcal{F})$, the corresponding element F is $F_0 \cup \{\bigcup S\}$, and hence F can actually be constructed from S. It is interesting to note how compact the representation $D(\mathcal{F})$ is in Figure 2.8 as compared to the Hasse diagram of $\mathcal{F}$ in Figure 2.5.

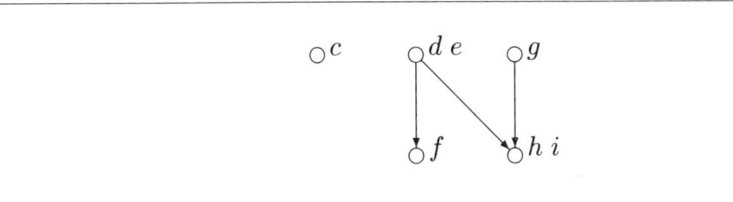

Figure 2.8: The partial order $D(\mathcal{F})$ for $\mathcal{F}$

2.4.3 The Minimal Differences Are Found on Chains

The partial order $D(\mathcal{F})$ provides a compact representation of $\mathcal{F}$, but its elements, the minimal differences of $\mathcal{F}$, are defined from the (generally hard to obtain) irreducible elements of $\mathcal{F}$, or worse, by the (huge) set of symmetric differences of elements of $\mathcal{F}$. Hence, we have no indication so far that minimal differences are easy to find, although we know there are at most $|B|$ of them, since by Lemma 2.4.1 (page 80), no element of B is in more than one minimal difference. In this section we show that the minimal differences show up repeatedly and in a predictable way in $\mathcal{F}$, and this will be the key to efficiently finding them in $P(\mathcal{M})$. Before launching into the technical content, we examine a suggestive example.

Example Consider again the Hasse diagram in Figure 2.5 (page 77). On each edge connecting an element F' with its immediate predecessor F, we have shown the set $F' \setminus F$. The interesting point to note is that each of these differences is a minimal difference of $\mathcal{F}$. In this section we will prove that this is true for any ring of sets; this will make it possible to identify the minimal differences of a ring of sets without knowing its irreducible elements, and that will be crucial in efficiently building $\Pi(\mathcal{M})$, our desired representation of $\mathcal{M}$.

A *chain* $C = \{C_1, \ldots, C_q\}$ in $\mathcal{F}$ is an ordered set of elements of $\mathcal{F}$ such that C_i is an immediate predecessor of C_{i+1}, for each i $1 \leq i \leq q - 1$. An F_0-*chain* is a chain that extends from the minimal element of $\mathcal{F}$, F_0, and a *maximal F_0-chain*, or maximal chain for short, is a chain that extends from F_0 to the maximal element F_z of $\mathcal{F}$.

Lemma 2.4.4 *Let F and F' be any elements of $\mathcal{F}$ (not necessarily irreducible), and suppose F is an immediate predecessor of F' in $\mathcal{F}$. Then $F' \setminus F$ is a minimal difference of $\mathcal{F}$, that is, it is an element of $D(\mathcal{F})$.*

Proof Suppose $F' \setminus F = D$, and let $\bar{F}$ be a minimal element of $\mathcal{F}$ that contains D. It is then immediate that $\bar{F} \subseteq F'$, that $\bar{F} \cup F = F'$, and that $\bar{F} \not\subseteq F$, so $\bar{F} \neq F_0$. Now if $F(a)$ is not $\bar{F}$ for some given element $a \in D$, then $F(a) \subset \bar{F}$, and $F \subset (F \cup F(a)) \subset (F \cup \bar{F}) = F'$, contradicting the assumption that F is an immediate predecessor of F'. Hence $F(a) = \bar{F}$ for every $a \in D$, so $\bar{F}$ is an irreducible element of $\mathcal{F}$, and $D \subseteq D(\bar{F})$. Now if $D \subset D(\bar{F})$, then $F' = (F \cup D) \subset (F \cup D(\bar{F})) \subseteq (F \cup \bar{F}) = F'$, an impossibility. Hence $D = D(\bar{F})$, and so D is a minimal difference of $\mathcal{F}$. $\square$

If D is the difference between two consecutive elements on a chain C in $\mathcal{F}$, then we say that that C *contains* the difference D, and D *appears* on C. Note that by Lemma 2.4.4, D is a minimal difference of $\mathcal{F}$. The following theorem is another reflection of the way that the structure of $\mathcal{F}$ is determined and expressed by its minimal differences.

Theorem 2.4.2 *If F' and F are any two elements in $\mathcal{F}$ such that F precedes F', then every chain from F to F' in $\mathcal{F}$ contains exactly the same set of minimal differences, although in a different order. In particular, if $F = F_0$, then every F_0-chain ending at F' contains the same set of minimal differences.*

Proof Let C be a chain that leads from F to F'. Clearly, $F' \setminus F$ is the union of the consecutive (minimal) differences along C. But by Corollary 2.4.1, this set of minimal differences must be unique, and the theorem follows. $\square$

Corollary 2.4.3 *If C is any maximal chain in $\mathcal{F}$, then each difference of consecutive elements on C is a minimal difference of $\mathcal{F}$, and each minimal difference of $\mathcal{F}$ appears exactly once as a difference of consecutive elements on C.*

Corollary 2.4.4 *Every maximal chain in $\mathcal{F}$ has exactly $|D(\mathcal{F})| + 1$ elements.*

Corollary 2.4.3 will be the key to efficiently finding the minimal differences of $P(\mathcal{M})$, without needing to know in advance the matchings in $I(\mathcal{M})$.

Theorem 2.4.2 and its corollaries are very clearly illustrated in Figure 2.5. For example, there are three chains from F_2 to F_{13}. Each contains the minimal differences $\{f\}$, $\{g\}$, and $\{h, i\}$, but in a different order on each chain. The theorem will have an interesting generalization in our discussion of the stable roommates problem in Chapter 4.

2.4.4   Relating Chains to Closed Subsets

Theorem 2.4.2 establishes a one-one correspondence between the elements of $\mathcal{F}$ and *certain* subsets of $D(\mathcal{F})$. However, the main theorem of section 2.4.2, Theorem 2.4.1 (page 83), establishes a one-one correspondence between the elements of $\mathcal{F}$, and the *closed* subsets of $D(\mathcal{F})$. It is natural then to ask how these two correspondences relate to each other. The answer is that they are identical.

Theorem 2.4.3 *The set of minimal differences along any F_0-chain C is a closed subset of $D(\mathcal{F})$. Conversely, if S is a closed subset of $D(\mathcal{F})$ corresponding to element $F \in \mathcal{F}$, then the F_0-chain in $\mathcal{F}$ ending at F contains exactly the elements of S.*

Proof   Let C end with element $F \in \mathcal{F}$. Clearly, F is the union of F_0 and the differences of consecutive elements on C. Now by Corollary 2.4.3, each of these consecutive differences is a minimal difference of $\mathcal{F}$, so F is the union of F_0 and a set of minimal differences of $\mathcal{F}$. But by Lemma 2.4.2, F can be expressed in only one such way, and so by Theorem 2.4.1 the minimal differences on C must be the minimal differences in the closed subset of $D(\mathcal{F})$ that generates F. Conversely, if S is a closed subset of $D(\mathcal{F})$ corresponding to element $F \in \mathcal{F}$, and C is any chain in $\mathcal{F}$ ending at F, then F equals F_0 unioned with the minimal differences in S, and also equals F_0 unioned with the minimal differences along C. Then by Lemma 2.4.2, these sets of minimal differences must be the same. $\square$

As an example of Theorem 2.4.3, in Figure 2.5 every chain from F_0 to F_9 contains the minimal differences $\{d, e\}$, $\{g\}$, and $\{f\}$, and these minimal differences indeed form the closed subset of $D(\mathcal{F})$ that corresponds to F_9.

With Theorem 2.4.3 we can now establish a direct connection between the precedence relation on $D(\mathcal{F})$ and the order that the minimal differences appear on chains in $\mathcal{F}$. This relationship will be one of the keys to efficiently deducing the precedence relation on $D(\mathcal{M})$, even when the associated matchings in $I(\mathcal{M})$ are unknown.

Theorem 2.4.4 *Let F_i and F_j be two nonzero irreducible elements of $\mathcal{F}$. Then $D(F_i)$ precedes $D(F_j)$ in $D(\mathcal{F})$ if and only if $D(F_i)$ appears before $D(F_j)$ on every maximal chain in $\mathcal{F}$.*

Proof Suppose $D(F_i)$ appears before $D(F_j)$ on every maximal chain in $\mathcal{F}$. Then by Theorem 2.4.3, $D(F_i)$ is in every closed subset of $D(\mathcal{F})$ that contains $D(F_j)$, and in particular, the closed subset consisting of all the predecessors of $D(F_j)$. Hence $D(F_i)$ does precede $D(F_j)$ in $D(\mathcal{F})$.

Conversely, suppose that $D(F_i)$ precedes $D(F_j)$ in $D(\mathcal{F})$, and hence any closed subset of $D(\mathcal{F})$ containing $D(F_j)$ also contains $D(F_i)$. Now suppose there is an F_0-chain C in which $D(F_i)$ appears before $D(F_j)$, and let S be the set of minimal differences on C ending with $D(F_i)$. Then by Theorem 2.4.3, S is a closed subset of $D(\mathcal{F})$ that contains F_i but not F_j, a contradiction. □

Example Consider the minimal differences $\{d,e\}, \{c\}$, and $\{h,i\}$ in the partial order $D(\mathcal{F})$ of Figure 2.8. The minimal difference $\{d,e\}$ precedes $\{h,i\}$ in $D(\mathcal{F})$ and, as shown in Figure 2.5, $\{d,e\}$ appears before $\{h,i\}$ on every maximal chain in $\mathcal{F}$. Also in that figure, there are chains in which $\{c\}$ appears before $\{d,e\}$, and chains where it appears after $\{d,e\}$; as required by Theorem 2.4.4, these two minimal differences are incomparable in $D(\mathcal{F})$.

2.5   Representing the Stable Matchings by Differences

In this section we return to examining the structure of the set of stable matchings in the stable marriage problem. We will specialize the representation $D(\mathcal{F})$ to the case in which $\mathcal{F}$ is the ring of P-sets $P(\mathcal{M})$ for a marriage lattice $\mathcal{M}$.

We have seen that every ring of sets $\mathcal{F}$ over a base-set B is represented by the partial orders $I(\mathcal{F})$ and $D(\mathcal{F})$, each of at most $|B|$ elements. We have also seen that the minimal differences are found on every maximal chain of $\mathcal{F}$, and this suggests a way to find the minimal differences, if we can find a maximal chain in $\mathcal{F}$. However, we have not seen in general how to find such a chain. Further, we have not seen how to deduce the precedence relation on the minimal differences without first knowing $I(\mathcal{F})$. Nor have we seen how to find $I(\mathcal{F})$ in an arbitrary ring of sets without explicitly knowing all the elements of $\mathcal{F}$.

There are good reasons for these omissions: to carry out these tasks, we must specify how $\mathcal{F}$ is represented and how information about $\mathcal{F}$ is obtained, and those details vary with each particular ring of sets.

In the special case of stable marriage, $D(P(\mathcal{M}))$ can surely be constructed in $O(n^5)$ time, since $I(\mathcal{M})$ can be constructed in that time bound. However, this bound can be greatly improved: we will show, in this chapter and the next, that the minimal differences of $\mathcal{M}$ can be constructed from the preference lists in $O(n^2)$ time, and that a "sufficient" (in a sense made precise later) subset of the precedence relations on $D(P(\mathcal{M}))$ can also be constructed in $O(n^2)$ time. This improvement in efficiency, from $O(n^5)$ to $O(n^2)$, is enough in itself to make the representation of $\mathcal{M}$ based on minimal differences of value, but later we will see other algorithmic advantages of $D(P(\mathcal{M}))$ as well. For ease of notation, we will hereafter write $D(\mathcal{M})$ in place of $D(P(\mathcal{M}))$.

We start by introducing the concept of a rotation and end by transforming the partial order $D(\mathcal{M})$ into $\Pi(\mathcal{M})$, a partial order defined on the rotations. Rotations embody the special structure that the ring $P(\mathcal{M})$ possesses; they express in a more direct and algorithmic way what the minimal differences between matchings are.

2.5.1 Rotations

Let M be a stable matching. For any man m let $s_M(m)$ denote the first woman w on m's list such that w strictly prefers m to $p_M(w)$ (her partner in M). Let $next_M(m)$ denote the partner in M of woman $s_M(m)$. Note that since M is stable, m prefers $p_M(m)$ to $s_M(m)$. Note also that $s_M(m)$ might not exist. For example, if M is the woman optimal matching, then $s_M(m)$ does not exist for any man.

Example As an example, consider the stable matching M_1 from Figure 2.2 on page 70. Figure 2.9 shows $s_{M_1}(m)$ and $next_{M_1}(m)$ for each man m.

1:	3	2
2:	8	1
3:	1	6
4:	8	1
5:	2	7
6:	5	3
7:	5	3
8:	2	7

Figure 2.9: Woman $s_{M_1}(m)$ and man $next_{M_1}(m)$ for each man m

There is another way to think about $s_M(m)$ and $next_M(m)$ that is motivated by the extended version of the Gale-Shapley algorithm discussed in Section 1.2.4 on page 15. Suppose for each woman w we delete all pairs (m', w) such that w prefers $p_M(w)$ to m'. It is easy to see that in the resulting lists, which we call *reduced lists*, $p_M(w)$ is the last entry in w's list, and $s_M(m)$ is the entry just following $p_M(m)$ in m's list. It is also true that $p_M(m)$ is the first entry in m's list (hence $s_M(m)$ is the second entry), for if any woman w' remains above $p_M(m)$ after the deletions, then w' prefers m to her partner in M, and (m, w') would block M. So, after the deletions, $p_M(m)$, $s_M(m)$, and $p_M(w)$ are easy to identify, and $next_M(m)$ is also easy to find, since it is the last entry on $p_M(m)$'s new list; equivalently, $next_M(m)$ is the man m' such that $p_M(m)$ is the first entry on the reduced list of m'.

Note that when $M = M_0$, the reduced lists are the MGS-lists defined and discussed in Section 1.2.4 (page 15). The use of reduced lists will streamline the presentation of certain algorithms to be discussed later. As an example, Figure 2.10 shows the reduced lists of the men when M is the stable matching M_1 of Figure 2.2 (page 70).

1:	8	3			
2:	3	6			
3:	5	1	6	2	
4:	6	8	5		
5:	7	2	1	3	6
6:	1	5	2	3	
7:	2	5	7	8	1
8:	4	2	6		

Figure 2.10: The reduced lists of the men for stable matching M_1

Let $\rho = (m_0, w_0), (m_1, w_1), \ldots, (m_{r-1}, w_{r-1})$ be an ordered list of pairs in a stable matching M such that for each i $(0 \leq i \leq r-1)$, m_{i+1} is $next_M(m_i)$, where $i+1$ is taken modulo r. Then ρ is called a *rotation (exposed)* in M, and we say that m (or w) is *in* rotation ρ if there is a pair (m, w) in the ordered list defining ρ. From this point on, it will be assumed that whenever we refer to an element m_i or w_i in a rotation $(m_0, w_0), (m_1, w_1), \ldots, (m_{r-1}, w_{r-1})$, the value of the subscript i is taken modulo r.

Example   It is easy to see from Figure 2.10 that the ordered list of pairs $(1,8)$, $(2,3)$, $(4,6)$ is an exposed rotation in matching M_1, as is the ordered list $(3,5)$, $(6,1)$. There are no other rotations exposed in M_1.

Note that a rotation may be exposed in more than one matching, and hence the definition does not associate a rotation with a unique matching. However, no ordered set of pairs is a rotation unless it satisfies the above definition for at least one stable matching of $\mathcal{M}$. As a first indication of the utility of rotations, and their connection to minimal differences, we prove the following.

Lemma 2.5.1 *If $\rho = (m_0, w_0), (m_1, w_1), \ldots, (m_{r-1}, w_{r-1})$ is a rotation, and for some i $(0 \le i \le r - 1)$, w is any woman strictly between w_i and w_{i+1} in man m_i's list, then (m_i, w) is not a stable pair, i.e., it is never a pair in any stable matching of $\mathcal{M}$.*

Proof Let M be any stable matching in which ρ is exposed. Then in m_i's list, w is strictly between w_i (which is $p_M(m_i)$) and w_{i+1} (which is $s_M(m_i)$), and by the definition of $s_M(m_i)$, w prefers her partner in M to m_i. Now suppose (m_i, w) is a pair in stable matching M'. Then both m_i and w prefer their partners in M to their partners in M', violating Theorem 1.3.1 (page 18). $\square$

Example In rotation $(1, 8), (2, 3), (4, 6)$, which is exposed in matching M_1 of Figure 2.2, m_0 is man 1, and woman 4 is between woman $w_0(8)$, and woman $w_1(3)$. So, the pair $(1, 4)$ cannot be in any stable matching for the preferences of Figure 2.1 (page 69).

If M is a stable matching, and $\rho = (m_0, w_0), (m_1, w_1), \ldots, (m_{r-1}, w_{r-1})$ is a rotation exposed in M, then M/ρ is defined to be the matching in which each man not in ρ stays married to his partner in M, and each man m_i in ρ marries $w_{i+1} = s_M(m_i)$. The matching M/ρ essentially differs from M by a one place cyclic shift of each man in ρ to the M-partner of the next man in ρ; hence it is easy to verify that it is a matching, i.e., it is one-one. The transformation of M to M/ρ is called the *elimination* of ρ from M.

Example The elimination of rotation $(1, 8), (2, 3), (4, 6)$ from M_1 yields the matching M_2 of Figure 2.2, and the elimination of $(3, 5), (6, 1)$ from M_1 yields M_3.

The following two central lemmas further demonstrate the utility of rotations; for example, they immediately imply that M_0 can be transformed to M_z through a sequence of stable matchings, by successively finding and eliminating *any* exposed rotation in each successive matching.

Lemma 2.5.2 *If ρ is any rotation exposed in a stable matching M, then M/ρ is a stable matching dominated by M.*

Proof Suppose (m, w) blocks M/ρ. All the women either have the same or better partners in M/ρ than in M, and w prefers m to her partner in

M/ρ, so she also prefers m to her partner in M. But then m must be in ρ or else (m, w) would block M. So w is strictly above $s_M(m)$ in m's list and she prefers m to $p_M(w)$, contradicting the definition of $s_M(m)$ as the first woman in m's list who prefers m to her partner in M. $\square$

Lemma 2.5.3 *If M is any stable matching other than the woman optimal matching M_z, then there is at least one rotation exposed in M.*

Proof Let m be any man who has different partners in M and M_z, and let w be m's partner in M_z. Since M_z is woman-optimal and man-pessimal, m strictly prefers his partner in M to w, and w strictly prefers m to her partner in M. Hence $s_M(m)$ exists. Also, if $s_M(m)$ exists and $m' = next_M(m)$ (the partner in M of woman $s_M(m)$), then $s_M(m')$ exists also. Otherwise, m' and $s_M(m)$ would be partners in M_z, so m would prefer $s_M(m)$ to his partner in M_z, and $s_M(m)$ would prefer m to her partner in M_z, contradicting the stability of M_z.

Now let $H(M)$ be a directed graph with a node for each man m who has different partners in M and M_z. Direct an edge from the node for m to the node for $next_M(m)$, which, as shown above, must also be in $H(M)$. Then, every node in $H(M)$ has out-degree exactly one, and so there must be a simple cycle in $H(M)$. Any such simple cycle defines the men in a rotation exposed in M, in the order that they appear in the rotation; for any man m in the cycle, $(m, p_M(m))$ is a pair in the associated rotation. $\square$

Figure 2.11 shows the graph $H(M_1)$ for the stable matching M_1 of Figure 2.2.

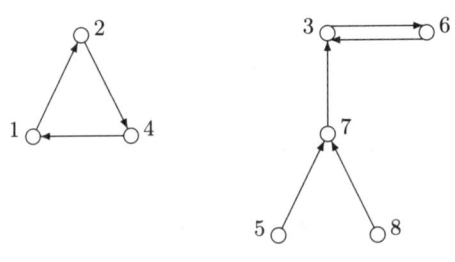

Figure 2.11: The graph $H(M)$

The above proof gives a simple way to find a rotation exposed in M: starting from any man m, traverse the *unique* path in $H(M)$ from m until

m or some other node is visited twice. If ρ is the rotation discovered by this traversal, we say that m *leads to* rotation ρ; if m leads to ρ but is not in ρ, then the path in $H(M)$ from m to the first man in ρ is called a *tail* of ρ. Note that a rotation can have several tails. The following is now immediate.

Corollary 2.5.1 *If m has different partners in M and M_z, then m leads to exactly one exposed rotation in M, so m is either in exactly one rotation exposed in M or is in exactly one tail.*

The following lemma is an extension of Lemma 2.5.1 and is proved in essentially the same way. We leave the details to the reader.

Lemma 2.5.4 *If ρ is exposed in M and m is a man on a tail of ρ in $H(M)$, then (m, w) cannot be a stable pair if w is strictly between $p_M(m)$ and $s_M(m)$.*

2.5.2 Rotations and Minimal Differences

In this section, we will exhibit a one-one correspondence between the rotations and the minimal differences of $P(\mathcal{M})$. Then, given Lemmas 2.5.2 and 2.5.3 above, and the fact that all the minimal differences are found along any maximal chain of $P(\mathcal{M})$, we will be able to identify all the minimal differences and all the rotations by successively finding and eliminating exposed rotations, myopicly following any maximal chain in $\mathcal{M}$ from M_0 to M_z. The following is a central technical lemma.

Lemma 2.5.5 *If M strictly dominates M', and ρ is exposed in M, then either all the men in ρ have the same partners in M and in M', or none of them does. In the latter case, M/ρ dominates M'. Similarly, if a man m is on a tail of ρ, and m has different partners in the two matchings, then so does every man in ρ, and again M/ρ dominates M'.*

Proof By Lemma 2.5.1, if $m_i \in \rho$ has a different partner w in M' than in M, then w must either be $s_M(m_i)$ or a woman below her in m_i's list. In either case, $s_M(m_i)$ must not be matched in M' to m_{i+1}, her partner in M, for if $s_M(m_i)$ and m_{i+1} are partners in M', then either $s_M(m_i)$ has two partners in M', or the pair $(m_i, s_M(m_i))$ blocks M'. Hence m_{i+1} must also have a different partner in M' than in M, and it follows that all men in ρ have different partners in M and M' if any one of them does. In the case that the men of ρ have different partners in the two matchings, Lemma 2.5.1 implies that M/ρ dominates (possibly equals) M', since the only men with different partners in M and M/ρ are the men in ρ. The case when m is on a tail of ρ is proved in essentially the same way, using Lemma 2.5.4 in place of Lemma 2.5.1. $\square$

Example In Figure 2.2, M_1 dominates both M_4 and M_5, among other matchings, and the rotation $(1,8),(2,3),(4,6)$, which we will call ρ_1, is exposed in M_1. In matching M_5, every man in ρ_1 has the same partner he has in M_1, while in M_4 every man in ρ_1 has a different partner. Further, $M_2 = M_1/\rho_1$ and M_2 dominates M_4, as required by the lemma.

Theorem 2.5.1 *If ρ is exposed in M, then M is an immediate predecessor of M/ρ in $\mathcal{M}$, and $P(M/\rho) \setminus P(M)$ is a minimal difference of $P(\mathcal{M})$.*

Proof It is immediate from Lemma 2.5.5 that there is no stable matching M' such that M dominates M', and M' dominates M/ρ, so M immediately precedes M/ρ. Then by Lemma 2.4.4, $P(M/\rho) \setminus P(M)$ is a minimal difference of $P(\mathcal{M})$. $\square$

For rotation $\rho = (m_0, w_0), (m_1, w_1), \ldots, (m_{r-1}, w_{r-1})$, we define $d(\rho)$ to be the set of all pairs (m_i, w), where $m_i \in \rho$ and w is either w_{i+1} or a woman strictly between w_i and w_{i+1} in m_i's list.

Example When $\rho = (3,5),(6,1)$, which is a rotation in the example from Figure 2.2 (page 70), then $m_0 = 3, m_1 = 6, w_0 = 5, w_1 = 1$, and so it can be seen from the preference lists of Figure 2.1 (page 69) that $d(\rho) = \{(3,1),(6,6),(6,7),(6,5)\}$.

Notice that rotation ρ is completely determined by the set of pairs $d(\rho)$ and the preference lists, and that ρ can be constructed from $d(\rho)$ as follows: for each man m in a pair $(m, w) \in d(\rho)$, let $w(m)$ be the woman m most prefers among the women w such that (m, w) is in $d(\rho)$; let $\hat{w}(m)$ be the woman immediately before $w(m)$ in m's preference list. Then ρ consists of all pairs $(m, \hat{w}(m))$, such that m is in a pair $(m, w) \in d(\rho)$. The order of the pairs in ρ is easily determined from these pairs and the preference lists. We leave the details to the reader.

Lemma 2.5.6 *If rotation ρ is exposed in distinct matchings M and M', then $P(M/\rho) \setminus P(M) = P(M'/\rho) \setminus P(M') = d(\rho)$.*

Proof The difference $P(M/\rho) \setminus P(M)$ consists of all pairs (m_i, w), where w is either w_{i+1} or a woman strictly between w_i and w_{i+1} in m_i's list. Clearly this set of pairs depends only on ρ and the preference lists, and not on M. Hence, $P(M/\rho) \setminus P(M) = P(M'/\rho) \setminus P(M')$, and they both are $d(\rho)$. $\square$

Combining Lemma 2.5.6 and Theorem 2.5.1, we have the following.

Theorem 2.5.2 *For any rotation ρ, the set of pairs $d(\rho)$ is a minimal difference of $P(\mathcal{M})$, and so each rotation ρ maps to a unique minimal difference $d(\rho)$. Further, $d(\rho)$ can be constructed directly from ρ and the preference lists.*

Our goal now is to show the converse of Theorem 2.5.2, i.e., that every minimal difference of $P(\mathcal{M})$ is $d(\rho)$ for exactly one rotation ρ. We will do this through the use of Algorithm *minimal-differences*, shown in Figure 2.12. This algorithm will find all the minimal differences of $P(\mathcal{M})$, and all the rotations of $\mathcal{M}$, using only the preference lists of the problem instance.

Algorithm *minimal-differences*

find the man- and the woman-optimal matchings M_0, M_z;
$i := 0$;
while $M_i \neq M_z$ do
begin
    find an exposed rotation ρ_i in M_i;
    $M_{i+1} := M_i/\rho_i$;
    $d(\rho_i) := P(M_{i+1}) \setminus P(M_i)$;
    $i := i + 1$;
end

Figure 2.12: Algorithm to find all the minimal differences and rotations

Theorem 2.5.3 *Every minimal difference of $P(\mathcal{M})$ is the set $d(\rho_i)$ for exactly one rotation ρ_i generated by Algorithm minimal-differences and every rotation in $\mathcal{M}$ is generated exactly once by Algorithm minimal-differences.*

Proof By Lemmas 2.5.2 and 2.5.3, each M_i generated by the algorithm is a stable matching, and there is an exposed rotation in each matching until the woman optimal matching is reached. Further, by Theorem 2.5.1, each M_i is an immediate predecessor in $\mathcal{M}$ of M_{i+1}. Hence the sequence of stable matchings generated by the algorithm must be a maximal chain in $\mathcal{M}$ from the man optimal matching to the woman optimal matching. Now by Corollary 2.4.3, every minimal difference of $\mathcal{M}$ appears exactly once as a consecutive difference of matchings along any maximal chain in $\mathcal{M}$; hence, every minimal difference of $\mathcal{M}$ is $d(\rho_i)$ for exactly one ρ_i generated by the algorithm.

For the second claim, let ρ be any rotation, and let M be any stable matching in which it is exposed. By Lemma 2.5.6 $d(\rho) = P(M/\rho) \setminus P(M)$, which is a minimal difference, by Theorem 2.5.1. Hence $d(\rho) = d(\rho_i)$, for some ρ_i found by the algorithm. But since $d(\rho)$ uniquely determines ρ, it follows that $\rho = \rho_i$. $\square$

We will say that a rotation ρ is *on* a chain in $\mathcal{M}$, and that the chain *contains* ρ, if the minimal difference $d(\rho)$ is on the corresponding chain in $P(\mathcal{M})$. Then, combining the results of this section with Theorem 2.4.2 we have the main result of this section.

Theorem 2.5.4 *There is a one-one correspondence $\rho \leftrightarrow d(\rho)$ between the rotations of $\mathcal{M}$ and the minimal differences of $P(\mathcal{M})$. Further, if M dominates M', then every chain in $\mathcal{M}$ between M and M' contains exactly the same set of rotations. Hence every rotation of $\mathcal{M}$ appears exactly once on every maximal chain of $\mathcal{M}$.*

Example We will demonstrate Algorithm *minimal-differences* on the problem instance shown in Figure 2.1. In the example, we will use reduced preference lists, as discussed on page 87. This will keep the lists smaller, and make it easier to recognize exposed rotations. Also, we will display only the reduced lists of the men, as all information can be extracted from their reduced lists. To verify that the reduced lists of the men are maintained correctly, the reader can check the successive changes against the original preference lists shown in Figure 2.1. To start, the MGS-lists for the man-optimal matching M_0 are shown in Figure 2.13.

1:	5	8	3				
2:	3	8	6				
3:	8	5	1	6	2		
4:	6	8	5				
5:	7	2	1	3	6	8	4
6:	1	5	2	3			
7:	2	5	7	8	1		
8:	4	5	2	6			

Figure 2.13: The MGS lists

There is one exposed rotation $\rho_0 = (1,5),(3,8)$ in M_0, and $M_0/\rho_0 = M_1$. The reduced lists for M_1 were used in an earlier example and appear in Figure 2.10 on page 88. As noted before, there are two exposed rotations in M_1. Suppose the

1:	3				
2:	6				
3:	5	1	2		
4:	8	5			
5:	7	2	1		
6:	1	5	2		
7:	2	5	7	8	1
8:	4	2			

Figure 2.14: The reduced lists of the men for stable matching M_2

algorithm picks rotation $\rho_1 = (1,8),(2,3),(4,6)$ at this point. Then $M_1/\rho_1 = M_2$; the reduced lists of the men for M_2 are shown in Figure 2.14.

In M_2 there is one exposed rotation, $\rho_2 = (3,5),(6,1)$, and $M_2/\rho_2 = M_4$ (note that we are using the name of the matching given in Figure 2.2 rather than the name given by Algorithm *minimal-differences*). The reduced lists for M_4 are shown in Figure 2.15.

1:	3			
2:	6			
3:	1	2		
4:	8			
5:	7	2	1	
6:	5	2		
7:	2	7	8	
8:	4	2		

Figure 2.15: The reduced lists of the men for stable matching M_4

The rotation $\rho_3 = (7,2),(5,7)$ is exposed in M_4, and $M_4/\rho_3 = M_6$. The reduced lists are shown in Figure 2.16.

Rotation $\rho_4 = (3,1),(5,2)$ is exposed in M_6, and $M_6/\rho_4 = M_7$, the woman-optimal matching. The final reduced lists are shown in Figure 2.17.

Even without additional implementation detail, it is easy to establish that Algorithm *minimal-differences* needs no more than $O(n^3)$ time to find all the rotations. In the next chapter we will implement Algorithm *minimal-differences* to run in $O(n^2)$ time.

The reader should now be able to see that rotations can be more useful for algorithmic purposes than are minimal differences. Any stable matching M other than M_z has an exposed rotation ρ that defines a minimal difference

1:	3	
2:	6	
3:	1	2
4:	8	
5:	2	1
6:	5	2
7:	7	8
8:	4	2

Figure 2.16: The reduced lists of the men for stable matching M_6

1:	3	
2:	6	
3:	2	
4:	8	
5:	1	
6:	5	2
7:	7	8
8:	4	2

Figure 2.17: The reduced lists of the men for woman-optimal matching

$d(\rho)$, and both ρ and $d(\rho)$ are easy to find from the reduced lists for M. Hence rotations allow one to focus on a *single* stable matching M, knowing that $d(\rho)$ is a minimal difference of $\mathcal{M}$, whereas the definition of a minimal difference involves a very particular stable matching, an irreducible one, or involves two stable matchings. The existence of rotations is the special, algorithmically valuable feature of $P(\mathcal{M})$ that does not exist in a general ring of sets.

2.5.3 The Rotations Generate All Stable Matchings

We know that the minimal differences of $P(\mathcal{M})$ can be used to generate all the stable matchings, and that the rotations can be used to generate the minimal differences. Hence, the rotations can surely be used to generate all the stable matchings. In this section we will establish a more direct approach to thinking about and using rotations for this purpose.

Lemma 2.5.7 *Let M be an immediate predecessor of M' in $\mathcal{M}$, and let ρ be the rotation such that $d(\rho) = P(M') \setminus P(M)$. Then ρ is exposed in M, and $M/\rho = M'$.*

Proof It is immediate from the definition of $d(\rho)$, and the way that ρ is uniquely determined from $d(\rho)$, that if ρ is exposed in M, then $M' = M/\rho$. Every man $m' \in \rho$ has different partners in M and M_z, so by Corollary 2.5.1, m' leads to some rotation ρ' exposed in M. Now since m' has a different partner in M than in M', Lemma 2.5.5 implies that each man $m \in \rho'$ must also have different partners in M' and M. Let w be m's partner in M, and let w' be the woman just following w in m's list. Then (m, w') must be in the minimal difference $P(M') \setminus P(M) = d(\rho)$. But (m, w') must also be in $d(\rho')$, so it must be that $d(\rho) = d(\rho')$ which can only happen when $\rho' = \rho$, hence ρ is exposed in M. $\square$

Corollary 2.5.2 *For any stable matchings M and M', where M dominates M', let C be a chain between M and M' in $\mathcal{M}$. Then M' can be generated from M by successively exposing and eliminating the rotations on C, in their order on C. Further, every sequence of rotation eliminations transforming M to M' contains exactly the same set of rotations, although in a different order.*

Proof The first statement follows inductively from Lemma 2.5.7. The second statement follows from the fact that any sequence of rotation eliminations follows a chain in $\mathcal{M}$, and Theorem 2.4.2. $\square$

Specializing Corollary 2.5.2 to the case when $M = M_0$ gives the next theorem.

Theorem 2.5.5 *Every stable matching M' can be generated by a sequence of rotation eliminations, starting from M_0, and every such sequence contains exactly the same rotations.*

That is, chains in $\mathcal{M}$ not only indicate how to transform one matching to another by unioning the minimal differences along the corresponding chain in $P(\mathcal{M})$, but they also indicate how to transform matchings by successive rotation eliminations.

Example Every edge in Figure 2.2 on page 70 is labeled with the name of one of the rotations obtained by Algorithm *minimal-differences*. If M is an immediate predecessor of M', then the edge (M, M') is labeled with the rotation ρ such that $d(\rho) = P(M') \setminus P(M)$. Corollary 2.5.2 is very clearly illustrated in that figure.

Characterizing stable pairs

At this point, we have the tools to characterize the stable pairs of any problem instance.

Theorem 2.5.6 *i) A pair (m, w) is a stable pair if and only if it is a pair in M_z or it is a pair in some rotation. Equivalently, (m, w) is stable if and only if it is a pair in M_0, or for some rotation $(m_0, w_0), (m_1, w_1), \ldots, (m_{r-1}, w_{r-1})$ and some i, $m = m_i$ and $w = w_{i+1}$.*
ii) A pair is a fixed pair if and only if it is in both M_0 and M_z, or equivalently, it is in M_0 but not in any rotation.

Proof i) The "if" part is by definition. For the "only if" part, let (m, w) be a stable pair in a stable matching $M \neq M_z$. Then by Corollary 2.5.2, there is a chain C in $\mathcal{M}$ from M to M_z, and M_z can be obtained by eliminating the rotations on this chain in order. Since $p_{M_z}(m) \neq w$, there must be some rotation ρ on C whose elimination changes m's partner from w to some other woman. But then, (m, w) must be in ρ.

The proof of ii) is immediate. □

By Theorem 2.5.4, every rotation is contained on every maximal chain in $\mathcal{M}$, so combined with Theorem 2.5.6 we have the following observation.

Corollary 2.5.3 *The stable matchings on any maximal chain in $\mathcal{M}$ contain all the stable pairs of $\mathcal{M}$.*

2.5.4 The Rotation Poset

Given the one-one correspondence between the minimal differences of $P(\mathcal{M})$ and the rotations of $\mathcal{M}$, we can finally define the long awaited representation $\Pi(\mathcal{M})$ of $\mathcal{M}$ based on rotations.

The *rotation poset* of $\mathcal{M}$, denoted $\Pi(\mathcal{M})$, is the partial order,on the rotations on the rotations of $\mathcal{M}$ defined by replacing each minimal difference $d(\rho)$ in the partial order $D(\mathcal{M})$ by the rotation ρ. The precedence relation on $\Pi(\mathcal{M})$ corresponds exactly to that on $D(\mathcal{M})$: ρ' precedes ρ in $\Pi(\mathcal{M})$ if and only if $d(\rho')$ precedes $d(\rho)$ in $D(\mathcal{M})$. Note that $\Pi(\mathcal{M})$ is isomorphic to the partial order $I(\mathcal{M})$ after the removal of M_0 from $I(\mathcal{M})$.

Example The rotation poset $\Pi(\mathcal{M})$ for the lattice $\mathcal{M}$ from Figure 2.2 is shown in Figure 2.18.

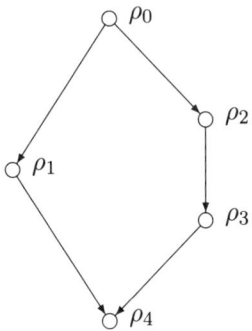

Figure 2.18: The rotation poset for $\mathcal{M}$

As expected, we have

Theorem 2.5.7 *i) There is a one-one correspondence between the closed subsets of $\Pi(\mathcal{M})$ and the stable matchings of $\mathcal{M}$.*
ii) S is the closed set of rotations of $\Pi(\mathcal{M})$ corresponding to a stable matching M if and only if S is the (unique) set of rotations on every M_0-chain in $\mathcal{M}$ ending at M. Further, M can be generated from M_0 by eliminating the rotations in their order along any of these paths, and these are the only ways to generate M by rotation eliminations starting from M_0.
iii) If S and S' are the unique sets of rotations corresponding to distinct stable matchings M and M', then M dominates M' if and only if $S \subset S'$.

We end this chapter here, having completely defined our desired representation $\Pi(\mathcal{M})$, but not having shown how it can be efficiently constructed. That is the first topic discussed in the next chapter, which is devoted to algorithms rather than to the primarily structural matters of this chapter.

2.6   Notes and References

The fundamental, classical theorem behind our approach to the structure of stable matchings is Birkhoff's representation theorem for finite distributive lattices [2], [30, pages 73–74]: Every finite distributive lattice $\mathcal{L}$ is *isomorphic* to a ring of sets $R(\mathcal{L})$. In more detail, Birkhoff defines a *meet irreducible* element of a distributive lattice $\mathcal{L}$ as either the minimal element of $\mathcal{L}$ (the zero of $\mathcal{L}$), or an element that has exactly one immediate predecessor in $\mathcal{L}$. Then the base set of $R(\mathcal{L})$ is the set of nonzero irreducible elements of $\mathcal{L}$, and the isomorphism in the theorem associates each element of $\mathcal{L}$ with the set of nonzero irreducible elements of $\mathcal{L}$ that precede it in $\mathcal{L}$. This family of subsets of the irreducible elements of $\mathcal{L}$ forms a ring of sets that is isomorphic to $\mathcal{L}$. Further, if we define $\mathcal{P}$ as the partial order, under the lattice relation, of the nonzero irreducible elements of $\mathcal{L}$, then Birkhoff's theorem also says that the closed subsets of $\mathcal{P}$ are in one-one correspondence with the elements of $R(\mathcal{L})$ and hence with those of $\mathcal{L}$. And, as expected, a closed subset C of $\mathcal{P}$ generates an element of $R(\mathcal{L})$ by unioning together the base elements of $R(\mathcal{L})$ contained in C, and every element of $R(\mathcal{L})$ can be generated in this way.

It is easy to prove that the nonzero irreducible elements of a ring of sets $\mathcal{F}$ (as defined in this chapter), have the property that they have exactly one immediate predecessor in $\mathcal{F}$. Further, any element of $\mathcal{F}$ or $\mathcal{M}$ that has only one immediate predecessor is irreducible in the terms of this chapter. Hence the irreducible elements of this chapter are exactly the meet irreducible elements of Birkhoff's theorem.

Birkhoff's theorem could therefore have been used explicitly to prove the existence of $I(\mathcal{M})$ and $I(\mathcal{F})$, and could have been the basis for proving the existence and properties of $D(\mathcal{F})$. We now explain why we chose not to base this chapter directly on Birkhoff's theorem, and why we developed our own exposition on rings of sets, rather than following well established expositions from the mathematics literature.

For algorithmic applications, Birkhoff's theorem is not the ideal tool to use to develop the structure of stable matchings, or for other problems whose solutions form a distributive lattice. The problem is that Birkhoff's theorem starts with the distributive lattice $\mathcal{L}$, and then defines the partial-order representation of $\mathcal{L}$ in terms of elements with a structural property, the property of having exactly one immediate predecessor. For algorithmic purposes, this is a backwards viewpoint. In the stable marriage problem (and other combinatorial problems), we are not given a lattice — we are given the input to a problem whose solutions form a distributive lattice. We cannot afford to construct the lattice first and then look for those elements with exactly one immediate predecessor. In short, while Birkhoff's theorem shows the existence of a partial order representing the distributive lattice, the theorem by itself does not suggest when, or how, the partial order can be computed efficiently from the problem input, or even when it will be small. These are serious omissions, for the partial order is valuable precisely when it is small and can be computed efficiently from the problem input. Hence, for algorithmic applications, we need an approach that is based on what is given as input —the problem instance — not on a feature of the output. The rings-of-sets approach developed in this chapter satisfies this requirement in three ways.

First, in the problems of interest, such as stable marriage and others that will be discussed in Chapter 3, the problem solutions have a natural description as a ring of sets over a base set B, where B is *easily identified from the input* to the problem. Given the ring of sets description of the solutions, we then have a characterization of the irreducible elements of the ring (and hence of the distributive lattice), in terms of the input data rather than in terms of a structural feature of the lattice: an element F of $\mathcal{F}$ is irreducible if for some element $a \in B$, F is the smallest element in $\mathcal{F}$ containing a. For the problems of interest, it is easy to find such an F given an $a \in B$, and the partial-order relation on them is just set containment, so we have a general, simple method for constructing the partial order on the irreducible elements *without first knowing* the full distributive lattice. As mentioned above, these irreducible elements are actually the meet irreducible elements of Birkhoff's theorem, but this characterization of them avoids the need to have the lattice in hand.

Second, for the problems of interest, not only is the base set B easily expressed in terms of the input to the problem, but its size is polynomial in the size of the input. In fact, for all the problems we know of, the size of B equals the size of the input. This immediately says that the partial-order representation of the set of all solutions to the problem has size that is polynomial in the size of the input to the problem, although, for the problems of interest, the number of solutions can grow exponentially in the size of the input. Hence the partial-order representation of the problem solutions is guaranteed to be, in the worst case, exponentially smaller than the lattice of solutions. For algorithmic purposes, this is a crucial property. Further,

we need the ring of sets viewpoint for this property, for the only bound on
the size of the partial-order representation given by Birkhoff's theorem is
the number of nonzero meet irreducible elements of the lattice, and that
number can be nearly equal to the number of elements of the lattice.

Finally, for greatest efficiency in building the partial-order representation,
we use minimal differences between problem solutions, not irreducible solutions themselves. Clearly, to be able to consider set differences between
solutions we need to think of solutions as sets over some set, and this is easy
to do in the context of a ring of sets.

The exposition of rings of sets is our own, as is the definition of the
irreducible elements of a ring of sets, and the representation $I(\mathcal{F})$ based on
them; as explained above, this definition is really a characterization of the
meet irreducible elements of a a ring of sets $\mathcal{F}$ in terms of the sets, and not
the structure of $\mathcal{F}$. We have not seen this crucial characterization elsewhere,
but discussions that are similar in spirit have appeared in [44] and [78], and
the viewpoint in this chapter was influenced by those papers. The view of
the set of stable matchings as a ring of P-sets, the representations $I(\mathcal{M})$
and $I(\mathcal{F})$, Theorems 2.2.1 and 2.3.1, and the connection between rotations
and minimal differences (Theorems 2.5.1, 2.5.3, 2.5.4 for example) are all
new.

The representation $\Pi(\mathcal{M})$ was first defined and derived by Irving and
Leather [48], who proved Theorem 2.5.7 strictly in the context of the stable
marriage problem, without reference to rings of sets or lattices. Their work
solved one of of Knuth's twelve open problems [59], namely to characterize
and represent the set of all stable matchings without enumerating them all,
i.e., without explicitly constructing the lattice of stable matchings. Most of
the fundamental lemmas concerning rotations (Lemmas 2.5.1, 2.5.2, 2.5.3,
2.5.5) were first proved by Irving and Leather in [48]. The fact that every
rotation is contained on every maximal chain in $\mathcal{M}$, and every stable pair is
in those matchings (Corollary 2.5.3) was proved strictly in terms of stable
matchings by Gusfield [35]; a version of Algorithm *minimal differences* was
also developed there to find all the rotations, but not the minimal differences.
Theorems 2.5.5 and 2.5.6 were first shown by Irving and Leather [48], again
using arguments strictly in terms of stable marriage.

Chapter 3

Building and Exploiting the Representation of All Stable Matchings

3.1   Introduction

In this Chapter we move from the purely structural and representation issues of Chapter 2 to algorithmic issues involving the rotation poset $\Pi(\mathcal{M})$. We first show how to efficiently construct $\Pi(\mathcal{M})$ from the preference lists alone, and provide the implementation details to find all the rotations in $O(n^2)$ time. In so doing, we will also define the digraph $G(\mathcal{M})$, a very useful sparse representation of $\Pi(\mathcal{M})$. We then exploit the rotation poset $\Pi(\mathcal{M})$ and the digraph $G(\mathcal{M})$ to obtain complexity results and efficient algorithms for a range of problems derived from the basic stable marriage problem.

We start the exploitation of $\Pi(\mathcal{M})$ by examining three questions that can be easily and efficiently solved using the rotations and $\Pi(\mathcal{M})$: finding all stable pairs, determining if a *set* of pairs is stable (defined in Section 3.4.2), and optimally decomposing a problem instance into independent subinstances. We then show how to enumerate all the stable matchings in $O(n)$ time per matching (after the first matching is found) and $O(n^2)$ space, which is clearly time and space optimal. We next examine the harder problem of efficiently computing stable matchings that are more equitable than the man-optimal or woman-optimal matchings; we give three related solutions to this problem. After that, we examine a relationship between linear programming and the stable marriage problem. Next we look at the relationship between the marriage lattice and arbitrary distributive lattices, and between the rotation poset and arbitrary partial orders. Finally, we show that the stable marriage problem is "structurally equivalent" to other well-known combinatorial problems, yielding, as a side consequence, certain *NP*-hardness results. In each of these applications, we will see the central role played by the existence of the compact representation $\Pi(\mathcal{M})$ and the efficient construction of digraph $G(\mathcal{M})$.

3.2   Constructing the Rotation Poset

We have seen that all the elements of $\Pi(\mathcal{M})$, the rotations, can be found by Algorithm *minimal-differences*, which takes as input only the preference lists and ranking arrays (which can be obtained from the preference lists). We will later implement this algorithm to run in $O(n^2)$ time. However, a much more important algorithmic issue that we have ignored is how to efficiently construct the precedence relation on $\Pi(\mathcal{M})$. We do not want to base the algorithm solely on the definition of the relation, since its definition, given in Chapter 2, ultimately relies on the precedence relation on $I(\mathcal{M})$, which we don't know. It is not obvious that the relation on $\Pi(\mathcal{M})$ can be deduced without knowing the irreducible matchings, $I(\mathcal{M})$; indeed, for a general ring of sets $\mathcal{F}$, one cannot construct the partial order on $D(\mathcal{F})$ from the set $D(\mathcal{F})$ alone, that is, without $I(\mathcal{F})$. However, in the case of the stable marriage problem, we will show how to determine the precedence relation on $\Pi(\mathcal{M})$ using only the rotations and the preference lists, justifying the claim made at the start of Chapter 2 that $\Pi(\mathcal{M})$ can be constructed without knowing $I(\mathcal{M})$ or $\mathcal{M}$.

The idea is that we will efficiently find a subset $G(\mathcal{M})$ of the pairs of rotations in the partial order $\Pi(\mathcal{M})$, such that the transitive closure of $G(\mathcal{M})$ is the full partial order $\Pi(\mathcal{M})$. It will turn out that for most of the algorithmic applications in this chapter, $G(\mathcal{M})$ can be used in place of $\Pi(\mathcal{M})$, and this substitution will be a key to efficient algorithms.

Let $\rho = \{(m_0, w_0), (m_1, w_1), \ldots, (m_{r-1}, w_{r-1})\}$ be a rotation. We say that ρ *moves* m_i *down* from w_i to w_{i+1}, and *moves* w_i *up* from m_i to m_{i-1}. If w is either w_i or is strictly between w_i and w_{i+1} in m_i's list, then ρ *moves* m_i *below* w. Similarly, ρ *moves* w_i *above* m if m is m_i, or is strictly between m_i and m_{i-1} in w_i's list.

These definitions simply reflect what happens to each person in ρ when ρ is eliminated from a matching M in which it is exposed. Note that a rotation moves a man m below w if and only if $(m, w) \in d(\rho)$. However, the concept of a rotation moving a woman above a man has no such simple interpretation, and it is not generally true that when ρ moves m below w, ρ moves w above m. In fact, it is true if and only if (m, w) is in ρ. Notice that between a person's partners in M_0 and M_z, the moves that the rotations make divide the person's preference list into contiguous intervals that share only their endpoints, a fact implied by the lemmas below.

Lemma 3.2.1 *For any man m and woman w, there is at most one rotation that moves m down to w, and w up to m. Further, there is at most one rotation that moves m from w.*

Proof If two rotations, ρ and ρ', move m to w, then (m, w) is in $d(\rho) \cap d(\rho')$ contradicting Lemma 2.4.1 (page 80). Further, a rotation moves m to w if and only if it moves w to m, so the first claim follows. For the second claim, let w' be the woman immediately following w in m's list. If ρ and ρ' both move m from w, then $(m, w') \in d(\rho) \cap d(\rho')$, again a contradiction. □

Corollary 3.2.1 *Every man-woman pair (m, w) is in at most one rotation. Hence there are at most $n(n-1)/2$ rotations in an instance of the stable marriage problem of size n.*

Lemma 3.2.2 *For any man m and woman w, there is at most one rotation that moves w to a man strictly above m in w's list.*

Proof The case when w is moved from m has been covered by Lemma 3.2.1, so assume that rotation ρ_1 moves w from a man $m_1 \neq m$ to a man above m, and that rotation $\rho_2 \neq \rho_1$ moves w from a man $m_2 \neq m$ to a man above m. By Lemma 3.2.1 $m_1 \neq m_2$, so suppose without loss of generality that w prefers m_1 to m_2, hence ρ_2 moves w above m_1. Then there can be no chain of rotation eliminations that includes both ρ_1 and ρ_2: if ρ_1 is eliminated first, then w moves to a man above m_2, and so ρ_2 cannot thereafter be exposed; similarly, if ρ_2 is eliminated first, then w moves above m_1, and ρ_1 cannot become exposed. But by Theorem 2.5.4, every maximal chain of $\mathcal{M}$ contains all the rotations, and by Corollary 2.5.2 the rotations along any chain can be exposed and eliminated in their order on the chain; hence only one rotation moves w above m. □

Type 1 and Type 2 Pairs of $\Pi(\mathcal{M})$

We will now define the directed, acyclic graph $G(\mathcal{M})$, called the *rotation digraph*, whose edges correspond to a subset of the pairs of $\Pi(\mathcal{M})$, and show that its transitive closure is $\Pi(\mathcal{M})$. In the next section we will show that $G(\mathcal{M})$ can be explicitly constructed in $O(n^2)$ time.

Suppose (m, w) is in rotation ρ. If ρ' is the (unique) rotation that moves m to w, then (ρ', ρ) is a directed edge in $G(\mathcal{M})$. In this case, ρ' is called a *type 1* of ρ. Note that ρ has no type 1 predecessor if ρ is exposed in M_0.

If ρ moves m below w, and $\rho' \neq \rho$ is the (unique) rotation that moves w above m, then (ρ', ρ) is a directed edge in $G(\mathcal{M})$. In this case, ρ' is called a *type 2* predecessor of ρ.

Example Figure 3.1 shows the rotation digraph $G(\mathcal{M})$ for the lattice $\mathcal{M}$ of Figure 2.2. The type(s) of each edge are shown on the edge. Note that an edge can be both type 1 and type 2. Rotation ρ_0 is a type 2 predecessor of ρ_1 because of the pair $(2, 8)$; ρ_1 is a type 2 predecessor of ρ_4 because of pair $(3, 6)$; ρ_2 is a type 2 predecessor of ρ_3 because of pair $(7, 5)$.

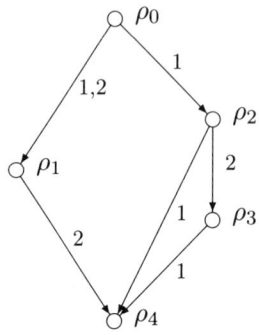

Figure 3.1: The rotation digraph

Another View of the Precedence Relation

Our goal is to show that the transitive closure of $G(\mathcal{M})$ is $\Pi(\mathcal{M})$. In particular, $G(\mathcal{M})$ is a subset of the pairs of $\Pi(\mathcal{M})$ containing all pairs (ρ', ρ), where ρ' is an immediate predecessor of ρ in $\Pi(\mathcal{M})$. To do this, we need to introduce a different view of the precedence relation on $\Pi(\mathcal{M})$. We first restate Theorem 2.4.4 (page 86) in terms of rotations instead of minimal differences.

Theorem 3.2.1 *Rotation ρ' precedes rotation ρ in $\Pi(\mathcal{M})$ if and only if ρ' appears before ρ on every maximal chain in $\mathcal{M}$.*

Theorem 3.2.2 *For any two rotations ρ' and ρ, rotation ρ' precedes ρ in $\Pi(\mathcal{M})$ if and only if ρ' is eliminated in every sequence of eliminations that starts at M_0 and ends at a stable matching in which ρ is exposed. Informally, ρ' precedes ρ if and only if ρ cannot be exposed unless ρ' has been eliminated.*

Proof Suppose ρ' precedes ρ in $\Pi(\mathcal{M})$, but that there exists a sequence of rotation eliminations starting from M_0 that does not contain ρ', and that ends at a matching M in which ρ is exposed. This sequence of eliminations corresponds to an M_0-chain ending at M which does not contain ρ'. Now M dominates M_z, so there exists a chain from M to M_z, and hence there is a maximal chain through M from M_0 to M_z. Now all maximal chains contain all the rotations, so in this maximal chain ρ appears before ρ', violating Theorem 3.2.1. Hence, if ρ' precedes ρ, then ρ cannot be exposed unless ρ' is eliminated.

Conversely, by Corollary 2.5.2, the rotations along any maximal chain in $\mathcal{M}$ can be exposed and eliminated in order, starting from M_0. So if ρ' must be eliminated on any sequence of eliminations starting from M_0 before ρ is exposed, then ρ' must appear before ρ on every maximal chain in $\mathcal{M}$, and by Theorem 3.2.1, ρ' precedes ρ in $\Pi(\mathcal{M})$. $\square$

Now we return to the main goal of this section, proving that the transitive closure of $G(\mathcal{M})$ is $\Pi(\mathcal{M})$.

Lemma 3.2.3 *If (ρ', ρ) is an edge in $G(\mathcal{M})$, then the pair (ρ', ρ) is a pair in the partial order $\Pi(\mathcal{M})$. Hence a pair in the transitive closure of $G(\mathcal{M})$ is a pair in the partial order $\Pi(\mathcal{M})$.*

Proof Let ρ' be a type 1 predecessor of ρ. Then ρ' moves some man m to w, where (m, w) is a pair in ρ. Let M be any matching in which ρ is exposed, and let C be any M_0-chain in $\mathcal{M}$ ending at M. Clearly, (m, w) is a matched pair in M. Now M is created by eliminating the rotations along C, and ρ' is the unique rotation that moves m to w. Hence ρ' must be in C, and so by Theorem 3.2.1, ρ' precedes ρ in $\Pi(\mathcal{M})$.

Now suppose that ρ' is a type 2 predecessor of ρ. That is, suppose that for some pair $(m_i, w_i) \in \rho$, ρ moves m_i below a woman $w \neq w_i$, and that $\rho' \neq \rho$ is the unique rotation that moves w above m_i. Again let C be any M_0-chain ending with a matching M in which ρ is exposed. If ρ' is not in C, then ρ could not be exposed in M, for then m_i prefers w to w_{i+1} and w prefers m_i to her partner in M, contradicting the definition of $w_{i+1} \equiv s_M(m_i)$. So ρ' precedes ρ in C, and hence is a pair in $\Pi(\mathcal{M})$. $\square$

Lemma 3.2.4 *If ρ' is an immediate predecessor of ρ in $\Pi(\mathcal{M})$, then (ρ', ρ) is an edge in $G(\mathcal{M})$. Hence the transitive closure of $G(\mathcal{M})$ contains all the pairs of $\Pi(\mathcal{M})$.*

Proof We first show that there is a stable matching M' in which ρ' is exposed, such that ρ is not exposed in M', but ρ is exposed in M'/ρ'. Consider the closed subset S of rotations consisting of all the strict predecessors in $\Pi(\mathcal{M})$ of ρ; let S' be $S \setminus \{\rho'\}$, and let S'' be $S \cup \{\rho\}$. S' is also closed in

$\Pi(\mathcal{M})$ since ρ' is an immediate predecessor of ρ, and S'' is closed because it consists of ρ and all of ρ's predecessors; let M, M' and M'' be the stable matchings corresponding to S, S' and S''. Now $P(M) \setminus P(M') = d(\rho')$, and $P(M'') \setminus P(M) = d(\rho)$, so M' is an immediate predecessor of M, and M is an immediate predecessor of M'' in $\mathcal{M}$, and hence by Lemma 2.5.7, ρ' is exposed in M', and ρ is exposed in M. Now M' can be obtained from M_0 by successively exposing and eliminating the rotations in S', so ρ cannot be exposed in M', for otherwise ρ would be exposed before ρ' is eliminated, violating Theorem 3.2.2.

Now since ρ is not exposed in M' but it is exposed in $M = M'/\rho'$, there must be a man m_i in ρ such that either (m_i, w_i) is not a pair in M', and ρ' moves m_i down to w_i, or there is a woman w strictly between w_i and w_{i+1} in m_i's list, and ρ' moves w from a man strictly below m_i to a man strictly above m_i in her list. But in the first case, ρ' is a type 1 predecessor of ρ, and in the second case it is a type 2 predecessor of ρ, hence the edge (ρ', ρ) is in $G(\mathcal{M})$. $\square$

Combining and summarizing the above two Lemmas, we have the main result of this section.

Theorem 3.2.3 *The transitive closure of $G(\mathcal{M})$ is $\Pi(\mathcal{M})$.*

Hence, to build the precedence relations of $\Pi(\mathcal{M})$ we need only find the edges of $G(\mathcal{M})$ and then take the transitive closure. Since the edges of $G(\mathcal{M})$ can be determined by looking only at the moves made by the rotations, $\Pi(\mathcal{M})$ can be constructed without knowing $I(\mathcal{M})$.

We will see in the next section that $G(\mathcal{M})$ can be completely constructed in $O(n^2)$ time (and hence it is very sparse). For most of the algorithmic problems we discuss, $G(\mathcal{M})$ can be used in place of $\Pi(\mathcal{M})$. The key to this replacement is the following immediate corollary of Theorem 3.2.3.

Corollary 3.2.2 *Any subset of rotations is closed in $\Pi(\mathcal{M})$ if and only if it is closed in $G(\mathcal{M})$.*

3.3   Efficient Construction

In this section we complete the details needed for the most efficient construction of $G(\mathcal{M})$, and hence of $\Pi(\mathcal{M})$.

3.3.1   Finding All the Rotations in $O(n^2)$ Time

We will show that Algorithm *minimal-differences* can be implemented to run in $O(n^2)$ time, and hence all the rotations of $\mathcal{M}$ can be found in that time bound. Recall that the algorithm traverses a maximal chain in $\mathcal{M}$ from M_0 to M_z, encountering all the rotations of $\mathcal{M}$ along the chain. There are two repeated operations in the algorithm, finding an exposed rotation ρ_i in the current matching M_i, and eliminating ρ_i, creating the next stable matching M_{i+1}. These operations are iterated until there is no man whose partner in the current matching differs from his partner in M_z.

The elimination of a rotation, once it has been located, is straightforward. The only detail of interest is that we will maintain the *reduced* preference lists, discussed in Section 2.5.1 (page 87), and these will be updated after each rotation elimination. We use reduced preference lists, rather than the original preference lists, in order to facilitate the search for exposed rotations and to streamline the description and analysis of the implementation.

Each rotation elimination takes time proportional to the number of men in the rotation, and an elimination moves each man in the rotation at least one place down his original list; hence the total work in the algorithm for eliminating all the rotations is $O(n^2)$. Each rotation elimination also moves an equal number of women up their lists, and the time to update the reduced preference lists after a rotation elimination is proportional to the total number of men that the women move above, during that elimination. By Lemma 3.2.2, at most one rotation moves any given woman above any given man, so the total work to maintain reduced lists is also $O(n^2)$.

To find an exposed in M_i, we follow the general method suggested by the proof of Lemma 2.5.3 (page 90), where it was shown that an exposed rotation exists in any matching M other than M_z. However, direct implementation of that method would lead at best to a $O(n^3)$ running time for Algorithm *minimal-differences*. We will speed up this direct implementation by avoiding extraneous work and by not duplicating work done at any earlier stage of the algorithm. In particular, when searching for an exposed rotation in stable matching M_i, we do not explicitly build the graph $H(M_i)$ and then look for a cycle in it; rather we search for a cycle as the (implicit) graph is being built. To avoid duplicating work, after each cycle C is found, we start the next search with the most recently visited man who is not in cycle C; we use a stack to facilitate locating that man. If no such man exists (the stack is empty), then the search begins with the lowest numbered man whose current partner is not his partner in M_z. Details of the implementation are given in Figure 3.2.

find M_0 and M_z, and create the GS-lists; {using the extended Gale-Shapley algorithm}
$i := 0$;
set up an empty stack;
$x := 1$;
while $x \leq n$ do
begin
      if stack empty then
          begin
              while $(p_{M_i}(x) = p_{M_z}(x))$ and $(x \leq n)$ do
                  $x := x + 1$;
              if $x \leq n$ then
                  push x onto stack
          end; {x is the lowest numbered man such that $p_{M_i}(x) \neq p_{M_z}(x)$}
      if stack not empty then
      begin
          $m :=$ man on top of stack;
          $m := next_{M_i}(m)$;
          while m not in stack do
          begin
              push m onto stack;
              $m := next_{M_i}(m)$
          end;
          $m' :=$ top of stack;
          pop stack;
          set up list ρ_i containing the pair $(m', p_{M_i}(m'))$;
          while $m \neq m'$ do
          begin
              $m' :=$ top of stack;
              pop stack;
              add the pair $(m', p_{M_i}(m'))$ to the head of ρ_i
          end;
          output ρ_i;
          $M_{i+1} := M_i/\rho_i$;
          $i := i + 1$;
          update reduced preference lists
      end
end

Figure 3.2: Implementation of Algorithm *minimal-differences*

3.3.2   Correctness and Time Analysis

Let $R(\mathcal{M})$ denote the set of rotations associated with the stable matchings $\mathcal{M}$, and let $r(\mathcal{M})$ denote $|R(\mathcal{M})|$. We divide the execution of the algorithm into $r(\mathcal{M})$ iterations, where iteration k $(k = 0, \ldots, r(\mathcal{M}) - 1)$ begins when i is set to k.

Lemma 3.3.1 *At the start of iteration k (starting just after i is set to k), let m' be an arbitrary man in the stack, other than the top, and let m'' be the man above m' in the stack. Then $next_{M_{k+1}}(m') = next_{M_k}(m') = m''$.*

  Proof The only men who have different partners in M_k and M_{k+1} are the men in rotation ρ_k, discovered in iteration k. No men is in the stack at the end of iteration k are in ρ_k, hence each of these men have the same partner in M_k and M_{k+1}; let Q denote the set of these men. It follows that the M_k-partners of the men in Q each have the same reduced preference list at the start of iteration $k + 1$ and the start of iteration k. Hence the first and second entries of each man in Q are unchanged during iteration k, and the lemma follows. $\square$

  The high-level outline of the algorithm given in Figure 3.2 is the same as given in Figure 2.12 (page 93), and the only subtle implementation detail is how the search for an exposed rotation is conducted. In the earlier version of Algorithm *minimal-differences* (Figure 2.12), the search for an exposed rotation in M_k begins with any man m who has different partners in M_k and M_z. In the version in Figure 3.2, the search begins with the man m at the head of the stack, if the stack is not empty. Given Lemma 3.3.1, that search simulates a possible search in the Figure 2.12 version, and hence the correctness of the implementation follows from the correctness of the earlier version.

  For the time analysis, note first that the total work to update the reduced lists is $O(n^2)$, and because reduced lists are used, $next_M(m)$ for any M and m, can be found in constant time. Next, note that no man m can be in the stack twice at any given time, and each time m is popped from the stack, he is in the rotation being formed. Then, since no pair appears in more than one rotation, the total number of times the stack is popped is bounded by $n(n - 1)$, and so the total work is $O(n^2)$.

3.3.3   Building $G(\mathcal{M})$ in $O(n^2)$ Time

Lemma 3.3.2 *The digraph $G(\mathcal{M})$ can be constructed from the preference lists in $O(n^2)$ time.*

Proof We have already seen how to find all the rotations in $O(n^2)$ time. Given the rotations, the type 1 edges and type 2 edges are determined as follows: scan each rotation ρ, and for each pair $(m, w) \in \rho$, associate the label ρ with woman w in m's list. Each such label is called a *type 1 label*. Similarly, scan each rotation ρ, and for each pair (m, w) such that ρ moves w from below m to above m in her list, associate the label ρ with woman w in the list of man m. These labels are called *type 2* labels. Then scan each man's preference list from top to bottom, keeping track of the most recently encountered type 1 label, using a variable, say ρ^*, to indicate the the most recently encountered type 1 label. During the scan, when a type 1 label ρ is encountered, create a type 1 edge in $G(\mathcal{M})$ from ρ^* to ρ, and set ρ^* to ρ. When a type 2 label ρ is encountered, create the type 2 edge in $G(\mathcal{M})$ from ρ to ρ^*. It is clear from the definitions of type 1 and type 2 predecessors that all the required edges of $G(\mathcal{M})$ will be found after scanning the lists of all the men.

For the time analysis, note first that, by Corollary 3.2.1, no man-woman pair is in more than one rotation; hence the type 1 labels are unique and can be written in $O(n^2)$ time. For the type 2 labels, note that if $\rho = (m_0, w_0), (m_1, w_1), \ldots, (m_{r-1}, w_{r-1})$, then ρ moves w_i up from m_i to m_{i-1}, and hence ρ moves w_i over an easily identified contiguous interval of men in her list. One type 2 label is generated for each man in the interior of this interval, so the labels generated by the move can be determined in time proportional to the number of them. By Theorem 3.2.2, at most one rotation moves any given woman above any given man, so the total time to write the type 2 labels is $O(n^2)$. The scans down the men's lists can easily be done within that time bound, so the type 2 edges of $G(\mathcal{M})$ can also be constructed in $O(n^2)$ time in total. $\square$

Since the time to construct $G(\mathcal{M})$ is bounded by $O(n^2)$, and since it takes at least one time unit to construct each edge, $G(\mathcal{M})$ is "sparse" in the following worst case sense.

Corollary 3.3.1 *Digraph $G(\mathcal{M})$ can have at most $O(n^2)$ edges, although it may have as many as $n(n-1)/2$ nodes, since its nodes correspond to rotations in $\Pi(\mathcal{M})$.*

Notice that the only bound on the number of pairs in the precedence relation on $\Pi(\mathcal{M})$ is $O(n^4)$, so $G(\mathcal{M})$ is indeed more "sparse", in a worst case sense, than is $\Pi(\mathcal{M})$. We have put quotes around "sparse" because for any particular problem instance, $G(\mathcal{M})$ may have just as many edges as does $\Pi(\mathcal{M})$, although it can obviously never have more.

Digraph $\tilde{G}(\mathcal{M})$

The above guaranteed "sparsity" of $G(\mathcal{M})$ will be crucial for the worst case efficiency of several of the algorithms in this chapter. However, an additional form of sparsity is needed for the algorithm to efficiently enumerate all stable matchings. For that algorithm, we require that no node have outdegree more than n, i.e. no node has more than n edges coming out of it. Unfortunately, $G(\mathcal{M})$ does not have that property in general. However, there is an easily obtained subgraph $\tilde{G}(\mathcal{M})$ of $G(\mathcal{M})$ whose transitive closure is still $\Pi(\mathcal{M})$, and which does have this additional sparsity. To obtain $\tilde{G}(\mathcal{M})$, we modify the rules for building $G(\mathcal{M})$ as follows: for each man m and for each rotation ρ, during the scan of m's list, ignore any type 2 label of ρ, if it is preceded in m's list by an earlier label of ρ, either as a type 1 or a type 2 label.

Theorem 3.3.1 *i)* *The outdegree of any node in* $\tilde{G}(\mathcal{M})$ *is at most n.*
ii) $\tilde{G}(\mathcal{M})$ *and* $G(\mathcal{M})$ *have the same transitive closure, namely* $\Pi(\mathcal{M})$.
iii) *A subset of rotations is closed in* $G(\mathcal{M})$ *if and only if it is closed in* $\tilde{G}(\mathcal{M})$.

Proof i) For any man m, no rotation ρ can appear twice as a type 1 label in m's labeled list, so at most one type 1 edge out of ρ is created by a scan of m's list. Similarly, since a type 2 label of a rotation ρ is ignored if it is preceded by an earlier label of ρ, at most one type 2 edge out of ρ is created by the scan. Finally, a type 2 label of ρ cannot precede a type 1 label of ρ in m's list, so at most one edge out of ρ, of either type, is created by the scan of m's list.
ii) Since, by Lemma 3.2.2, the transitive closure of $G(\mathcal{M})$ is $\Pi(\mathcal{M})$, and the edges of $\tilde{G}(\mathcal{M})$ are a subset of the edges of $G(\mathcal{M})$, it suffices to show that if edge (ρ, ρ') is in $G(\mathcal{M})$ but not in $\tilde{G}(\mathcal{M})$, then there is a path from ρ to ρ' in $\tilde{G}(\mathcal{M})$. Suppose edge (ρ, ρ') in $G(\mathcal{M})$ was created by a scan of man m's list. Clearly, the type 1 edges of both modified and unmodified scans are the same, so ρ is a type 2 predecessor of ρ' in $\Pi(\mathcal{M})$. Since (ρ, ρ') is not created by the modified scan of m's list, the first ρ label appears before the unique type 1 ρ' label. Therefore, in the modified scan of m's list, an edge (ρ, ρ'') is created, where ρ'' appears as a type 1 label before the type 1 ρ' label. Now in $\tilde{G}(\mathcal{M})$ there is a path from ρ'' to ρ' via type 1 edges, hence there is a path from ρ to ρ' in $\tilde{G}(\mathcal{M})$.
iii) From ii), the precedence relation on $\Pi(\mathcal{M})$ is the relation on both $G(\mathcal{M})$ and $\tilde{G}(\mathcal{M})$, so a subset of rotations is closed in $\Pi(\mathcal{M})$ if and only if it is closed in both $G(\mathcal{M})$ and $\tilde{G}(\mathcal{M})$, and iii) follows immediately. $\square$

It is clear that $\tilde{G}(\mathcal{M})$ can be constructed in $O(n^2)$ time, the same time bound for constructing $G(\mathcal{M})$.

3.4   Three Problems with "Easy" Solutions

In this section we discuss three problems that have efficient solutions obtained almost directly from $\Pi(\mathcal{M})$, $G(\mathcal{M})$ and proven properties of those structures. The first problem, finding all the stable pairs, was essentially already solved in Section 2.5.3; the second problem generalizes stable pairs to stable sets; and the third problem is to find the finest decomposition of a stable marriage instance into smaller instances. Although these problems are solved fairly easily using $\Pi(\mathcal{M})$ and $G(\mathcal{M})$, they were not efficiently solved problems before the introduction of $\Pi(\mathcal{M})$ and $G(\mathcal{M})$. Hence these problems illustrate the algorithmic power of those structures and ideas leading to them.

3.4.1   Stable Pairs

Theorem 3.4.1 *All the stable pairs can be found in $O(n^2)$ time.*

Proof   This theorem follows immediately from Theorem 2.5.6, which characterizes the stable pairs, together with the facts that the man-optimal matching and all the rotations for an instance can be found in $O(n^2)$ time. □

With Theorem 3.4.1, all the stable pairs can be found as quickly as the Gale-Shapley algorithm finds a single stable matching. This comparison is more interesting when combined with Theorems 1.5.1 and 1.5.2, that $\Omega(n^2)$ time is necessary to determine if even one given pair is stable or not. Hence one can answer all n^2 stability questions for the necessary price of one — a true quantity discount.

3.4.2   Efficient Tests for Set Stability

In this section we generalize the question of whether a single pair is stable to sets of pairs. We define a set of pairs Q to be a *stable set* if there is some stable matching M such that every pair in Q is a pair in M. We envision situations where, in an effort to find stable matchings that meet some complex conditions, a set of disjoint pairs will be specified, and the task will be to determine whether or not the pairs form a stable set. In fact, as is usual in complex optimization problems, many sets may be proposed, so it is reasonable to allow some preprocessing of the preferences before the sequence of sets is specified. Obviously, the stability of any set can be determined in $O(n^2)$ time, but with preprocessing, we can do better than that for the typical case that $|Q|$ is smaller than n.

For each pair (m, w) that is in Q but not in M_0, define $\tau(m, w)$ to be the unique rotation that moves m *to* w. Similarly for each pair (m, w) that is in Q but not in M_z, define $\phi(m, w)$ be the unique rotation that moves m *from* w. For $(m, w) \in M_0$, $\tau(m, w)$ does not exist, and for $(m, w) \in M_z$, $\phi(m, w)$ does not exist.

Theorem 3.4.2 *A set Q of pairs is a stable set if and only if each of the pairs is stable, and there are no two pairs (m, w) and (m', w') in Q such that $\phi(m, w) \prec \tau(m', w')$ in $\Pi(\mathcal{M})$.*

Proof   Clearly, each individual pair must be stable if Q is stable. If $\tau(m', w')$ exists, and M is any stable matching that contains (m', w'), then the unique closed subset S of $\Pi(\mathcal{M})$ corresponding to M must contain the rotation $\tau(m', w')$. Now if rotation $\phi(m, w)$ precedes $\tau(m', w')$ in $\Pi(\mathcal{M})$, then $\phi(m, w)$ must be in S, so (m, w) cannot be a pair in M. Hence the necessary side of the theorem is proved.

Conversely, suppose that for no pairs in Q does the ϕ-rotation of one pair precede the τ-rotation of the other. Let S be the closed subset of $\Pi(\mathcal{M})$ consisting of the τ-rotations of all of the pairs in Q that are not in M_0 (these have τ-rotations), plus all the rotations that precede those τ-rotations in $\Pi(\mathcal{M})$. That is, those τ-rotations are the maximal rotations in S. Let M be the stable matching that corresponds to S. Clearly, every pair in Q that is not in M_0 is in M. That is, every pair (m, w) whose τ-rotation is a maximal rotation in S is a matched pair in M. Now a pair (m, w) in both Q and M_0 will be in M unless $\phi(m, w)$ is in S. But then $\phi(m, w)$ would precede the τ-rotation of some other pair in Q, which is assumed not to happen. $\square$

Given Theorem 3.4.2, the obvious preprocessing of the problem instance is to identify the stable pairs, to completely construct $\Pi(\mathcal{M})$, and to determine $\tau(m, w)$ and $\phi(m, w)$ for each stable pair (m, w). Finding the stable pairs can be done in $O(n^2)$ time, determining the τ-rotations and ϕ-rotations for all the stable pairs can easily be done in $O(n^2)$ time, and $\Pi(\mathcal{M})$ can be fully constructed by taking the transitive closure of $G(\mathcal{M})$, as follows. From each rotation ρ in $G(\mathcal{M})$ find, by any straightforward search method, all the rotations that are reachable from ρ. As $G(\mathcal{M})$ has only $O(n^2)$ edges, each such search can be done in that time, hence the full construction of $\Pi(\mathcal{M})$ can be computed in $O(r(\mathcal{M})n^2) = O(n^4)$ total time. This is the only algorithmic problem in the book where $\Pi(\mathcal{M})$ is explicitly needed, and can't be replaced by $G(\mathcal{M})$ or $\tilde{G}(\mathcal{M})$.

When a set Q is specified, we identify $\tau(m, w)$ and $\phi(m, w)$ for each pair (m, w) in Q by table lookup, and then check that none of the ϕ-rotations precedes any of the τ-rotations in $\Pi(\mathcal{M})$. For $|Q| = k$, this last task takes no more than $k(k-1)$ checks, but may be faster because several of the pairs in Q may have the same τ-rotation or the same ϕ-rotation. In summary, we have the following theorems.

Theorem 3.4.3 *After $O(r(\mathcal{M})n^2) = O(n^4)$ preprocessing time, the stability of any set Q of k pairs can be determined in $O(k^2)$ time.*

Corollary 3.4.1 *After preprocessing, the stability of any matching can be checked in $O(r(\mathcal{M})^2)$ time.*

We don't know the expected number of rotations in a random problem instance, but our experience suggests that the number is often much smaller than $n(n-1)/2$, and hence Corollary 3.4.1 may provide a substantial speedup in practice over more direct methods not involving $\Pi(\mathcal{M})$.

Note that by Theorems 1.5.1 and 1.5.2, without preprocessing, checking the stability of even a *single* pair requires $\Omega(n^2)$ time, so checking whether a set is stable certainly also requires that time, even when k is smaller than n. Hence the use of $\Pi(\mathcal{M})$ allows a significant speed up in situations where preprocessing is permitted.

3.4.3 Optimal Decomposition

In this section, we consider whether a stable marriage instance can be decomposed into two or more subinstances in such a way that the set $\mathcal{M}$ of stable matchings for the original instance is the cartesian product of the sets of stable matchings for the subinstances. We show how to use the GS-lists to obtain, in $O(n^2)$ time, the finest possible decomposition (if one exists at all). The decomposition method will not use the rotation poset, but the proof of optimality will. We first state the problem precisely with the following definitions.

Given a stable marriage instance of size n, a *(P,Q) subinstance* consists of a subset P of the men and a subset Q of the women, and sets of (possibly incomplete) preference lists, where the men in P rank only women in Q, and the women in Q rank only men in P. Note that it is not necessary for each man in P to rank each woman in Q and vice versa. Note also that the definition does not require that the preference list of a person bear any resemblance to his/her preference list in the original instance, although for the (P,Q) subinstances that we will use, there will be a certain correspondence. For a (P,Q) subinstance, we use $\mathcal{M}(P,Q)$ to denote the set of stable matchings for that instance.

Given the set of initial preference lists, if $\mathcal{M}$ is the set of stable matchings for the instance, a *decomposition* of the instance is a partition of the people into two or more (P, Q) subinstances, $\{(P_i, Q_i), i = 1, \ldots, k\}$, so that the set $\mathcal{M}$ is the cartesian product of the sets $\mathcal{M}(P_i, Q_i), i = 1, \ldots, k$. That is, if we arbitrarily take one stable matching from each of the k subinstances of the decomposition, then the union of these matchings is a stable matching in $\mathcal{M}$, and every stable matching in $\mathcal{M}$ can be obtained in this way.

For example, the instance shown in Figure 3.3 has six stable matchings, shown in Figure 3.4. A decomposition of the instance into two subinstances is shown in Figure 3.5. The first subinstance has three stable matchings, and the second has two, as shown in Figure 3.6. It is easy to verify that the cartesian product of those stable matchings is the set of stable matchings of the original instance.

1	2	5	1	3	4		1	5	4	2	1	3
2	1	3	4	2	5		2	2	5	3	1	4
3	1	3	2	4	5		3	1	3	2	4	5
4	3	2	4	1	5		4	1	2	4	3	5
5	5	2	1	3	4		5	3	4	2	5	1

Men's Preferences	Women's Preferences

Figure 3.3: Problem instance before decomposition

Men	1	2	3	4	5
	2	1	3	4	5
	3	1	2	4	5
Matchings	3	4	2	1	5
	3	4	5	1	2
	3	1	5	4	2
	2	4	3	1	5

Figure 3.4: The six stable matchings of the problem instance

A decomposition is interesting partly for the way it exhibits the structure of $\mathcal{M}$, but it has a more important, practical consequence because each of the subinstances can be treated independently, allowing faster solutions in practice to a variety of problems. For example, in this chapter we will see how to efficiently find stable matchings other than the man-optimal or

1	2	3			2	5	3	1
3	3	2	5		3	1	3	
5	5	2			5	3	5	

Sub-Instance 1

2	1	4		1	4	2
4	4	1		4	2	4

Sub-Instance 2

Figure 3.5: Decomposition with two subinstances

Men	1	3	5		2	4
	2	3	5		1	4
Matchings	3	2	5		4	1
	3	5	2			

Figure 3.6: The stable matchings of the two subinstances

woman-optimal matchings, and in each of these cases, the original problem instance can be solved by unioning the solutions from each of the independent subinstances. In these algorithms, the running time is a (greater than linear) function of the number of people in the instance, so when decomposition is possible, the decomposed instance will be solved faster than the original one.

The Component Decomposition

Recall that the GS-lists for a problem instance are obtained from the original preference lists by removing every pair (m, w) where either w is below m's partner in M_0, or m is below w's partner is M_z. We saw in Chapter 1 that the set of stable matchings for the GS-lists of an instance is exactly the same as for the original complete lists.

Given the GS-lists for an instance of the stable marriage problem, we define the GS-graph as a bipartite graph containing one node for each person, and an edge between a man m and a woman w if and only if w is on m's GS-list. Let $K_i, i = 1, ..., k$, denote the i'th connected component of the GS-graph.

Our proposed decomposition consists of k subinstances as follows: for $i = 1, \ldots, k$, P_i consists of all the men, and Q_i consists of all the women, who are in the connected component K_i. The preference list of each person is simply his or her GS-list. We will call this proposed decomposition the *component decomposition*.

Example For example, the decomposition shown in Figure 3.5 is the component decomposition of the problem instance described in Figure 3.3. The GS-lists of the instance are shown in Figure 3.7. In the GS-graph obtained from those lists, men 2 and 4 are in a connected component with women 1 and 4, while men 1, 3, and 5 are in a separate connected component with women 2, 3, and 5.

1	2	3		1	4	2	
2	1	4		2	5	3	1
3	3	2	5	3	1	3	
4	4	1		4	2	4	
5	5	2		5	3	5	

Men's Lists   Women's Lists

Figure 3.7: The GS-lists for the decomposition example

For a stable matching $M \in \mathcal{M}$, define M_i to be M restricted to $P_i \cup Q_i$. That is, the pairs of M_i are the pairs of M that are contained in the i'th subinstance of the component decomposition.

Lemma 3.4.1 *M_i is a matching of the people in $P_i \cup Q_i$.*

Proof If (m, w) is a pair in M, then it is stable, and m is on w's GS-list, so m and w are in the same component of the GS-graph, and hence in the same subinstance. Every person has a partner in M, so every person in (P_i, Q_i) is matched in M_i. □

Theorem 3.4.4 *The component decomposition is a decomposition.*

Proof First, each person is in exactly one component of the GS-graph; hence the component decomposition partitions the people into subinstances. Now for any $M \in \mathcal{M}$, each matching M_i is a stable matching in the (P_i, Q_i) subinstance, since any pair that blocks M_i would also block M. So any stable matching in $\mathcal{M}$ is in the cartesian product of stable matchings in the k subinstances.

Conversely, let M be a matching obtained by unioning together k stable matchings M^i, $i = 1, \ldots, k$, where M^i is from $\mathcal{M}(P_i, Q_i)$. If M is not stable for the full preference lists, then it is not stable for the GS-lists, since the stable matchings of the GS-lists are the same as for the full lists. So there must be a blocking pair (m, w) that is a pair in the GS-lists. But then m and w would be in the same component of the GS-graph, and hence must both be part of some subinstance (P_i, Q_i). It follows then that (m, w) would block M^i for subinstance (P_i, Q_i), contradicting the assumption that M^i is stable for that instance. $\square$

It is not difficult to show that there is a decomposition of a problem instance with stable matchings $\mathcal{M}$ if and only if $\Pi(\mathcal{M})$ contains more than one connected component. Further, the rotation posets of the subinstances in the component decomposition are simply the connected components of $\Pi(\mathcal{M})$.

Now we show that component decomposition is the finest possible decomposition. In particular, any people who are in the same subinstance of the component decomposition must be in the same subinstance of every decomposition.

Lemma 3.4.2 *Suppose man m is in rotation ρ_m and woman w is in rotation ρ_w, where ρ_w precedes ρ_m in $\Pi(\mathcal{M})$. Then in any decomposition of the original instance, m and w are together in the same subinstance.*

Proof Suppose that ρ_w moves w from m', and that ρ_m moves m to w'. Then (m', w) and (m, w') are stable pairs in $\mathcal{M}$, so in any decomposition, m' and w are together in one subinstance and m and w' are also together in one subinstance. Further, each pair must be a stable pair in its respective subinstance. Now suppose that m and w are in different subinstances of some decomposition, so that (m', w) is a stable pair in one subinstance, and (m, w') is a stable pair in another subinstance. Then by the definition of a decomposition, there must be a stable matching $M \in \mathcal{M}$ containing both pairs (m', w) and (m, w'). Now ρ_m is the unique rotation that moves m to w', so ρ_m must be on any chain in $\mathcal{M}$ that leads to M. But ρ_w precedes ρ_m in $\Pi(\mathcal{M})$, so it must be eliminated on this chain also, making it impossible for (m', w) to be a pair in M. Hence no stable matching in $\mathcal{M}$ can contain both pairs (m', w) and (m, w'), so m and w must be in the same subinstance in any decomposition. $\square$

Theorem 3.4.5 *The component decomposition partitions the people into subinstances as finely as possible.*

Proof We will show first that if (m, w) is an edge in the GS-graph, then m and w must be in the same subinstance in any decomposition. By successively applying this fact, any two people who are in the same component of the GS-graph must be in the same subinstance in any decomposition, and the theorem follows.

If (m, w) is a stable pair, then m and w are always in the same subinstance of any decomposition, so suppose that (m, w) is not a stable pair. Since the first entry on m's GS-list is his M_0-partner, and the last entry on his GS-list is his M_z-partner, w must be neither of these entries. Hence w is in a rotation ρ_w, such that the elimination of ρ removes w from m's list. Further, ρ_w must precede the rotation, ρ_m say, that moves m to his M_z-partner. So by Lemma 3.4.2 above, m and w are in the same subinstance in any decomposition. $\square$

Given Theorem 3.4.5, the only way that the decomposition might be improved is to reduce the number of people on a preference list of the decomposition. However, the running times of the algorithms of interest are not much improved by such list reductions, and we leave the possibility of this improvement for the reader to puzzle out. As a first observation, although the list of person x must include y if (x, y) is a stable pair in $\mathcal{M}$, it is not true that x's list should contain y only if (x, y) is a stable pair in $\mathcal{M}$.

3.5 Efficient Enumeration of All Stable Matchings

In this section we give a time- and space-optimal algorithm for enumerating all stable matchings (set $\mathcal{M}$) in a problem instance of size n, using only $O(n^2 + n|\mathcal{M}|)$ total time and $O(n^2)$ space, where n is the size of the problem instance. That is, after $O(n^2)$ time is spent to find matching M_0 and to build the graph $\tilde{G}(\mathcal{M})$ (defined in Section 3.3.3, page 113), each successive stable matching is found in $O(n)$ time. Considering the time needed just to output a matching, and the space needed just to store the preference lists, this time and space use is clearly necessary, and hence the result is time and space optimal. The efficiency of the method is dependent on the existence and structural properties of $\Pi(\mathcal{M})$ and $\tilde{G}(\mathcal{M})$.

The enumeration problem has been considered by several people, and there are several published enumeration methods that are not based on rotations or any of the structural material of Chapter 2. The best of these methods runs in $O(n^3|\mathcal{M}|)$ time, and can be shown to take at least $\Omega(n^3|\mathcal{M}|/\log^2|\mathcal{M}|)$ time. Therefore, we have another example where the insights obtained from studying and developing $\Pi(\mathcal{M})$ lead to a dramatic improvement in running time over earlier methods.

3.5.1   A Straightforward Method

Perhaps the most direct enumeration method that is based on the structural material of Chapter 2 is the following: starting with M_0, find all the rotations $\rho_1, ..., \rho_t$ exposed in M_0; then branch from M_0 in t ways, eliminating ρ_i from M_0 on branch i, creating a stable matching for each branch out of M_0; then recurse on each of the matchings created.

It is immediate that every matching created will be stable, and from Theorem 2.5.5, that every stable matching will be created by the method. However, most of the stable matchings will be enumerated more than once by this method. In fact, the method generates each stable matching M once for each distinct chain in the lattice $\mathcal{M}$ from M_0 to M. The number of such chains can certainly grow exponentially as a function of n.

The duplicated enumeration in the above method is easily remedied. We associate with each stable matching M a list of exposed rotations in M that are *forbidden* to be eliminated from M. Any forbidden rotation exposed in M will remain exposed in any stable matching generated from M, and we will insist that all forbidden rotations in M remain forbidden in any stable matching generated from M. At the start of the enumeration, none of the rotations $\rho_1, ..., \rho_t$ exposed in M_0 will be forbidden. When branching out of M_0, we eliminate each exposed rotation ρ_i, creating matching M_i say, and then declare rotations $\rho_1, \rho_2, \ldots, \rho_{i-1}$ to be forbidden rotations in M_i; these rotations therefore will not be eliminated on any path of rotation eliminations starting from M_i. In general, when branching out of a stable matching M, which has a list of *permitted* (nonforbidden) exposed rotations $L = \rho_1, ..., \rho_q$, we eliminate each rotation ρ_i on branch i out of M and then declare all the rotations before ρ_i in L to be forbidden in the resulting matching.

The method enumerates every stable matching exactly once, and with some additional ideas, it is possible to implement the method so that each stable matching is obtained in $O(n^2)$ time. The dominant time for the method is due to the work needed to find the exposed rotations in the matchings and to the work needed to maintain and check the lists of forbidden rotations.

3.5.2   Speeding Up the Enumeration

The $O(n^2)$ time bound for the above enumeration method is already an improvement over the methods not based on rotations, but the desired result is $O(n)$ time, an order of magnitude faster. To speed up the enumeration, we will use the graph $\tilde{G}(\mathcal{M})$ (defined in Section 3.3.3) to avoid duplicating work involved in searching for exposed rotations, and to avoid any maintenance of lists. After all, all of the rotations in $\mathcal{M}$ have already been found, and, as we will show below, using $\tilde{G}(\mathcal{M})$ it is easy to identify the exposed rotations in any stable matching.

For a closed subset S of rotations (nodes) in $\mathcal{M}$, we define $M(S)$ to be the matching generated by S (as in Theorem 2.5.7), and define $\tilde{G}_S(\mathcal{M})$ to be the graph obtained from $\tilde{G}(\mathcal{M})$ by removing all the rotations in S from $\tilde{G}(\mathcal{M})$.

Lemma 3.5.1 *The exposed rotations in $M(S)$ are exactly the minimal rotations of $\tilde{G}_S(\mathcal{M})$, i.e. rotations with in-degree zero.*

Proof Suppose ρ is a minimal rotation in $\tilde{G}_S(\mathcal{M})$. Then $S \cup \{\rho\}$ is a closed set of rotations in $\Pi(\mathcal{M})$, and so $S \cup \{\rho\}$ generates a stable matching M'. The closed sets generating M and M' differ by exactly one rotation, so M is an immediate predecessor of M', and by Lemma 2.5.7 (page 97), ρ must be exposed in M.

Conversely, suppose ρ is exposed in M. Then, by Theorem 3.2.2, the only rotations that precede ρ in $\Pi(\mathcal{M})$ must be in S, so ρ is certainly a minimal rotation in $\tilde{G}_S(\mathcal{M})$. □

For a rotation ρ we define $N(\rho)$ to be the set of *out-neighbors* of ρ in $\tilde{G}(\mathcal{M})$. That is, ρ' is in $N(\rho)$ if and only if there is an edge in $\tilde{G}(\mathcal{M})$ from ρ to ρ'. Then, by Theorem 3.3.1, $|N(\rho)| < n$ for any rotation ρ. Hence if ρ is deleted from $\tilde{G}_S(\mathcal{M})$, then the minimal rotations of the resulting graph consist of the minimal rotations of $\tilde{G}_S(\mathcal{M})$, excluding ρ, together with the rotations of $N(\rho)$ that have degree one in $\tilde{G}_S(\mathcal{M})$; these are the exposed rotations in $M(S \cup \{\rho\})$. Being able to quickly identify exposed rotations in this way is one of the keys to speeding up the enumeration method.

Suppose that, for a given stable matching M, the exposed rotations have been partitioned into a set of forbidden rotations and a set of nonforbidden, or permitted, rotations. A stable matching M' will be called a *permitted descendant* of M if M' is strictly dominated by M and none of the forbidden rotations exposed in M is on a chain from M to M' in $\mathcal{M}$; that is, if M' can be obtained from M without eliminating any of the forbidden rotations[1].

We will enumerate all the stable matchings exactly once using the recursive procedure *GetStableMatchings* shown in Figure 3.8. The algorithm

---

[1]Recall from Theorem 2.5.4 (page 94) that every chain between a stable matching M and a matching M' dominated by M contains exactly the same set of rotations.

makes use of N, the out-neighbor relation defined above, as a global static array, and takes three parameters, which are also global variables:

- M $(= M(S))$, the current stable matching.

- L, a list containing the permitted rotations exposed in M.

- D, an array containing the in-degree in $\tilde{G}_S(\mathcal{M})$ of each rotation.

The variables M, L, and D are global, and so need not actually be passed to the procedure, but we include them in the procedure header to emphasize their role. In the exposition, but not in the procedure itself, we will use M^* to refer to the value of M on entry to the procedure; similarly, we use L^* for the entry value of L.

The procedure generates, exactly once, all the permitted descendants of M. Hence, if called initially with $M = M_0$, $L =$ a list of *all* rotations exposed in M_0, and $D =$ the in-degrees in $\tilde{G}(\mathcal{M})$ of the rotations, the procedure will generate exactly once all the stable matchings (provided M_0 itself is output separately).

Note that, in the procedure, we write $M * \rho$ for the unique stable matching M' such that $M = M'/\rho$, that is, $*$ represents rotation *restoration*, the inverse operation to rotation elimination. Clearly, $M * \rho$ can be constructed from M and ρ in $O(n)$ time.

Explanation and Correctness

In block 1 of the procedure, a permitted rotation ρ is removed from the head of L, and is eliminated from M, and M^*/ρ is output. Then D is updated and all the exposed rotations in M^*/ρ that are not exposed in M^*, are appended to the current list L. Block 1 ends with a recursive call to find all the permitted descendants of $M = M^*/\rho$.

To better understand Block 2, keep in mind that one of the goals of this implementation is to use no more than $O(n^2)$ space; therefore M, L, and D are global variables. In Block 2 we find all the permitted descendants of M^* that can be reached without eliminating ρ. Therefore, we need to call the procedure with variables M and L set to M^* and $L^* \setminus \{\rho\}$, and with D set accordingly. However, M^* and L^* are unavailable, and must be inferred from the current state of the variables M, L, and D. This is what Block 2 does.

Restoring M^* from the global M and the local ρ is immediate. To set D correctly, we simply add one to the in-degree of each out-neighbor of ρ. To set L correctly, note that ρ is already gone from L, so the only thing that must be done is to remove from L all those rotations that were appended

---

begin
        find and output M_0;
        construct $\tilde{G}(\mathcal{M})$; $\{S := \emptyset\ \}$
        $D_0 :=$ in-degree of each rotation in $\tilde{G}(\mathcal{M})$;
        $L_0 :=$ list of rotations exposed in M_0;
                $\{$Each is identified by a node of in-degree zero in $\tilde{G}(\mathcal{M})\}$
        GetStableMatchings (M_0, L_0, D_0);
end.

procedure GetStableMatchings (M, L, D);
$\{$The procedure generates, exactly once, each permitted descendant of the stable matching
$M = M(S)$, where list L contains the permitted rotations exposed in M, D contains
the in-degree in $\tilde{G}_S(\mathcal{M})$ of each rotation; ρ is a local variable, but M, L and D are global$\}$
begin $\{$This is the start of block 1$\}$
        if L is nonempty then
        begin
                remove rotation ρ from head of L;
                $M := M/\rho$; $\{S := S \cup \{\rho\}\}$
                output M;
                for each rotation π in $N[\rho]$ do
                begin
                        $D[\pi] := D[\pi] - 1$;
                        if $D[\pi] = 0$ then append π to the end of L
                            $\{D[\pi] = 0 \implies \pi$ is minimal in $\tilde{G}_S(\mathcal{M})$, and so is exposed in $M\}$
                end;
                GetStableMatchings(M, L, D); $\{$end of block 1$\}$
                $\{$Now restore M to M^*, update D and L for the next
                branch out of M, and recurse; this is the start of block 2$\}$
                for each rotation π in $N[\rho]$ do
                begin
                        $D[\pi] := D[\pi] + 1$;
                        if $D[\pi] = 1$ then remove the last rotation from L
                end;
                $M := M * \rho$; $\{S := S \setminus \{\rho\}\}$
                GetStableMatchings(M, L, D); $\{$This is the end of block 2$\}$
                restore ρ to head of L
        end
end;

Figure 3.8: Algorithm to generate all the stable matchings

to it in Block 1. These were out-neighbors of ρ whose in-degree dropped
from one to zero when D was changed in Block 1, so they are now the out-
neighbors of ρ whose in-degree is one. The code to remove these rotations is
a little indirect, because rotation $\pi \in N(\rho)$ is not necessarily removed in the
same iteration that $D[\pi]$ is found to have value one. However, one rotation
is removed for each such iteration, and the rotations to be removed from the
end of L are contiguous in L, so we need only remove the correct number of
rotations to get the correct set of removals. Hence, Block 2 correctly sets the
variables to find all the permitted descendants of M^* that can be reached
without eliminating ρ. The end of Block 2 is the actual recursive call to find
these stable matchings.

The last step in the procedure adds ρ back to the head of the global L,
so that on exit, L has the value of L^*. That is, the end of each execution of
the procedure restores L to what it had been on entry to the procedure.

Theorem 3.5.1 *The execution of GetStableMatchings (M_0, L_0, D_0) enumerates every stable matching exactly once.*

Proof Certainly, every matching produced is stable, since it is obtained
by eliminating a chain of successively exposed rotations. Suppose that, in
a general call of procedure *GetStableMatchings(M,L,D)*, ρ is in the list L
of permitted rotations for input stable matching $M(= M^*)$. Then every
permitted descendant of M^* is either

i) M^*/ρ; or

ii) a permitted descendant of M^*/ρ relative to list L, where L is obtained
from L^* by removing ρ and adding all rotations that are exposed
in M^*/ρ but not in M^*; these are precisely the rotations in $N(\rho)$
that have in-degree one in $\tilde{G}_S(\mathcal{M})$ (and therefore in-degree zero in
$\tilde{G}_{S\cup\{\rho\}}(\mathcal{M})$); or

iii) a permitted descendant of M^* relative to list L, where L is obtained
from L^* by removing ρ, i.e. where ρ is forbidden.

By Theorem 2.5.2 (page 97), two stable matchings are the same only
if, starting from M_0, the set of rotations eliminated to obtain them is the
same. Hence, the above three categories of permitted descendants of M are
disjoint. Further, each is handled by procedure *GetStableMatchings*, (i) by
the output statement, and (ii) and (iii) by the recursive calls in block 1 and
2 respectively. Hence, each permitted descendant of M is generated exactly
once during the execution of *GetStableMatchings(M,L,D)*; setting M to M_0
proves the theorem. $\square$

Time Analysis

Each call of the recursive procedure outputs one stable matching. The number of operations within each call is dominated by the "for" loops and the elimination and restoration of ρ. Each "for" loop involves $O(n)$ operations, since $|N(\rho)| < n$ for all ρ, and rotation elimination and restoration are $O(n)$ operations, since each rotation contains at most n pairs. Hence there is a $O(n)$ time bound on the generation of each stable matching.

The time to find M_0 and $\tilde{G}(\mathcal{M})$ has already been shown to be $O(n^2)$, and it is straightforward to set up N and to initialize L_0 and D_0 in $O(n^2)$ time. Therefore, overall, the time complexity of our stable matching enumeration algorithm is $O(n^2 + n|\mathcal{M}|)$, as claimed.

Space Analysis

Each call of the recursive procedure, before termination, restores the values of M, L and D, the three parameters, to exactly the values that they had when that call was made. Hence no local copy of any of these parameters is necessary. Each call of the procedure stores a local rotation ρ, but at any point in the execution of the algorithm, if ρ is the local rotation in the currently invoked procedure, then it cannot be the local rotation of any of the procedure calls whose completion is pending, for those rotations are the rotations along some maximal chain in $\mathcal{M}$. Then, since the total number of pairs in all rotations is at most $n(n-1)$, $O(n^2)$ space suffices for all of the pending, stored ρs. The (static) array N contains one list entry for each edge in $G(\mathcal{M})'$, and so $O(n^2)$ entries in total, and the single copies of M, L and D also use $O(n^2)$ space. Hence the total space requirement of the algorithm is $O(n^2)$.

3.6 Finding Fair Stable Matchings

We have seen that the classical Gale-Shapley algorithm can be used to find either the man-optimal or the woman-optimal stable matching, but no other stable matchings. We have also seen that these two matchings treat the two sexes very asymmetrically: the optimal matching for one sex is pessimal for the other. So, given the requirement that a matching must be stable, there could not be any better matching than the man-optimal matching for the men as a whole, or for any individual man, nor could there be any worse matching for the woman as a whole, or for any individual woman. For that reason, we are interested in efficiently finding other stable matchings that are more equitable than are the man or woman-optimal matchings. In particular, we would like a stable matching where each individual is treated equally, regardless of sex.

In the next three sections we consider several different, but related, definitions of stable matchings that treat the sexes and the individuals more equitably than do the man or woman-optimal matchings. In the first two approaches, each person is treated equally, and in the third approach we consider a continuum of stable matchings that establish trade-offs between the preferences of the men and those of the women. In each of these three approaches, we give efficient algorithms to find the desired stable matching or matchings.

3.6.1 Egalitarian Stable Marriage

Recall that $mr(m, w)$ is the position of woman w in man m's list, and $wr(w, m)$ is the position of m in w's list. The man-optimal matching minimizes

$$\sum_{(m,w)\in M} mr(m, w)$$

and maximizes

$$\sum_{(m,w)\in M} wr(w, m)$$

over all stable matchings in $\mathcal{M}$. The woman-optimal matching does the reverse.

We define $w(M)$, the *weight* of matching M, to be

$$\sum_{(m,w)\in M} [mr(m, w) + wr(w, m)],$$

and define an *egalitarian* stable matching to be a stable matching with minimum possible weight, taken over all stable matchings.

An egalitarian stable matching treats the men and women symmetrically and treats each individual equally, since the egalitarian stable matching optimizes an objective function that has a symmetric term for each individual, regardless of gender.

In this section we will show that an egalitarian stable matching can be found in $O(n^4)$ time. The efficiency of the method relies heavily on the structure of $\Pi(\mathcal{M})$ and special properties of the digraph $G(\mathcal{M})$.

For a rotation $\rho = (m_0, w_0), (m_1, w_1), \ldots, (m_{r-1}, w_{r-1})$, define the *weight* of ρ, denoted $w(\rho)$, to be

$$w(\rho) = \sum_{i=0}^{r-1} [mr(m_i, w_i) - mr(m_i, w_{i+1})] + \sum_{i=0}^{r-1} [wr(w_i, m_i) - wr(w_i, m_{i-1})],$$

The weight of a rotation ρ is just the change in the weight of a matching after ρ is eliminated from it. We see this more precisely below.

Lemma 3.6.1 *If ρ is exposed in a stable matching M, then $w(M/\rho) = w(M) - w(\rho)$.*

Proof The proof is immediate from the definition of $w(\rho)$, and Lemma 2.5.6 which says that $M(\rho) \setminus M = d(\rho)$. $\square$

Corollary 3.6.1 *If S is the (unique) closed subset of $\Pi(\mathcal{M})$ associated with stable matching M, then*

$$w(M) = w(M_0) - \sum_{\rho_i \in S} w(\rho_i),$$

where M_0 is the man-optimal matching.

Proof This follows by repeatedly applying Lemma 3.6.1 to the rotations in S. $\square$

In the light of this corollary, the following theorem is now immediate.

Theorem 3.6.1 *An egalitarian stable matching is the matching generated by a closed subset of $\Pi(\mathcal{M})$ of maximum total weight, where the weight of a set is the sum of the weights of the rotations in it.*

Example For the problem instance of Figure 2.1 (page 69), we see that $w(\rho_0) = -1, w(\rho_1) = -1, w(\rho_2) = +1, w(\rho_3) = -1, w(\rho_4) = -3$, and there are two closed subsets of the rotation poset in Figure 2.18 (page 99) whose total weight is maximum. One subset is the empty set (corresponding to the man-optimal matching), with weight zero, and the other is the set $\{\rho_0, \rho_2\}$. It is not always the case that the man-optimal (or woman-optimal) matching is also a solution to the egalitarian stable marriage problem.

By Lemma 3.2.2 (page 108), the closed subsets of $\Pi(\mathcal{M})$ and of $G(\mathcal{M})$ are the same; hence the egalitarian stable matching problem can be solved by finding a maximum-weight closed subset of $G(\mathcal{M})$. The use of the digraph $G(\mathcal{M})$ in place of $\Pi(\mathcal{M})$ will be crucial in solving this problem efficiently.

Finding a maximum-weight closed subset in $\Pi(\mathcal{M})$

We have reduced the egalitarian stable matching problem to that of finding a maximum-weight closed subset of the weighted digraph $G(\mathcal{M})$. The general problem of finding a maximum-weight closed subset of a weighted poset, or of a digraph, is a classical problem that has numerous applications, and there are several known methods that solve this problem using network flow or related techniques. However, without making use of special structure of $G(\mathcal{M})$, these methods at best yield $O(n^6)$ time algorithms for the egalitarian stable matching problem. The method we will present follows the general outline of the other methods, but it is much faster because it exploits the "sparsity" of $G(\mathcal{M})$ described in Corollary 3.3.1: although $G(\mathcal{M})$ can have $\Omega(n^2)$ nodes, it can never have more than $O(n^2)$ edges.

The flow network $\vec{G}(\mathcal{M})$

A node ρ in $G(\mathcal{M})$ is called a *negative node* if $w(\rho) < 0$, and is called a *positive node* if $w(\rho) > 0$. We let $\mathcal{P}$ denote the set of positive nodes and let $\mathcal{N}$ denote the set of negative nodes of $G(\mathcal{M})$. For a set S of rotations, we define the *weight of S*, denoted $w(S)$ to be the sum of the weights of the rotations in S.

Given a weighted, directed network G with designated nodes s and t, an *s-t cut* is a partition of the nodes of G into two sets (U, V), with $s \in U$ and $t \in V$. The capacity of the cut, denoted $C(U, V)$, is the sum of the weights on the edges which cross from nodes of U to nodes of V. A minimum *s-t* cut is an *s-t* cut of minimum total weight.

Given $G(\mathcal{M})$, we define the following capacitated *s-t* flow network $\vec{G}(\mathcal{M})$. A source node s and a terminal node t are added to digraph $G(\mathcal{M})$. A directed edge is added from s to every negative node ρ_i in $G(\mathcal{M})$; the capacity of directed edge (s, ρ_i) is set to $|w(\rho_i)|$. A directed edge is added to node t from every positive node ρ_j; the capacity of edge (ρ_j, t) is $w(\rho_j)$. Note that $\vec{G}(\mathcal{M})$ contains neither edge (s, ρ) nor (ρ, t) if $w(\rho) = 0$. The capacity of every original edge in $G(\mathcal{M})$ is set to be infinite.

Example Figure 3.9 shows the network $\vec{G}(\mathcal{M})$ derived from the rotation digraph $G(\mathcal{M})$ of Figure 2.18 (page 99). In this particular example, $\vec{G}(\mathcal{M})$ could be trimmed down to contain just the nodes s, t, ρ_0 and ρ_2, since any negative node that does not precede a positive node can be deleted, for it will never be in a maximum-weight closed subset. Also, any positive node that has no negative predecessors can be deleted, for it will always be in a maximum-weight closed subset.

Theorem 3.6.2 *Let K be the set of edges crossing a minimum s-t cut in $\vec{G}(\mathcal{M})$, and let $\mathcal{P}_K$ be the positive nodes of $\vec{G}(\mathcal{M})$ whose edges into t are not in K. Then the nodes $\mathcal{P}_K$ and all nodes that reach them in $\vec{G}(\mathcal{M})$ (their predecessors), define a maximum-weight closed subset of $G(\mathcal{M})$. Further, $\mathcal{P}_K$ is exactly the set of positive nodes of this closed subset of $G(\mathcal{M})$.*

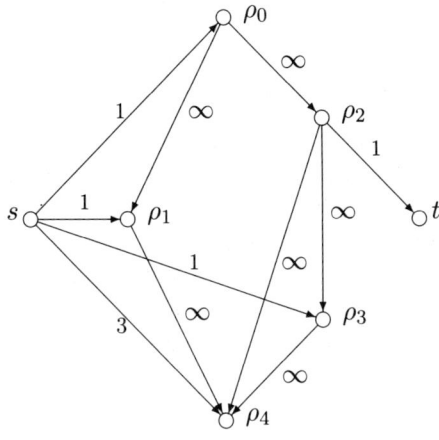

Figure 3.9: The network $\vec{G}(\mathcal{M})$

Proof Let $C(K)$ denote the summed capacities of the edges that cross from the s-side of K to the t-side of K. For any subset S of $\mathcal{P}$, let $\mathcal{N}[S]$ be the set of all negative predecessors of S in $G(\mathcal{M})$ (and hence in $\vec{G}(\mathcal{M})$). Any negative node in a maximum-weight closed subset Q of $G(\mathcal{M})$ must precede at least one positive node in Q; hence the set of positive nodes in the maximum weight closed subset of $G(\mathcal{M})$ is the subset S of $\mathcal{P}$ that maximizes $[w(S) - |w(\mathcal{N}[S])|]$ over all subsets of $\mathcal{P}$. But then the same subset *minimizes* $w(\mathcal{P}) - [w(S) - |w(\mathcal{N}[S])|]$ over all subsets of $\mathcal{P}$. Hence the problem of finding the maximum-weight closed subset can be solved by minimizing $w(\mathcal{P} \setminus S) + |w(\mathcal{N}[S])|$ over all subsets $S \subseteq \mathcal{P}$.

Now note that for an arbitrary subset S of $\mathcal{P}$, if every edge in $\vec{G}(\mathcal{M})$ from s to a node in $\mathcal{N}[S]$ is cut, and every edge from a node in $\mathcal{P} \setminus S$ to t is also cut, then all paths from s to t are cut. Hence $C(K) \leq Min[w(\mathcal{P} \setminus S) + |w(\mathcal{N}[S])| : S \subseteq \mathcal{P}]$. Conversely, if we let $S^* \subseteq \mathcal{P}$ consist of the positive nodes whose edges to t are not in K, then, by definition, K cuts all edges to t from nodes in $\mathcal{P} \setminus S^*$, and so K must cut all the edges from s to nodes in $\mathcal{N}[S^*]$, since K is an s-t cut of finite capacity, and all original edges in $\vec{G}(\mathcal{M})$ have infinite capacity. Hence $C(K) = w(\mathcal{P} \setminus S^*) + |w(\mathcal{N}[S^*])| \geq Min[w(\mathcal{P} \setminus S) + |w(\mathcal{N}[S])| : S \subseteq \mathcal{P}]$, and the theorem is proved. $\square$

Example In the network in Figure 3.9, there are two minimum s-t cuts, and in each there is exactly one edge across the cut. In one cut, $K = (s, \rho_0)$, and in the other cut, $K = (\rho_2, t)$. In the first case $Q_K = \rho_2$, and the associated closed subset is $\{\rho_0, \rho_2\}$. In the second case, $\mathcal{P}_K = \emptyset$, and so the associated closed subset is also the empty set. These are the same two sets that were observed earlier to be the maximum-weight closed subsets of the underlying rotation poset.

The fastest-known algorithms for finding a minimum s-t cut in a network with N nodes and E edges run in $O(N^3)$ time as a function of N alone, while several others run in time $O(NE \log N)$, as a function of both N and E; other more recent algorithms find a minimum cut in time $O(NE \log \frac{N^2}{E})$, which is never worse than $O(NE \log N)$, and is better for certain combinations of N and E. However, we will use the simpler expression of $O(NE \log N)$ as the time bound, parameterized on N and E, for finding a minimum s-t cut. Now for $\vec{G}(\mathcal{M})$, $N = r(\mathcal{M}) = O(n^2)$, and $E = O(n^2)$ also. Hence, we have established the following theorem.

Theorem 3.6.3 *A minimum s-t cut in the network $\vec{G}(\mathcal{M})$ can be found in either $O(r(\mathcal{M})^3)$ or $O(n^4 \log n)$ time.*

We now reduce the latter time bound to $O(n^4)$, as follows.

Lemma 3.6.2 *The minimum s-t cut in $\vec{G}(\mathcal{M})$ has capacity bounded by $O(n^2)$.*

Proof The minimum cut is certainly bounded by $\sum_{\rho \in \mathcal{P}} w(\rho)$, and we will show that this is $O(n^2)$. Each term $w(\rho)$ consists of a negative part representing the net change of the men when rotation ρ is eliminated, and a positive part representing the net change of the women; for each rotation ρ, let $f(\rho)$ denote the positive (female) part. Then $\sum_{\rho \in \mathcal{P}} w(\rho) < \sum_{\rho \in \mathcal{P}} f(\rho)$. But, $f(\rho) = \sum_{w_i \in \rho} [wr(w_i, m_i) - wr(w_i, m_{i-1})]$, the total number of men that are passed over by the moves made by ρ. Now by Lemma 3.2.2, at most one rotation moves a given woman w above a given man m, so $\sum_{\rho \in \mathcal{P}} f(\rho)$ is bounded by $O(n^2)$. $\square$

Theorem 3.6.4 *A maximum flow and minimum s-t cut in $\vec{G}(\mathcal{M})$ can be found in $O(n^4)$ time.*

Proof When all the edge capacities of a network with E edges are integral, the running time of the Ford-Fulkerson algorithm (or any of the many subsequent algorithms) is $O(E \times C(K))$, where $C(K)$ is the weight of a minimum s-t cut. Since all the capacities in $\vec{G}(\mathcal{M})$ are integral, and both E and $C(K)$ are $O(n^2)$, the theorem follows. $\square$

Combining Theorems 3.6.2 and 3.6.4, all the positive nodes of a maximum-weight closed subset of $\Pi(\mathcal{M})$ can be found in $O(n^4)$ time, so all that remains is to find the predecessors of these nodes.

Lemma 3.6.3 *Given the positive nodes S^* in a maximum-weight closed subset of $G(\mathcal{M})$, the entire closed subset can be found in $O(n^2)$ time.*

Proof Reverse the edges of $G(\mathcal{M})$ and determine, by depth-first search say, all the nodes of $G(\mathcal{M})$ that are reachable from any node in S^*. Such nodes are the predecessors of S^* and fill out the desired closed subset of $\Pi(\mathcal{M})$. Depth-first search runs in time proportional to the number of edges in $G(\mathcal{M})$, hence in $O(n^2)$ time. □

Putting the pieces together

Summarizing the above discussion, we solve the egalitarian stable marriage problem in $O(n^4)$ time as follows. First use Algorithm *minimal-differences* to find all the rotations in $O(n^2)$ time; then build $G(\mathcal{M})$, and from it $\vec{G}(\mathcal{M})$, in $O(n^2)$ time; find a minimum s-t cut K in $\vec{G}(\mathcal{M})$ in $O(n^4)$ time; use K to find the maximum weight closed subset S of $G(\mathcal{M})$ in $O(n^2)$ time, and then obtain the egalitarian stable marriage, either by eliminating the rotations in S^* from M_0 or by forming and unioning the minimal differences associated with S^*.

Note that, other than the $O(n^4)$ time network flow computation, the above method runs in $O(n^2)$ time; hence any speedup in the flow computation would immediately speed up the overall solution. Such an improvement seems probable, and finding such a speed up is a natural and attractive open problem.

3.6.2 Optimal Stable Marriage

The egalitarian stable marriage problem can be generalized to a weighted version, called the *optimal* stable marriage problem. In this version of the problem, instead of a rank-ordered preference list, each person p provides a real number weight $c(p, q)$ for each person q of the opposite sex; then p prefers q to s if and only if $c(p, q) < c(p, s)$, and the definition of stability remains unchanged.

An *optimal stable matching* is a stable matching M minimizing

$$\sum_{(m,w)\in M} [c(m, w) + c(w, m)].$$

This weighted version of the egalitarian stable marriage problem allows each person to specify the structure of his/her preferences in more detail, and hence may give more useful solutions. In addition, there are several problems that can be modeled and solved by the appropriate selection of weights. For example, if M is a stable matching, and $V(M)$ is a vector of length n in which the i'th element indicates the number of people who get their i'th choice in M, then we can pick weights so that the solution to the resulting optimal stable marriage problem solves the problem of finding a stable matching M that makes $V(M)$ lexicographically maximum, i.e., one that maximizes the number of people who get their first-choice mate, and within that maximizes the number of people who get their second choice mate, and within that ... etc. This is done by the standard trick of assigning a weight of $n^{(n-i)}$ for each person's i'th choice in their list, and then finding the stable matching M *maximizing* $\sum\limits_{(m,w)\in M} [c(m,w) + c(w,m)]$. This weighted maximization problem can be solved by reducing it to an instance of the optimal stable marriage problem by subtracting each weight from a large enough constant. This works because the weight of each stable matching involves exactly $2n$ of these constant terms, and so the weight of each stable matching is changed by exactly the same amount, preserving the original order of the stable matchings.

In addition to the uses suggested above, the optimal stable marriage problem will be a key subproblem in our final approach below to finding fairer compromises between the men's and women's preferences.

Theorem 3.6.5 *An optimal stable matching can be found in $O(r(\mathcal{M})^3)$ or $O(n^2 r(\mathcal{M}) \log r(\mathcal{M})) = O(n^4 \log n)$ time.*

Proof The general method is the same as for the egalitarian stable marriage problem, but now the weight of a rotation depends on the weighted preferences in the obvious way. With these weights, the edge capacities of $\vec{G}(\mathcal{M})$ are no longer necessarily integral, nor is the minimum cut bounded by $O(n^2)$. However, the $O(N^3)$ and $O(NE \log N)$ time bounds of algorithms mentioned earlier are correct for any edge capacities, and $\vec{G}(\mathcal{M})$ has $N = r(\mathcal{M}) = O(n^2)$ nodes and $E = O(n^2)$ edges as before. $\square$

We note at this point a fact that follows from our solution of the optimal stable marriage problem. This fact will be discussed again in Section 3.8.

Theorem 3.6.6 *For any instance of the optimal stable marriage problem, there is a one-one correspondence between the set of optimal stable matchings for the instance, and the set of minimum s-t cuts in $\vec{G}(\mathcal{M})$.*

A note on $\Pi(\mathcal{M})$ verses $I(\mathcal{M})$

Up to now, the principal advantage of $\Pi(\mathcal{M})$ over the conceptually simpler representation $I(\mathcal{M})$, was that the digraphs $G(\mathcal{M})$ and $\tilde{G}(\mathcal{M})$, which are based on $\Pi(\mathcal{M})$, can be built in $O(n^2)$ time, and their use allows faster solutions to certain algorithmic problems. In contrast, the direct approach (discussed in Section 2.2) to building $I(\mathcal{M})$ might require $\Omega(n^5)$ time. In the egalitarian and optimal stable marriage problems we see another advantage of $\Pi(\mathcal{M})$ over $I(\mathcal{M})$, namely that we do not know how to directly solve these problems using $I(\mathcal{M})$. The major difficulty in trying to use $I(\mathcal{M})$ to solve the optimal stable marriage problem is that we know of no nice way to express the weight of a stable matching M in terms of $\hat{U}(M)$, the weights of the closed subsets of matchings in $I(\mathcal{M})$ that generate M. Given a closed subset S of $I(\mathcal{M})$, the only way we know to compute the weight of the stable matching $M = \bigvee S$ is to first explicitly form M, and then calculate its weight from the preference data. Hence we do not have a nice way to express the "best" stable matching M, in terms of the data associated with $I(\mathcal{M})$, so we do not have a tractable way to express the optimal stable marriage problem as a problem of selecting a "best" closed subset of $I(\mathcal{M})$.

In contrast to $I(\mathcal{M})$, the weight of the stable matching corresponding to a closed subset S of rotations of $\Pi(\mathcal{M})$ is simply the weight of M_0 minus the sum of the weights of the rotations in S. This allows the formulation of the optimal stable marriage problem as a problem of finding a maximum weight closed subset of $\Pi(\mathcal{M})$, which is a problem well known to be tractable. Thus this is another definite advantage of $\Pi(\mathcal{M})$ over $I(\mathcal{M})$.

We should note that it is possible to transform the absolute costs of the matchings of $I(\mathcal{M})$ to marginal costs of the type associated with rotations, so that the cost of the matching associated with a closed subset $S \subseteq I(\mathcal{M})$ is the sum of the marginal costs of the matchings in S. This transformation can be done in $O(n^4)$ time, but it just creates something akin to $\Pi(\mathcal{M})$. Further, the resulting structure is not guaranteed to be sparse, so again, $\Pi(\mathcal{M})$ and $G(\mathcal{M})$ have great advantages over $I(\mathcal{M})$.

3.6.3 Parametric Stable Marriage

Given the extreme asymmetry between the man-optimal and woman-optimal stable matchings produced by the Gale-Shapley algorithm, it is of interest to see how the optimal stable matching changes as favor is continuously shifted from one sex to the other. This approach generalizes the egalitarian and optimal stable marriage problems, identifying a continuum of compromises between the preferences of the men and the women. In this section we define such a continuum and show how to find it efficiently. In fact, it will turn out rather surprisingly that *all* the stable matchings in the continuum can be found in the same time bound established to solve just one instance of the optimal stable marriage problem.

For a fixed value of parameter λ and a stable matching M, define

$$C_M(\lambda) \equiv \lambda \times \sum_{(m,w)\in M} c(m,w) + \sum_{(m,w)\in M} c(w,m).$$

Then as a function of parameter λ, we define

$$F(\lambda) \equiv min\{C_M(\lambda) : M \in \mathcal{M}\}.$$

When $c(p,q) = r(p,q)$ for each ordered pair (p,q), we will refer to $F(\lambda)$ as $P(\lambda)$. Note that the values of $P(0), P(\infty)$, and $P(1)$ are attained for the woman-optimal, man-optimal, and egalitarian stable marriages, respectively. A matching M for which $F(\lambda) = C_M(\lambda)$ is called λ-*optimal*, and *uniquely* λ-*optimal* if it is the only such M.

Lemma 3.6.4 *The function $F(\lambda)$ (hence also $P(\lambda)$) is a piecewise linear, concave, nondecreasing function of λ.*

Proof As a function of λ, the cost of any stable matching M is a nondecreasing affine function of λ. Hence the function $F(\lambda)$ is the lower envelope of the superposition of the straight lines describing the costs of the stable matchings. Clearly then, the lower envelope must be piecewise linear, concave, and nondecreasing in λ. $\square$

Places where $F(\lambda)$ changes slope are called *breakpoints*, and it is easy to verify that a stable matching that is optimal in the interior of an interval between two successive breakpoints is optimal over the entire interval; similarly, M_z is optimal in the entire interval $[0, \lambda_1]$, and M_0 is optimal in the entire interval $[\lambda_t, \infty)$. A solution to the parametric stable marriage problem, for either $P(\lambda)$ or $F(\lambda)$, is a list of the breakpoints $\lambda_1, \ldots, \lambda_t$, together with an ordered list of stable matchings, $M_1, \ldots, M_{t-1}$ such that M_i is an optimal stable matching in the interval $[\lambda_i, \lambda_{i+1}]$.

A solution to the parametric stable marriage problem gives a wide range of stable matchings from which to choose, depending on how the preferences of the men are valued compared to the preferences of the women. In order to make this approach of practical significance, we must show that the number of breakpoints is not excessive, and that the optimal stable matchings between the breakpoints can be found efficiently.

We will show that despite the fact that the number of stable matchings can grow exponentially with n, the size of a problem instance, the number of breakpoints grows surprisingly slowly, and hence is in the practical range. We will then note that *all* the breakpoints of either $P(\lambda)$ or $F(\lambda)$, and their associated stable matchings, can be found in $O(n^4 \log n)$ time, the same time bound for computing just a *single* optimal stable matching.

3.6.4 The Number of Breakpoints

Breakpoints of $P(\lambda)$

Theorem 3.6.7 *There can be at most $O(n^{4/3})$ breakpoints of $P(\lambda)$.*

Proof Suppose that the breakpoints occur at $\lambda_1, \ldots, \lambda_t$, with $\lambda_1 < \cdots < \lambda_t$. Then there is a sequence $M_0, M_1, \ldots, M_t$ of distinct stable matchings such that, for each i $(0 \le i \le t)$, M_i is optimal in the range $[\lambda_i, \lambda_{i+1}]$, where $\lambda_0 = 0$ and $\lambda_{t+1} = \infty$. For each such M_i define $x_i = \sum_{(m,w)\in M_i} r(m, w)$, and $y_i = \sum_{(m,w)\in M_i} r(w, m)$. It is immediate that all the x_i and y_i lie between n and n^2, and that $x_{i+1} < x_i$ and $y_{i+1} > y_i$ for each i, since when λ is 0, the optimal stable matching is woman-optimal and man-pessimal.

For fixed k, the number of values of i for which $(x_i - x_{i+1}) + (y_{i+1} - y_i) = k$ is at most $k - 1$. For if $(x_i - x_{i+1}) = j$ and $(y_{i+1} - y_i) = (k - j)$, then since $\lambda_i x_i + y_i = \lambda_i x_{i+1} + y_{i+1}$, λ_i is the unique point $(k - j)/j$. Hence $(j, k - j)$ can occur at most once as a pair $(x_i - x_{i+1}, y_{i+1} - y_i)$.

Therefore it follows that

$$2(n^2 - n) \ge \sum_{i=1}^{t-1}\{(x_i - x_{i+1}) + (y_{i+1} - y_i)\} \ge \sum_{k=2}^{s} k(k - 1) = \frac{1}{3}(s - 1)s(s + 1)$$

where s is the largest integer such that $\sum_{k=2}^{s}(k - 1) \le t$, so that $\sum_{k=2}^{s+1}(k - 1) > t$. Hence $t < \frac{1}{2}s(s + 1)$, where $(s - 1)s(s + 1) \le 6n(n - 1)$. It follows easily that $t < (\frac{9}{2})^{\frac{1}{3}}n^{\frac{4}{3}} + O(n^{\frac{2}{3}})$. □

Using the fact that there can be no M_i, M_j such that $x_i = cx_j$ and $y_i = cy_j$, we can obtain the stronger inequalities $2(n^2 - n) \ge \sum_{k=2}^{s} k\phi(k)$ and $\sum_{k=2}^{s} \phi(k) \le t$, where ϕ is Euler's totient function. With a finer analysis based on these inequalities, and using the asymptotic result $\sum_{k=2}^{n} \phi(k) \sim \frac{3n^2}{\pi^2}$ and its easy consequence $\sum_{k=2}^{n} k\phi(k) \sim \frac{2n^3}{\pi^2}$, the constant in the bound for the number of breakpoints can be reduced from $(\frac{9}{2})^{\frac{1}{3}} \approx 1.65$ to $(\frac{3}{\pi})^{\frac{2}{3}} \approx 0.97$, but the exponent $\frac{4}{3}$ remains unchanged.

Breakpoints of $F(\lambda)$

The bound on the number of breakpoints of $F(\lambda)$ is based on the following key lemma and its corollary.

Lemma 3.6.5 *Let $\lambda_1 < \lambda_2$, and let M_1 and M_2 be stable matchings that are respectively λ_1- and λ_2-optimal. Then $M_1 \wedge M_2$ is λ_2-optimal.*

Proof Let S be the set of men who prefer their mates in M_1 to their mates in M_2, and let T be the set of women who are the mates in M_1 of the men in S. By the definitions of $M_1 \vee M_2$ and S, it follows that in $M_1 \vee M_2$, every man in S is married to his mate from M_2, and all other men are married to their mates from M_1. Hence, if we define $\Delta_S \equiv \sum_{m \in S}[c_{M_1}(m) - c_{M_2}(m)]$, and $\Delta_T \equiv \sum_{w \in T}[c_{M_1}(w) - c_{M_2}(w)]$, then $C_{M_1}(\lambda_1) - C_{Min(M_1,M_2)}(\lambda_1) = \lambda_1 \Delta_S + \Delta_T$. Now M_1 is λ_1-optimal, so $\lambda_1 \Delta_S + \Delta_T \leq 0$. Further, since $\Delta_S \leq 0$ and $\lambda_1 < \lambda_2$, it follows that $\lambda_2 \Delta_S + \Delta_T \leq 0$ also.

In $M_1 \wedge M_2$, every man in S is married to his mate in M_1 and every other man is married to his mate in M_2. So $C_{Max(M_1,M_2)}(\lambda_2) - C_{M_2}(\lambda_2) = \lambda_2 \Delta_S + \Delta_T \leq 0$ (the inequality is from the paragraph above). But $C_{(M_1 \wedge M_2)}(\lambda_2) - C_{M_2}(\lambda_2) \geq 0$, since M_2 is λ_2-optimal. Hence $C_{(M_1 \wedge M_2)}(\lambda_2) - C_{M_2}(\lambda_2) = 0$, and the lemma is proved. □

Corollary 3.6.2 *If M_1 is λ_1-optimal but not λ_2-optimal, where $\lambda_2 > \lambda_1$, then there exists a stable matching M that is λ_2-optimal and that dominates M_1. Certainly, $M_1 \wedge M_2$ is such a stable matching.*

As an interesting aside, a symmetric argument to Corollary 3.6.2 shows that $M_1 \vee M_2$ is λ_1-optimal. It follows that the set of stable matchings that are λ-optimal for a fixed value of λ form a distributive lattice under the dominance relation. Hence, these λ-optimal matchings can be compactly represented by a partial order. We leave to the reader the details of how to efficiently construct that partial order, and to work out its relationship to $\Pi(\mathcal{M})$.

We now bound the number of breakpoints of $F(\lambda)$.

Theorem 3.6.8 *If $r(\mathcal{M})$ is the number of rotations in an instance with marriage lattice $\mathcal{M}$, then there can be at most $r(\mathcal{M}) \leq n(n-1)/2$ breakpoints of $F(\lambda)$.*

Proof Let $\lambda_1, \lambda_2, \ldots, \lambda_k$ be the breakpoints of $F(\lambda)$. By Corollary 3.6.2, there exists a sequence of stable matchings $M_1, M_2, \ldots, M_t$ such that each M_i is λ_i-optimal, and such that M_{i+1} dominates M_i. Clearly, the length of such a sequence is bounded by the number of stable matchings on a maximal chain in $\mathcal{M}$, which by Corollary 2.4.4 is exactly $r(\mathcal{M})+1$, and so the number of breakpoints is bounded by $r(\mathcal{M})$. $\square$

It can be shown that the bound in Theorem 3.6.8 is tight, at least for n even. To show this, one needs to exhibit problem instances where the maximal chain has length $n(n-1)/2$, and where every matching on the chain is optimal for some value of λ. Hence the λ_i-optimal matching on the chain is an immediate predecessor in $\mathcal{M}$ of the λ_{i-1}-optimal matching on the chain. Corollary 3.6.2 applies to $P(\lambda)$ as well as to $F(\lambda)$, but it is interesting to note that since the number of breakpoints of $P(\lambda)$ is smaller than $n(n-1)/2$, even in the cases when the maximal chain is long, the successive optimal solutions to $P(\lambda)$ will often skip over an immediate predecessor.

3.6.5   Finding All the Breakpoints Efficiently

There is a general method, called the ES method, for finding all the breakpoints for *any* piecewise linear function. We will describe that method, given formally in procedure *Break* (shown in Figure 3.10), in terms of the function $F(\lambda)$. The primitive operation of the method is the *evaluation* of $F(\lambda)$, i.e. finding the value of $F(\lambda)$ for a fixed value of λ. Procedure *Break* takes as input two values of λ, $\lambda_i < \lambda_j$, a λ_i-optimal matching M_i, and a λ_j-optimal matching M_j; it produces all the breakpoints in the range $[\lambda_i, \lambda_j]$. We are interested in a continuum between the woman-optimal and the man-optimal stable matching, so we first set λ_i to be 0, and λ_j to be larger than $\sum_{(w,m)} c(w,m)$, where the man-optimal matching is certainly λ_j-optimal. To start the algorithm, evaluate and output $F(\lambda)$ at these two extremes, then call *Break* to find all the breakpoints between λ_i and λ_j.

Once the breakpoints have been found, the optimal stable matching for any interval between consecutive breakpoints can be obtained by finding any optimal stable matching at a value of λ strictly in the interior of the interval.[2] Hence, once the breakpoints are known, the desired continuum of egalitarian stable matchings can be found in $O(n^{4/3}n^4 \log n)$ time, and the continuum of optimal stable matchings can be found in $O(n^6 \log n)$ time. We will now show that all the breakpoints can be found in these times.

Lemma 3.6.6 *Letting k denote the number of breakpoints of $F(\lambda)$ for a given problem instance, procedure Break finds all the breakpoints of $F(\lambda)$ using exactly $2k - 1$ evaluations of $F(\lambda)$.*

---

[2]Actually, the needed stable matchings have already been computed during *Break*, and the procedure could be modified to produce both the breakpoints and the associated stable matchings at the same time. However, for the exposition, it is simpler to separate these tasks.

---

procedure $Break(\lambda_i, M_i; \lambda_j, M_j)$

begin
      if (M_i is λ_j-optimal) or (M_j is λ_i-optimal) then
          return; {no breakpoints in the interval (λ_i, λ_j)}
      set λ_{ij} to be the unique value of λ, where $C_{M_i}(\lambda) = C_{M_j}(\lambda)$;
      evaluate $F(\lambda_{ij})$;
      set M_{ij} to be the λ_{ij}-optimal matching found;
      if $C_{M_i}(\lambda_{ij}) = C_{M_{ij}}(\lambda_{ij})$ then {M_i is λ_{ij}-optimal} {step A}
          begin
              output λ_{ij}; {λ_{ij} is a breakpoint}
              return
          end
      else
          begin
              $Break(\lambda_i, M_i; \lambda_{ij}, M_{ij})$;
              $Break(\lambda_{ij}, M_{ij}; \lambda_j, M_j)$;
              return
          end;
end;

Figure 3.10: Procedure *Break*

Proof First, if in step A, $C_{M_i}(\lambda_{ij}) = C_{M_{ij}}(\lambda_{ij})$, for the current λ_{ij} and M_{ij}, then M_i is optimal at both λ_i and λ_{ij}, and so it must be optimal at all points in between. Similarly, since $C_{M_i}(\lambda_{ij}) = C_{M_j}(\lambda_{ij})$, M_j must be optimal from λ_{ij} to λ_j. But since M_i is not optimal to the right, and M_j is not optimal to the left of λ_{ij}, λ_{ij} must be a breakpoint; further, it is the only breakpoint in the interior of the interval $[\lambda_i, \lambda_j]$. Hence when *Break* finds an equality in step A, it correctly finds the breakpoints in the interval it was called with. It is also clear that if M_i is λ_j-optimal or M_j is λ_i-optimal, then there can be no breakpoints in the interior of $[\lambda_i, \lambda_j]$.

Note that when $C_{M_i}(\lambda_{ij}) \neq C_{M_{ij}}(\lambda_{ij})$ in step A, then M_{ij} cannot be optimal to the right of λ_j, for it has larger cost than M_j to the right of λ_j. So when λ_{ij} is not a breakpoint, the slope of the cost of M_{ij} must be larger than the slope of the cost of M_j.

Consider now the execution of the algorithm up to the first time that an equality is found in step A, and *Break* outputs a breakpoint. Each stable matching M_{ij} computed in this sequence of calls to *Break*, other than the last matching in the sequence, has a slope larger than its associated matching M_j, and M_{ij} is then passed as the M_j parameter in the next call of *Break*. So no matching in this sequence, except the last one, is computed twice during this sequence of calls of *Break*. Since the number of stable matchings is finite, the sequence must terminate, which happens when $C_{M_i}(\lambda_{ij}) = C_{M_j}(\lambda_{ij})$, for the current λ_{ij} and M_{ij}; *Break* then correctly returns the leftmost breakpoint of $F(\lambda)$, and it correctly determines the form of $F(\lambda)$ from the original λ_i to the current λ_j. The left end of the next interval called in *Break* is this λ_j, so the correctness of the entire algorithm follows by repeating the above argument each time that *Break* finds an equality in step A.

For the proof of the time bound, note that each call of *Break* requires one evaluation of $F(\lambda)$, and either finds exactly one breakpoint and returns, or it recursively calls *Break* twice and returns. Hence the tree of recursive calls is binary, and each leaf represents a call that finds a breakpoint. No breakpoint is found twice, since the λ intervals in the calls never overlap; so if there are k breakpoints, then the tree has exactly k leaves and exactly $2k - 1$ nodes, and since the method evaluates $F(\lambda)$ once for each node, it evaluates it exactly $2k - 1$ times. $\square$

Note that since $P(\lambda)$ is a special case of $F(\lambda)$, Lemma 3.6.6 holds for $P(\lambda)$ as well. Each evaluation of $F(\lambda)$ or $P(\lambda)$ is obtained by solving a single optimal stable marriage problem in $O(n^4 \log n)$ time, and only two evaluations are required before *Break* is first called, so applying Theorems 3.6.7 and 3.6.8, we have the following conclusion.

Theorem 3.6.9 *All the breakpoints of $F(\lambda)$ and their associated optimal stable matchings, can be found in $O(n^6 \log n)$ time, and all the breakpoints and associated matchings of $P(\lambda)$ in $O(n^{4/3}n^4 \log n)$.*

Finding Breakpoints Faster

Both of the above times can be reduced to $O(n^4 \log n)$, which is the best presently known time bound for computing even a single optimal matching. This is another example, similar to the problem of finding all the stable pairs, where a set of many related problems can be solved as quickly as can a single instance. The speed-up is due to a modification of a recent result on computing parametric minimum cuts.

Recall that in network $\vec{G}(\mathcal{M})$, each node ρ is associated with rotation ρ, and is adjacent to s if and only if $w(\rho) < 0$, and is adjacent to t if and only if $w(\rho) > 0$. Recall also that the weight of ρ is given by:

$$w(\rho) = \sum_{i=0}^{r-1}[mr(m_i, w_i) - mr(m_i, w_{i+1})] + \sum_{i=0}^{r-1}[wr(w_i, m_i) - wr(w_i, m_{i-1})].$$

We will call the first term $\delta_m(\rho)$ and the second term $\delta_w(\rho)$. Note that $\delta_m(\rho)$ is always negative, and $\delta_w(\rho)$ is always positive.

Now in the case of the parametric stable marriage problem, a rotation no longer has a fixed weight but has a weight that is a linear function of λ. In particular, the weight of ρ is give by the function $\lambda\delta_m(\rho) + \delta_w(\rho)$. For any fixed value of λ, the optimal stable matching can be found as before, but as a function of λ, the network on which the flow is computed is not fixed, since the weight of a rotation may be either positive or negative, depending on the particular λ. To account for this, we modify $\vec{G}(\mathcal{M})$ by connecting every node ρ to both s and t, and instead of giving these edges a fixed capacity, the capacity of edge (s, ρ) is set to $max[0, -(\lambda\delta_m(\rho) + \delta_w(\rho))]$, and the capacity of edge (ρ, t) is set to $max[0, (\lambda\delta_m(\rho) + \delta_w(\rho))]$; all other edges have infinite capacity, as before. We call this modified network $\vec{G}_\lambda(\mathcal{M})$. Hence, as a function of λ, the edges incident with s have monotonically nondecreasing capacities, and those incident with t have monotonically nonincreasing capacities, and all other edges have fixed capacities. We will call this the *monotonicity property*. It is easy to verify that for any fixed value of λ, the edges of $\vec{G}_\lambda(\mathcal{M})$ with nonzero capacity form the network $\vec{G}(\mathcal{M})$ used to compute the optimal stable matching for that value of λ.

Recently, Gallo, Grigoriadis, and Tarjan specialized the general ES method to the parametric minimum-cut problem, and showed that when the capacities of the edges incident with s and t are defined by *linear* functions of λ, and the network has the monotonicity property, then all the $k = O(N)$ breakpoints of the parametric minimum-cut function on a graph with N nodes and E edges can be found in $O(NE \log(N^2/E))$ time. This method, which we will call the GGT method, is a dramatic improvement over the ES method, since $O(NE \log(N^2/E))$ is the best time bound presently known for computing a minimum cut on such a graph, for even a single value of λ.

Unfortunately, the GGT method does not immediately apply to parametric stable marriage, because the parameterized capacities in $\vec{G}_\lambda(\mathcal{M})$ are not linear functions of λ but are *piecewise* linear functions of λ. However, a closer examination of the GGT method and its proof shows that the method works under more general conditions than were first observed: only the monotonicity property is required for the result. Hence, all of the minimum cut computations on $\vec{G}_\lambda(\mathcal{M})$ needed by procedure *Break* can be executed in $O(n^4 \log n)$ time, so all the breakpoints of $F(\lambda)$ and $P(\lambda)$ can be found in that time. For more details, see the papers mentioned in the notes and references section of this chapter (Section 3.10).

3.7 Linear Programming and Stable Marriage

In this section we examine a relationship between the stable marriage problem and linear programming. In particular, for any stable marriage instance of size n, we efficiently construct a set of linear inequalities, whose size is polynomial in n, such that there is a one-one correspondence between the stable matchings of the instance and the extreme points of the polytope defined by the inequalities. Hence, with those inequalities, stable matching problems, including the egalitarian, optimal, and parametric marriage problems, can be solved by general linear programming methods that give primal (extreme point) solutions.

3.7.1 Inequalities Based on Rotations

The simplest way to write a system of linear inequalities that describe all stable matchings is to to describe the closed subsets of $\Pi(\mathcal{M})$ by a system of *integer* linear inequalities. To do this, we create a variable $y(\rho)$ for each rotation ρ in $\Pi(\mathcal{M})$, and an inequality

$$y(\rho') - y(\rho) \leq 0$$

for each pair of rotations such that ρ precedes ρ' in $\Pi(\mathcal{M})$. We then add the constraint that for each rotation ρ, the value of $y(\rho)$ must be either zero or one. We call this system of inequalities system I.

With the intuitive interpretation that $y(\rho) = 1$ means that ρ is in a set of rotations, the constraints say that ρ cannot be in the set unless each of its predecessors is also in the set. Hence the following theorem is immediate.

Theorem 3.7.1 *Let S be any closed subset of $\Pi(\mathcal{M})$. Then setting $y(\rho) = 1$ if $\rho \in S$, and $y(\rho) = 0$ if $\rho \notin S$, gives a solution to system I. Conversely, given any solution to system I, if S is the set of rotations ρ such that $y(\rho) = 1$, then S is a closed subset of $\Pi(\mathcal{M})$.*

Given the one-one correspondence between the stable matchings and the closed subsets of $\Pi(\mathcal{M})$, the solutions to system I are clearly in one-one correspondence with the stable matchings. To actually obtain the stable matching from a solution to system I, we could eliminate the closed subset of rotations given by the solution. However, there is a more direct way to obtain the matching from a solution to system I. We create the variable $x(m, w)$ for each man-woman pair (m, w), and assign its value according to the following equations:

$$x(m, w) = 1 - y(\phi(m, w)) \text{ for } (m, w) \in M_0 \qquad (3.7.1)$$

and

$$x(m, w) = y(\tau(m, w)) \text{ for } (m, w) \in M_z \qquad (3.7.2)$$

and otherwise

$$x(m, w) = y(\tau(m, w)) - y(\phi(m, w)) \qquad (3.7.3)$$

where, as earlier, $\tau(m, w)$ is the unique rotation that moves m to w, and $\phi(m, w)$ is the unique rotation that moves m from w. It is easy to verify that these equations give the correct associated stable matching for a solution to system I.

System I describes the stable matchings. However, it is not a linear program, because of the integer constraints on each variable $y(\rho)$. We now define the system I' as the system I where each such integrality constraint on $y(\rho)$ is replaced by the less restrictive constraint $0 \leq y(\rho) \leq 1$.

System I' is a linear program and so can be solved by general linear programming methods, but although every stable matching clearly corresponds to a solution of I', the converse is no longer true. However, it is certainly true that every *integral* solution to I' is also a solution to I and so specifies a stable matching. We will see that the *extreme points* of system I' are integral and are in one-one correspondence with the stable matchings; hence, any *primal* solution (one corresponding to an extreme point) to system I' specifies a stable matching.

Integrality of System I'

Consider a general linear program specified by the constraints

$$Ay \leq b,$$

$$y \geq 0$$

where A is an integer matrix, b is an integer vector, and y is a vector of variables. Matrix A is defined to be *totally unimodular* if the determinant of every square submatrix of A is either $+1$, -1 or 0. The following well-known theorem indicates the importance of total unimodularity.

Theorem 3.7.2 *If A and b are integral, and A is totally unimodular, then every extreme point of the system $Ay \leq b$, $y \geq 0$ is integral. Hence, every primal solution to the system is integral.*

Further, the following well-known theorem gives a useful sufficient condition for a matrix to be totally unimodular.

Theorem 3.7.3 *A matrix whose entries are +1, -1 and 0 is totally unimodular if it contains no more than one +1 and one -1 in each row.*

Clearly, the system I' can be written as $Ay \leq b$, $y \geq 0$, where A and b are integral and A satisfies the conditions of Theorem 3.7.3. It follows then, by Theorem 3.7.2, that every extreme point of system I' is integral, and so each extreme point is also a solution to system I; therefore every extreme point of I' corresponds to a stable matching. Conversely, it is easy to see that every stable matching corresponds to an extreme point of system I', so the following is established.

Theorem 3.7.4 *For any problem instance, the extreme points of the polytope defined by I' are in one-one correspondence with the the stable matchings of the instance. Further, the association between the extreme points and the matchings is given by equations 3.7.1, 3.7.2, and 3.7.3 (on page 144).*

We will call the polytope defined by I' the *marriage polytope*.

Given Theorem 3.7.4, any linear programming method that finds primal solutions can be used to solve stable marriage problems. For example, to solve the optimal stable marriage problem, we minimize the following objective function subject to the constraints of system I':

$$\sum_{(m,w)\in M_0} c(m,w)[1-y(\phi(m,w))] + \sum_{(m,w)\in M_z} c(m,w)y(\tau(m,w))+$$

$$\sum_{(m,w)\text{ stable and }\notin M_0 \cup M_z} c(m,w)[y(\tau(m,w))-y(\phi(m,w))].$$

For the optimal stable marriage problem, it is an empirical question whether general linear programming methods are faster in practice than the network flow approach given in Section 3.6.1, although the worst-case time bound of the network flow approach is superior. However, even if the linear programming approach is less efficient, the integrality of the extreme points of I' may make it possible to efficiently solve, in practice, system I' together with interesting nonlinear objective functions.

In practice, we would not use the full system of inequalities I' but only the "sparse" system obtained from $G(\mathcal{M})$ (or $\tilde{G}(\mathcal{M})$), where each inequality comes from an edge in $G(\mathcal{M})$ (or $\tilde{G}(\mathcal{M})$). This system can clearly be written down in $O(n^2)$ time, which is faster than if $\Pi(\mathcal{M})$ is used and, being smaller, should allow a faster solution of the resulting linear program.

We should also note that one could use the representation $I(\mathcal{M})$ to obtain linear inequalities whose extreme points are in one-one correspondence with the stable matchings. Such inequalities simply define the nonempty closed subsets of $I(\mathcal{M})$ in the obvious way. Hence the easiest proof that we know of, that a polynomial bounded set of inequalities describes the stable marriage polytope, is given by the discussion of $I(\mathcal{M})$ in Section 2.2, followed by the discussion above on linear inequalities describing closed subsets, replacing rotations by their associated irreducible matchings.

3.7.2 More Direct Inequalities

Recently, John Vande Vate showed how to describe the marriage polytope with a system of inequalities containing only variables $x(m, w)$, that is, without variables for rotations. Let $P(m, w)$ be the set of women whom m strictly prefers to w, and let $\hat{P}(w, m)$ be the set of men such that w strictly prefers m to each man in $\hat{P}(w, m)$. Then let I'' be the following system of linear inequalities.

For each man m,

$$\sum_{w} x(m, w) = 1 \tag{3.7.4}$$

For each woman w,

$$\sum_{m} x(m, w) = 1 \tag{3.7.5}$$

For each pair (m, w),

$$x(m, w) \geq 0 \tag{3.7.6}$$

For each pair (m, w),

$$\sum_{m' \in \hat{P}(w, m)} x(m', w) - \sum_{w' \in P(m, w)} x(m, w') \leq 0 \tag{3.7.7}$$

The variables in I'' would have a simple intuitive interpretation *if* they were restricted to be integral. In that case, the meaning of $x(m, w)$ is that m is matched to w if and only if $x(m, w) = 1$. With such required integrality the first three inequalities would say that each person gets matched to exactly one person, and the last inequality says that if w is matched to a man she considers inferior to m, then for stability, m must be matched to a woman he prefers to w. The symmetric condition — if m is matched to someone inferior to w, then w must be matched to someone superior to m — is implied automatically from the other constraints. Hence it is easy to see that the *integral* solutions to the system I'' specify stable matchings, and the converse is also simple to establish. However, I'' does not have explicit integrality constraints, so the following theorem is quite surprising.

Theorem 3.7.5 *The extreme points of the system I'' are all integral, so that I'' describes the marriage polytope.*

We will not give the proof here, but we note that Vande Vate's proof is based on row operations on I'' which transform that system into system I'. Interestingly, I'' is not itself totally unimodular.

From an algorithmic standpoint, system I' is superior to I''. It has fewer variables and constraints; it can be constructed from the preference lists, via $G(\mathcal{M})$, in $O(n^2)$ time, while I'' takes $\Omega(n^3)$ time to write down; and being smaller and sparser, the solution of a linear program based on I' should be faster than one based on I''. In fact, not surprisingly, system I' can be transformed into a network flow problem (which can be solved much faster than general linear programs) by general methods that transform suitably structured linear programs into network flow problems. This conclusion can also be seen from the one-one correspondence between closed subsets of $\Pi(\mathcal{M})$ and the minimum s-t cuts in a suitably defined network, to be discussed in Section 3.8.3. Further, given Vande Vate's proof of Theorem 3.7.5, one can consider system I' to be an optimized version of system I''.

Conceptually, however, I'' is more natural, and more elegant than I', because it is written in terms of variables $x(m, w)$, which have a more direct connection with the data of the problem than do the variables $y(\rho)$ based on rotations. And, unlike I', one can write down system I'' without first finding any stable matchings. It is ironic that the more natural and direct reduction is less efficient than the reduction based on rotations and $G(\mathcal{M})$.

3.8 Equivalent Structures and Problems

In this section we address the following question: how special is the structure of the stable marriage problem? We will follow two approaches in answering this question. In the first approach, we will consider the structure of the stable marriage problem in terms of the structure of the stable matchings and hence in terms of the rotation poset, the ring of P-sets, and the marriage lattice. We will see that these structures contain, respectively, all partial orders, all rings of sets, and all distributive lattices. Therefore, for example, we cannot expect to find special structural properties that hold in general for marriage lattices but not for arbitrary distributive lattices.

However, when algorithmic complexity is considered, the above conclusion is not as compelling as it at first sounds: with the aid of the preference lists (the natural specification of an instance of the stable marriage problem), many algorithmic questions about marriage lattices can be answered much faster than for arbitrary distributive lattices. Therefore, in the second approach we include issues of problem representation and complexity: we consider polynomial time, structure-preserving reductions between the stable marriage problem and other combinatorial problems. In this approach we will again see that the stable marriage problem is just one of a large class of "structurally equivalent", known combinatorial problems.

3.8.1   The Rotation Posets Contain All Partial Orders

We have seen that for every instance of the stable marriage problem, the associated lattice of stable matchings $\mathcal{M}$ can be represented by a partial order, the rotation poset $\Pi(\mathcal{M})$. We now examine the converse question: is every partial order $\mathcal{P}$ isomorphic to the rotation poset for some instance of the stable marriage problem? That is, can every partial order be obtained as the rotation poset of some instance of the stable marriage problem, or are the rotation posets a special class of partial orders? Similarly, is every ring of sets isomorphic to a ring of P-sets, and is every distributive lattice isomorphic to a marriage lattice? We will show constructively that the answer to these three questions is "yes". We will also see that for any partial order $\mathcal{P}$, the size of the problem instance constructed is polynomial in the size of $\mathcal{P}$ and is in fact not much larger than the smallest possible problem instance whose rotation poset is isomorphic to $\mathcal{P}$; we will see analogous results for rings of sets and for distributive lattices. These results are of interest in their own right, and will be needed for efficient reductions later in this chapter.

Algorithm *construct-instance*

The algorithm shown in Figure 3.11 constructs an instance $I(\mathcal{P})$ of the stable marriage problem from the Hasse diagram of a partial order $\mathcal{P}$.

In general, the lists of $I(\mathcal{P})$ produced by the procedure will not be complete. If complete lists are desired, then after the procedure is finished, add any missing entries at the end of each list in arbitrary order. In what follows, we assume that $I(\mathcal{P})$ contains only the lists created by Algorithm *construct-instance*.

procedure construct-instance $(\mathcal{P}, k, I(\mathcal{P}))$;
{ From an arbitrary poset $\mathcal{P}$ with k elements, constructs a stable marriage
  instance $I(\mathcal{P})$ such that the rotation poset of $I(\mathcal{P})$ is $\mathcal{P}$ }
begin
        number the elements of $\mathcal{P}$ $1, \ldots, k$ so that each element has a larger
            number than any of its predecessors ; { a topological ordering }
        form $\mathcal{P}'$ from $\mathcal{P}$ by adjoining an element 0 that precedes all others
            and an element $k + 1$ that is a successor of all others ;
        $e' :=$ number of edges in the Hasse diagram $H(\mathcal{P}')$ of $\mathcal{P}'$;
        number the edges of $H(\mathcal{P}')$ $1, \ldots, e'$ arbitrarily;
        {The constructed stable marriage instance will be of size e'}
        for $j := 1$ to e' do
            place woman j and man j on each other's (initially empty) preference lists;
        {This completes iteration 0 }
        for $i := 1$ to k do
        begin
            $E(i) := (m_0^i, \ldots, m_{r-1}^i)$, an arbitrary ordering of the
                numbers on the edges of $H(\mathcal{P}')$ that are incident with node i;
            $W(i) := (w_0^i, \ldots, w_{r-1}^i)$, the ordered set of women such that
                w_j^i is (currently) last on m_j^i's list $(0 \le j \le r - 1)$;
            for $j := 0$ to $r - 1$ do
                place w_{j+1}^i at the end of man m_j^i's list
                   and m_j^i at the beginning of w_{j+1}^i's list; $\{j + 1 \text{ taken mod } r\}$
     end
end

Figure 3.11: Algorithm *construct-instance*

Example Consider the partial order $\mathcal{P}$ and its derived partial order $\mathcal{P}'$ shown in Figure 3.12. The problem instance given by executing Algorithm *construct-instance* on $\mathcal{P}$ is shown in Figure 3.13.

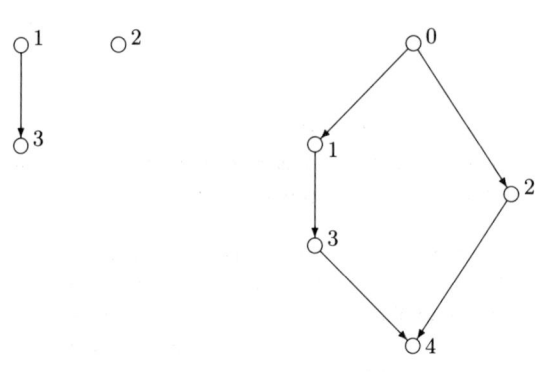

Figure 3.12: Partial orders $\mathcal{P}$ and $\mathcal{P}'$

1	1	3		1	5	3	1
2	2	4		2	4	2	
3	3	1	5	3	1	3	
4	4	2		4	2	4	
5	5	1		5	3	5	

Men's Preferences	Women's Preferences

Figure 3.13: The problem instance generated from $\mathcal{P}$

We let $\mathcal{M}(\mathcal{P})$ refer to the stable matchings of problem instance $I(\mathcal{P})$. We will prove that $\mathcal{P}$ is isomorphic to the rotation poset $\Pi(\mathcal{M}(\mathcal{P}))$, via the following lemmas.

Lemma 3.8.1 *After iteration i $(0 \leq i \leq k)$ of the algorithm, the mapping of each man to the last woman on his current list is a stable matching with respect to the preference lists of $I(\mathcal{P})$.*

Proof The proof is by induction on i. Clearly, for $i = 0$ the mapping is a matching, and it is stable, since each man gets his first choice woman in his $I(\mathcal{P})$ preference list. In each iteration thereafter, those men whose lists change merely permute among themselves the women at the end of their lists after the preceding iteration, so the new mapping is again a matching. It is stable with respect to $I(\mathcal{P})$, because each man who changes partners moves only one place down his $I(\mathcal{P})$ list, and each woman who changes partners moves to a partner she prefers to her previous partner. □

Given Lemma 3.8.1, we let M_i ($0 \leq i \leq k$) refer to the above stable matching after iteration i.

Lemma 3.8.2 *In the i'th iteration ($1 \leq i \leq k$), the ordered list of pairs $\rho_i = (m_0^i, w_0^i), ..., (m_{r-1}^i, w_{r-1}^i)$ is a rotation exposed in matching M_{i-1}, and $M_i = M_{i-1}/\rho_i$.*

Proof This follows directly from the stability of M_i and the fact that, for each j ($0 \leq j \leq r - 1$), woman w_{j+1}^i immediately follows w_j^i in the list of man m_j^i, and man m_j^i immediately precedes m_{j+1}^i in the list of woman w_{j+1}^i. □

We will use ρ_i to refer to the rotation associated with iteration i, and hence with element i of $\mathcal{P}$.

Lemma 3.8.3 *The set of rotations $\{\rho_i : 1 \leq i \leq k\}$ are all the rotations in the stable matchings of $\mathcal{M}(\mathcal{P})$.*

Proof All the man-woman pairs in $I(\mathcal{P})$ are either in the woman-optimal matching or are in one of the rotations of $\{\rho_i : 1 \leq i \leq k\}$. Since no pair can ever be in more than one rotation, and no pair in the woman-optimal matching can ever be in any rotation, the rotations of $I(\mathcal{P})$ are exactly $\{\rho_i : 1 \leq i \leq k\}$. □

Hence the rotation poset $\Pi(\mathcal{M}(\mathcal{P}))$ of $\mathcal{M}(\mathcal{P})$ has exactly k rotations, which is the number of elements of $\mathcal{P}$. We are now ready for the main result of this section.

Theorem 3.8.1 *If $\mathcal{P}$ is any partial order, then the rotation poset $\Pi(\mathcal{M}(\mathcal{P}))$ is isomorphic to $\mathcal{P}$.*

Proof We have already seen that $\mathcal{P}$ and $\Pi(\mathcal{M}(\mathcal{P}))$ have the same number of elements. The proposed isomorphism is given by associating element i in $\mathcal{P}$ with rotation ρ_i in $\Pi(\mathcal{M}(\mathcal{P}))$ ($1 \leq i \leq k$).

By construction, if rotation ρ_x is an immediate predecessor in $\Pi(\mathcal{M}(\mathcal{P}))$ of ρ_y, then there is a man m who is in both rotations, and m is the label on the edge (x, y) in $\mathcal{P}'$, where x and y are between 1 and k. Hence x and

y are both in $\mathcal{P}$ as well as in $\mathcal{P}'$, so x is an immediate predecessor of y in $\mathcal{P}$. Conversely, if x is an immediate predecessor of y in $\mathcal{P}$, then it is an immediate predecessor in $\mathcal{P}'$, and letting m be the man on edge (x, y), m must be in both ρ_x and ρ_y, and ρ_x must precede ρ_y in $\Pi(\mathcal{M}(\mathcal{P}))$. Now by construction, no man is contained in more than two of the sets $E(i)$, so given Lemmas 3.8.2 and 3.8.3, no man is contained in more than two rotations of $\Pi(\mathcal{M}(\mathcal{P}))$. Then, since m is contained in both ρ_x and ρ_y, ρ_x must be an immediate predecessor of ρ_y. It follows that $\mathcal{P}$ is isomorphic to $\Pi(\mathcal{M}(\mathcal{P}))$.
□

The size of the problem instance $I(\mathcal{P})$ is equal to the number of edges of $\mathcal{P}'$ which is at most twice the number of edges, e, of $\mathcal{P}$, so the size of instance $I(\mathcal{P})$ is at most $2e$. Further, each person gets included in at most two rotations, so the total size of the lists is $O(e)$, and Algorithm *construct-instance* runs in $O(e)$ time. The efficiency of this construction will be important in the next section.

Corollary 3.8.1 *Any ring of sets $\mathcal{F}$ is isomorphic is a ring of P-sets of some instance of the stable marriage problem.*

Proof For any partial order $\mathcal{P}$, the closed subsets of $\mathcal{P}$ are closed under union and intersection, and so define a ring of sets. Conversely, by Theorem 2.4.1, every ring of sets $\mathcal{F}$ is obtained from the closed subsets of the partial order $D(\mathcal{F})$. Hence there is a one-one correspondence between the set of rings of sets and the partial orders. But by Theorem 3.8.1, every $D(\mathcal{F})$ is isomorphic to the rotation poset for some instance of the stable marriage problem, and the corollary follows. □

The Marriage Lattices Contain All Finite Distributive Lattices

We can also settle the analogous question about marriage lattices and arbitrary distributive lattices. The stable matchings for any problem instance form a finite distributive lattice, the marriage lattice $\mathcal{M}$, under the dominance relation. Conversely, every distributive lattice is isomorphic to the marriage lattice for some instance of the stable marriage problem. The key fact we will need is Birkhoff's representation theorem for distributive lattices, Theorem 3.8.2 below.

For a partial order $\mathcal{P}$, let $L(\mathcal{P})$ denote the distributive lattice whose elements are the closed subsets of $\mathcal{P}$ under the relation of set containment.

Theorem 3.8.2 *Any distributive lattice L is isomorphic to $L(\mathcal{P})$ for exactly one partial order $\mathcal{P}$. Further, $\mathcal{P}$ is easily constructed from L.*

Clearly, $L(\mathcal{P})$ is a ring of sets, so every distributive lattice is isomorphic to a ring of sets. So Corollary 3.8.1 and Theorem 3.8.2 establish the following.

Theorem 3.8.3 *Every distributive lattice L is isomorphic to the marriage lattice $\mathcal{M}$ of some instance $I(L)$ of the stable marriage problem.*

To obtain $I(L)$, we find partial order $\mathcal{P}$ from L, as in Theorem 3.8.2, and then $I(L) = I(\mathcal{P})$.

The significance of Theorem 3.8.1 is that there is no special structure that holds in general for the set of rotation posets, that does not also hold for the set of all partial orders. The converse is, of course, true because a rotation poset is a partial order. Similarly, Corollary 3.8.1 and Theorem 3.8.3 imply that there is no special structure that holds in general for marriage lattices or for rings of P-sets that does not also hold for general distributive lattices or rings of sets. The converse statements are immediate.

The Generated Instances Are Small

It is interesting to note that for a given partial order $\mathcal{P}$, instance $I(\mathcal{P})$ may not be the smallest problem instance whose rotation poset is isomorphic to $\mathcal{P}$. However, the size of $I(\mathcal{P})$ is close to the size of the smallest possible instance, as we now show.

Theorem 3.8.4 *i) For any arbitrary partial order $\mathcal{P}$, suppose that the smallest stable marriage instance whose rotation poset is isomorphic to $\mathcal{P}$ is of size n. Then the instance $I(\mathcal{P})$ created by Algorithm construct-instance has size $O(n^2)$.*
ii) Let L be any finite distributive lattice, and suppose that the smallest instance whose marriage lattice is isomorphic to L is of size n. Then instance $I(L)$ has size $O(n^2)$.

Proof i) By assumption, $\mathcal{P}$ is isomorphic to the rotation poset of a problem instance of size n. Let $\mathcal{M}$ be the stable matchings of this instance. The Hasse diagram of $\mathcal{P}$ must be a subgraph of $G(\mathcal{M})$, since the transitive closure of $G(\mathcal{M})$ is $\mathcal{P}$ and the Hasse diagram of $\mathcal{P}$ is the (unique) minimal graph whose transitive closure is $\mathcal{P}$. Then, since $G(\mathcal{M})$ can have at most $O(n^2)$ edges (Lemma 3.3.1), the Hasse diagram of $\mathcal{P}$ has at most $O(n^2)$ edges as well. Now the size of instance $I(\mathcal{P})$ is proportional to the number of edges in the Hasse diagram of $\mathcal{P}$, so instance $I(\mathcal{P})$ has size at most $O(n^2)$. ii) Let $\mathcal{M}$ be the marriage lattice of the size n instance in question; by assumption, $\mathcal{M}$ is isomorphic to L. Let $\mathcal{P}$ be the unique partial order, discussed in Theorem 3.8.2, such that $L(\mathcal{P})$ is isomorphic to L and hence to $\mathcal{M}$. Under the relation of set containment, the closed subsets of $\Pi(\mathcal{M})$ form a distributive lattice isomorphic to $\mathcal{M}$ and hence to L. Therefore $\Pi(\mathcal{M})$ must be isomorphic to $\mathcal{P}$, and hence the Hasse diagram of $\mathcal{P}$ must have only $O(n^2)$ edges. Therefore, instance $I(L)$ is of size $O(n^2)$. $\square$

3.8.2   Problem Reduction and Equivalence

Theorem 3.8.3 says that the marriage lattices possess no special structure that does not exist for distributive lattices in general. But an instance of the stable marriage problem is not specified by its marriage lattice — it is specified by its preference lists. And given the preference lists of n men and n women, many questions are solvable in polynomial time as a function of n that are not efficiently solvable from the associated marriage lattice. For example, the question of whether a given matching is stable can be determined in $O(n^2)$ time given the preference lists, but given only $\mathcal{M}$, no such efficiency seems possible. Hence Theorems 3.8.1 and 3.8.3 do not satisfactorily answer the question of how special (for the purposes of finding efficient algorithms) is the structure of the stable marriage problem. That question is not answered by looking at the structure of the *solutions* to problems, but rather by looking at structure that is efficiently extracted from the natural *input* to the problems. We therefore should look for other problems with structural properties that are "equivalent" to those possessed by the stable marriage problem, where those properties can be efficiently exploited from the natural input to the problem. In particular, we should look for problems that admit efficient, structure-preserving reductions, to and from the stable marriage problem. Such problems are said to be *structurally equivalent* to the stable marriage problem, and it turns out that there are many such combinatorial problems; there are more problems that admit efficient structure-preserving reductions to (but not necessarily from) the stable marriage problem.

In this section we will discuss in detail the best-known and most important structurally equivalent problem, namely the minimum s-t cut problem. We emphasize the minimum-cut problem, because of its central role in combinatorial optimization. A huge number of problems can be cast as minimum-cut problems, or reduced, via structure-preserving reductions, to minimum-cut problems, and many problems concerning graph matching, matroids, polymatroids, submodular functions, and games are known to be structurally equivalent to the minimum-cut problem. In Section 3.10 we will list and reference some of these problems.

3.8.3   Stable Matchings and Minimum Cuts

We have already seen a reduction of the *optimal* stable marriage problem to a minimum-cut problem, with a one-one correspondence between the set of optimal stable matchings of $\mathcal{M}$ and the minimum s-t cuts in the network $\vec{G}(\mathcal{M})$. We will now show that there is a one-one correspondence between the set of *all* stable matchings of $\mathcal{M}$ (not just the optimal ones) and the minimum s-t cuts on a network related to $\vec{G}(\mathcal{M})$. We will also show the converse, reducing any arbitrary s-t network G to an instance $I(G)$ of the stable marriage problem, with a one-one correspondence between the minimum s-t cuts of G and the stable matchings of $I(G)$. Further, we will define a partial order on minimum s-t cuts of a network such that in each direction of the reduction, the minimum cuts form a partial order that is *isomorphic* to the lattice defined by the dominance relation on the set of associated stable matchings. Hence the stable marriage and the minimum-cut problems are structurally equivalent.

The Minimum Cuts as Stable Matchings

Recall that for a directed network G with designated nodes s and t, an s-t *cut* is a partition of the nodes of G into two sets (U, V), with $s \in S$ and $t \in T$. The capacity of a cut is the sum of the weights of the edges crossing from U to V. The crucial fact about the set of minimum s-t cuts for a given network G is stated in the following classical theorem.

Theorem 3.8.5 *If (U, V) and (U', V') are minimum s-t cuts of network G, then so are the cuts $(U \cup U', V \cap V')$ and $(U \cap U', V \cup V')$.*

It is immediate from Theorem 3.8.5 that the s-sides of the set of all minimum cuts of G form a ring of sets $\mathcal{F}$, where the base set B is the set of nodes of G. Further, since an s-t cut (U, V) partitions the nodes of G, V is completely determined by U and G, so one can loosely say that the minimum s-t cuts also form a ring of sets. From our discussion of rings of sets in Chapter 2 (Theorem 2.3.1), we know that $\mathcal{F}$ can be represented by the partial order $I(\mathcal{F})$ containing at most N elements of $\mathcal{F}$, where G has N nodes. In particular, the set $I(\mathcal{F})$ consists of the s-sides of the set of irreducible minimum cuts, where a minimum s-t cut (U, V) is irreducible if, for some node x, U is the (unique) minimal s-side set containing x, among all minimum s-t cuts. Also from Chapter 2 (Theorem 2.4.1), we know that $\mathcal{F}$ can be represented by the partial order $D(\mathcal{F})$ with at most N elements, constructed from the minimal differences between the s-sides of minimum s-t cuts. It is not difficult to find polynomial time bounded algorithms for constructing the irreducible s-t cuts of a network, and hence for constructing $I(\mathcal{F})$. However, as in the case of stable marriage, there exists a particularly fast way to find $D(\mathcal{F})$ for this problem; $D(\mathcal{F})$ can be constructed in the time needed to execute one maximum flow computation on G, plus $O(E)$ time, where E is the number of edges of G (see notes and references section 3.10 for appropriate citations).

Combining Algorithm *construct-instance* (and Theorem 3.8.1) with a fast algorithm to construct the partial order $D(\mathcal{F})$ representing the minimum s-t cuts, we have the following conclusion.

Theorem 3.8.6 *For any network G of N nodes, one can construct in $O(N^3)$ time an instance $I(G)$ of the stable marriage problem such that there is a one-one correspondence between the stable matchings of $I(G)$, and the minimum s-t cuts of G. Further, if stable matching M corresponds to the minimum cut (U, V) and M' corresponds to (U', V'), then M dominates M' if and only if $U \subseteq U'$.*

Hence there is a polynomial-time, structure-preserving reduction of the minimum-cut problem to the stable marriage problem. Therefore, at least with respect to polynomial time, there is no algorithmically useful structure in the stable marriage problem that does not exist, in some form, in the minimum-cut problem.

Stable Matchings as Minimum Cuts

Given the rotation digraph $G(\mathcal{M})$ for a problem instance, we obtain the following capacitated s-t flow network G. A source node s and a terminal node t are added to digraph $G(\mathcal{M})$. Then, for every node v in $G(\mathcal{M})$, we add a directed edge of capacity zero from s to v and a directed edge of capacity zero from v to t. The capacity of every original edge in $G(\mathcal{M})$ is set to infinity.

Theorem 3.8.7 *There is a one-one correspondence between the closed subsets of $G(\mathcal{M})$ and the minimum s-t cuts of G. Hence there is a one-one correspondence between the stable matchings of $\mathcal{M}$ and the minimum s-t cuts of G. Further, if stable matching M corresponds to the minimum cut (U, V) and M' corresponds to (U', V'), then M dominates M' if and only if $U \subseteq U'$.*

Proof Let S be a closed subset of $G(\mathcal{M})$, and let $\bar{S}$ be the set of nodes of $G(\mathcal{M})$ other than S. Then let $V = \{t\} \cup S$, and let $U = \{s\} \cup \bar{S}$. Since S is closed, the only edges crossing from U to V have capacity zero, so the partition (U, V) is a minimum s-t cut in G. Conversely, let (U, V) be a minimum s-t cut of G, so all edges from U to V must have capacity zero, and hence V must be a closed set in $G(\mathcal{M})$. The last claim in the Theorem follows immediately. □

Hence we have completed the claim that the stable marriage problem and the minimum s-t cut problem are structurally equivalent. Note that the reductions here serve a different purpose than do reductions commonly used in computer science. We do not reduce an instance of one problem to an instance of another problem in order to find *one* solution of the first problem. If that were the intent, then the time for the reduction must be faster than the time needed to solve the first problem directly. Rather, the (structure-preserving) reduction is used to establish that there are no structural features of the second problem that can be deduced faster (at least up to polynomial time) than they can be deduced for the first problem.

3.9 *NP*-**Hardness**

Given the efficient reductions discussed in the previous section, certain natural problems concerning stable marriage can now be shown to be *NP*-hard or #*P*-complete. These results imply that there are natural problems that we should not expect to solve efficiently, despite the existence and efficient construction of various elegant and compact representations of the set of stable matchings. In particular, we should not expect to determine in polynomial time the number of stable matchings for an arbitrary stable marriage instance.

An *antichain* Q in a partial order $\mathcal{P}$ is a set of elements of $\mathcal{P}$ such that no two elements in Q are comparable. The problem of counting the number of antichains in a partial order is known to be #*P*-complete.

Theorem 3.9.1 *The problem of counting the number of stable matchings in a problem instance is #P-complete.*

Proof There is a natural one-one correspondence between closed subsets and antichains in $\mathcal{P}$: given an antichain Q, let S be the closed set consisting of Q and all predecessors of Q in $\mathcal{P}$; given a closed set S, let Q be the antichain consisting of the maximal elements of S. Hence the problem of counting the number of closed subsets in a partial order is #*P*-complete. That problem can be reduced in polynomial time to the problem of counting the number of stable matchings, since $I(\mathcal{P})$ is constructed in polynomial time as a function of the size of $\mathcal{P}$. The correctness of this reduction follows immediately from Theorems 3.8.1 and 2.5.7. □

We have seen how to enumerate all stable matchings efficiently, how to find an optimal matching efficiently, and how to find a continuum of matchings between the man-optimal matching and the woman-optimal matching efficiently. A related natural problem is to find the k'th best stable matching M (or report that there are fewer than k stable matchings), according to the same criterion as in the egalitarian stable marriage problem, namely, according to the value of

$$\sum_{(m,w)\in M} [mr(m, w) + wr(w, m)].$$

However, when k is not a fixed number, this problem is *NP*-hard. If it could be solved in polynomial time, then we could use binary search to determine in polynomial time the number of stable matchings for a problem instance, since the number is bounded by $n!$, and $\log n! = O(n \log n)$.

3.10   Notes and References

The digraph $G(\mathcal{M})$ and its efficient construction was developed by Gusfield in [35] and used by Irving, Leather, and Gusfield [49]. Graph $\check{G}(\mathcal{M})$ was introduced in [35], and the $O(n^2)$ implementation to build $G(\mathcal{M})$ and $\check{G}(\mathcal{M})$ was shown there also. Theorem 3.2.2 and Corollary 3.2.1 were first proved by Irving and Leather [48]. Algorithm *minimal-differences* and its $O(n^2)$ time implementation is based on an algorithm to find all the rotations and all stable pairs in [35].

The application of $\Pi(\mathcal{M})$ to the stable set problem and to decomposition is new, and in particular, Theorems 3.4.4 and 3.4.5 are new. The issue of decomposition was raised first by Veklerov [123]; however he assumed (incorrectly) that in a decomposition, man m need be on woman w's list if and only if (m, w) is a stable pair, and his results are based on that assumption.

The enumeration method and time and space bounds discussed in this chapter were developed in [35], although the exposition here is different. Earlier, less efficient enumeration methods appear in [59], [71], and [125], and the lower bound of $\Omega(n^3|\mathcal{M}|/\log^2 |\mathcal{M}|)$ time for these methods appears in [34].

The solution of the egalitarian and optimal stable marriage problems is due to Irving, Leather, and Gusfield [49]. A better time bound of $O(n^3 \log n)$ for the egalitarian stable marriage problem has been claimed by T. Feder [15]. His general method is the same as described in this chapter, but the cut computation is claimed to be faster; no details of the speedup are yet available.

For an introduction to computing network flow and minimum cuts see [16] or [64]. Methods that compute a minimum s-t cut in $O(N^3)$ time as a function of N alone, and methods that run in $O(NE \log N)$ time as a function of both N and E, are discussed in [114] and [116]; a more recent algorithm that runs in $O(NE \log \frac{N^2}{E})$ time was introduced in [28]. The discussion of the parametric stable marriage problem is from Gusfield and Irving [36] and [37]. For a discussion of the totient function, used to reduce the constant in Theorem 3.6.7, see [40, page 268]. Theorem 3.6.5 and Corollary 3.6.2 are essentially simplifications of more general results about parametric optimization over submodular functions [44]. The ES method for finding breakpoints was developed by Eisner and Severance and appears in [13], and the results on parametric minimum cuts by Gallo, Grigoriadis, and Tarjan are in [25].

A different alternative to the man or woman-optimal matchings, called the *minimum-regret* stable matching, was discussed in [59], and a $O(n^4)$ time solution (attributed to S. Selkow) was given there. A minimum-regret stable matching is the best stable matching when the value of a matching is measured by the person who is worst off in it. A $O(n^2)$ time algorithm for this problem was given in [35]. An equally efficient algorithm for the more general problem of minimum-regret roommates matching will be discussed in Chapter 4. Two other approaches to finding compromises between the sexes are discussed in [74] and in [75]. The latter paper gives a $O(n^2)$ time algorithm for the following problem: given an ordered list $p_1, p_2, ..., p_{2n}$ of the people, find a stable matching in which p_1 matches with his or her best stable partner, and within that constraint, p_2 gets his or her best stable partner, etc. Note that when the first n people in the list are all men (women), then the solution is the man-optimal (woman-optimal) matching.

The explicit reduction of the stable marriage problem to general linear programming, and the system of inequalities I'', were developed by Vande Vate in [121]; the system of inequalities I', based on rotations, is new. Theorem 3.7.2 is due to Hoffman and Kruskal, and Theorem 3.7.3 is due to Camion. See [64] for an introduction to total unimodularity and for proofs of these theorems.

Algorithm *construct-instance*, which reduces any partial order to an instance of the stable marriage problem, is due to Irving and Leather [48]. Knuth [59], in the discussion associated with one of his twelve questions, asked whether every finite distributive lattice L is isomorphic to a marriage lattice for some instance. That question was first answered by Blair [4] who gave a constructive solution; however, if L has k elements, then

Blair's construction can have as many as 2^k people, so it was not suitable for polynomial time reductions. A reduction from L to an instance of at most k^2 people, based on Birkhoff's theorem [2] and [30], was developed in [38], where a weaker version of Theorem 3.8.4 was proved; a bound of $O(n^4)$ was established there rather than the better bound of $O(n^2)$ shown here.

The question of finding problems structurally equivalent to the stable marriage problem has not appeared in print before, although some aspects of the issue were discussed in a preprint of [121]. Theorem 3.8.5, establishing the minimum cuts as a ring of sets, is from [16]. A fast construction of $D(\mathcal{F})$ for the minimum-cut problem appears in [82], although with quite different terminology, and a version with a viewpoint closer to the ring of sets view is contained in [78]. The paper by Monma and Topkis [77] discusses the structural equivalence of the minimum s-t cut problem to problems involving the tight or active sets of a polymatroid, the solutions to convex games, submodular minimization, closure problems in graphs, and optimization problems on sublattices. All of these problems are hence structurally equivalent to the stable marriage problem. The relationship of many of these problems to the minimum-cut problem is further discussed in [3], [8], [18], [31], and [117]. The papers [25], [81], and [83] discuss many combinatorial problems that can be reduced to the minimum s-t cut problem, and hence to stable marriage via nontrivial, structure-preserving reductions.

In addition to problems closely related to the minimum-cut problem, there are many combinatorial problems whose solutions form a distributive lattice. Each of these problems is polynomially reducible to stable marriage by a structure-preserving reduction, and such a reduction in the other direction is likely but unknown to us at this time. For example, a *minimum cover* of a bipartite graph $G = (A, B, E)$ (A and B are the node sets of G) is a set of nodes of minimum size that touch every edge of G. If $C_1 = (A_1 \subseteq A, B_1 \subseteq B)$ and $C_2 = (A_2 \subseteq A, B_2 \subseteq B)$ are two minimum covers of G, then it is known [12] that $(A_1 \cup A_2, B_1 \cap B_2)$ and $(A_1 \cap A_2, B_1 \cup B_2)$ are also minimum covers of G. Hence the family of subsets of A nodes that are the A side of a minimum cover is closed under union and intersection, and so there is a partial order representation of the A sides of the minimum covers in G. This representation can be found in polynomial time (by finding the "A-side irreducible" covers), and hence there is a polynomial time, structure-preserving reduction from this node cover problem to the stable marriage problem. It is not clear what the relationship is between this family of node sets (the A sides of minimum covers) and minimum cuts in G, although there is a well-known one-one correspondence between minimum node covers in G (which include nodes on both sides of G) and the minimum cuts in a network derived from G. There are additional interesting families of sets arising out of combinatorial problems, which form a distributive lattice and are reducible to the stable marriage problem by structure-preserving reductions. Some of these sets and problems are discussed in [19], [20], [43], [44], [45], [66], [67], [73], [120], and [122], although this list is by no means exhaustive.

The $\#P$-completeness of counting the antichains in a partial order was shown in [86], and the $\#P$-completeness of counting stable matchings is from Irving and Leather [48]. Garey and Johnson [27] is the standard reference for the theory of NP-completeness, NP-hardness, and $\#P$-completeness, and it contains full explanations of all the relevant terms.

The Gale-Shapley algorithm runs in $O(m)$ time when unacceptable partners have been omitted from the preference lists and there are only m remaining entries in total. Similarly, the running time of the algorithms presented in this chapter can easily be expressed in terms of m: the time for algorithm *minimal-differences* is $O(m)$; digraphs $G(\mathcal{M})$ and $\tilde{G}(\mathcal{M})$ can be built in $O(m)$ time; all stable pairs can be found in $O(m)$ time; the preprocessing for the stable set problem can be done in $O(r(\mathcal{M})m) = O(m^2)$ time; the component decomposition can be found in $O(m)$ time; all the stable matchings can be enumerated in $O(m + n|\mathcal{M}|)$ time; the egalitarian stable marriage problem can be solved in $O(m^2)$ time; the optimal stable marriage problem can be solved in $O(m^2 \log n)$ time; and all the breakpoints of the parametric stable marriage problem can be found in $O(m^2 \log n)$ time.

Chapter 4

The Stable Roommates Problem

4.1 Introduction

The *stable roommates problem* is a generalization of the stable marriage problem in which each person in a set of even cardinality ranks *all* of the others in order of preference. In this setting, a *matching* is a partition of the set into disjoint pairs (of partners, or "roommates"). A matching is *unstable* if there are two persons, each of whom prefers the other to his partner in the matching. As in the stable marriage problem, if two such persons exist, they are said to *block* the matching. Otherwise, if there is no blocking pair, then the matching is said to be *stable*.

Much of the terminology that we shall use for the stable roommates problem is analogous to that used for the stable marriage problem. For example, a pair is *stable* if the members of the pair are partners in some stable matching; a person y is a *stable partner* of x if $\{x, y\}$ is a stable pair, etc. Note that, in the roommates case, pairs are unordered, in contrast to the ordered man-woman pairs of the stable marriage problem. Therefore we represent a typical pair using the notation $\{x, y\}$ rather than (x, y).

We shall follow convention and use masculine pronouns throughout when referring to the elements of a stable roommates instance.

The stable roommates problem can be viewed as a generalization of the stable marriage problem, as shown in the following lemma.

Lemma 4.1.1 *Given an instance of the stable marriage problem involving n men and n women, there is an instance (in fact there are many instances) of the stable roommates problem involving those 2n persons such that the stable roommates matchings are precisely the stable matchings for the original stable marriage instance.*

Proof Suppose that, for each person, all other members of the same sex are appended, in arbitrary order, to the end of his/her marriage preference list to produce a roommates instance.

No pair of the same sex can block a matching that was stable for the marriage instance, so all such man-woman matchings remain stable in the derived roommates instance. On the other hand, any matching that contains a pair $\{x, y\}$ of men must also contain a pair $\{u, v\}$ of women, and the pair consisting of either one of x, y, together with either one of u, v, blocks this matching. □

This lemma has a number of immediate consequences. For example, the fact that the maximum number of stable matchings for a stable marriage instance grows exponentially with the size of the problem implies an analogous result for stable roommates. Likewise, the result that counting stable matchings for stable marriage instances is #P-complete carries over to the stable roommates problem also.

Another obvious similarity between the stable marriage and stable roommates problems is that an arbitrary matching can easily be checked for stability in $O(n^2)$ time, for an instance of size n. It is straightforward to obtain from the marriage stability checking algorithm of Figure 1.2 on page 8 a version appropriate for roommates stability checking.

However, the most striking *difference* between the stable marriage problem and the stable roommates problem is that there are instances of the latter that admit no stable matching.

Example Consider the stable roommates instance defined by the preferences in Figure 4.1.

It is easy to see that the three matchings containing the pairs $\{1, 4\}$, $\{2, 4\}$, $\{3, 4\}$ are blocked by the pairs $\{1, 2\}$, $\{2, 3\}$, and $\{3, 1\}$ respectively, and that these are all the possible matchings.

1	3	2	4
2	1	3	4
3	2	1	4
4	arbitrary		

Figure 4.1: An unsolvable roommates instance

An instance of the stable roommates problem will be called *solvable* if it admits a stable matching; otherwise it is *unsolvable*.

Hence we are faced with the problem of determining, for a given roommates instance, whether it is solvable, and if so, how we can find a stable matching efficiently. We address this problem in Section 4.2, where we derive a $O(n^2)$-time algorithm for an instance of size n (i.e., involving n people).

In Section 4.3, we explore the structure of the set of all stable matchings for roommates instances, deriving, insofar as is possible, results analogous to those proved in Chapter 2 for the stable marriage problem. In Section 4.4, we exploit these structural results to solve problems of the kind addressed in Chapter 3 for the stable marriage problem. Finally, in Section 4.5, we study variations and extensions of the stable roommates problem. There we discuss one result that is particularly striking: in contrast to the case of stable marriage, where indifference can be easily handled, in the case of roommates with indifference allowed, the problem of determining whether a stable matching exists is NP-complete.

4.2   The Stable Roommates Algorithm

4.2.1   Overview

The general idea underlying the stable roommates algorithm is that entries are progressively deleted from the preference lists until one of two terminating conditions is satisfied — either some list becomes empty, indicating that no stable matching exists for that instance, or every list is reduced to a single entry, in which case these surviving entries constitute a stable matching. Throughout this reduction process, the deletion of x from y's list is invariably accompanied by the deletion of y from that of x, so that the lists remain mutually consistent throughout.

The algorithm consists of two phases. The first phase is quite similar to the extended Gale-Shapley algorithm of Section 1.2.4. No pair deleted from the preference lists during this phase can be stable; hence the original instance is solvable if and only if the reduced lists contain a stable matching. Phase 1 of the algorithm may terminate with some preference list empty, indicating that no stable matching exists. Otherwise it may happen, exceptionally, that all preference lists are already reduced to a single entry, in which case they represent the unique stable matching for that instance. But in general, at the end of phase 1 we can expect some of the lists to have more than one entry. In this case, unlike the corresponding situation in the Gale-Shapley algorithm, taking each person together with the first person on his (reduced) list does not even specify a matching, stable or otherwise.

Instead, we move on to the second phase of the algorithm, which resembles Algorithm *minimal-differences* of Chapters 2 and 3. Here, the preference lists are reduced further by the elimination of rotations, and this reduction continues until one of the two terminating conditions is satisfied. The second phase of the algorithm involves some nondeterminism in the choice of

rotation to be eliminated, and in cases where more than one stable matching
exists, the particular matching derived by the algorithm will depend on how
this nondeterminism is resolved.

4.2.2   Phase 1 of the Algorithm

Throughout, we assume that for any particular roommates instance of size
n, the persons are labeled $1, 2, \ldots, n$.

Bearing in mind that our stable roommates algorithm involves the deletion
of entries from the preference lists, we shall use the term *preference table* to
describe, for a given problem instance, a set of preference lists from which
zero or more entries have been deleted. Furthermore, we restrict the term
to apply only when the lists are *consistent*, i.e., when x is present in y's list
if and only if y is present in that of x. A pair *belongs* to a preference table
T if and only if each member of the pair is in the other's list in T. By the
deletion of a pair from a preference table, we mean the deletion of each from
the list of the other. We say that a preference table U or a matching R is
embedded in a preference table T if all the pairs of U (or R) belong to T. A
preference table U that is embedded in a preference table T is said to be a
subtable of T.

For a given preference table T and person x, we denote by $f_T(x)$, $s_T(x)$
and $l_T(x)$ the persons, if any, who are first, second, and last, respectively,
on x's list in T. The subscript T may be omitted if the preference table in
question is clear from the context.

As already observed, the first phase of the stable roommates algorithm
closely resembles the extended Gale-Shapley algorithm. However, in view
of the nonbipartite nature of the problem, each person will both make and
receive proposals. We will show that, as in the extended Gale-Shapley algorithm, a proposal from person x to person y implies that y cannot have a
partner worse than x in any stable matching, so no pair $\{y, x'\}$ such that y
prefers x to x' can be stable. Further, if all such pairs are deleted from the
table, no matching that is embedded in the reduced table is blocked by any
of them, so, from the point of view of finding stable matchings, nothing is
lost by such deletions.

Everyone is initially free, and each successive proposal in the algorithm
is made by some free person x to the person who is currently first in his
list, say y. As a result of this proposal, x ceases to be free and becomes,
instead, *semiengaged* to y. Note that the semiengagement relation, as its
name implies, is not symmetric, and it will not normally be the case that y
is semiengaged to x at this point; y may still be free, or may be semiengaged

to someone else. Note also that, as in the extended Gale-Shapley algorithm, there are no "immediate rejections" in the roommates algorithm; such rejections are preempted by the deletion of pairs from the preference table. To be precise, when x becomes semiengaged to y, all pairs $\{y, x'\}$ in the table such that y prefers x to x' are deleted, so that x becomes the last entry on y's list, as well as y being the first on x's list. If some other person z was previously semiengaged to y, then this semiengagement is broken, the pair $\{y, z\}$ is among those deleted, and z is set free as a result.

The first phase of the algorithm continues as long as some free person has a nonempty list (and can therefore make a further proposal). Phase 1 of the algorithm is outlined in Figure 4.2. The close resemblance to the extended Gale-Shapley algorithm of Figure 1.7 on page 16 is apparent.

```
assign each person to be free ;
while some free person x has a nonempty list do
begin
        y := first person on x's list ; {x proposes to y}
        if some person z is semiengaged to y then
            assign z to be free ; {y rejects z}
        assign x to be semiengaged to y ;
        for each successor x' of x on y's list do
            delete the pair {x', y} from the preference table
end
```

Figure 4.2: Phase 1 of the stable roommates algorithm

As described, phase 1 of the algorithm involves some nondeterminism, but, as in the case of the Gale-Shapley algorithm, this nondeterminism is of no consequence. The proof is similar to that of Theorem 1.2.2, but we give it here for completeness.

Lemma 4.2.1 *For a given instance of the problem, all possible executions of phase 1 of the algorithm yield the same reduced preference table.*

Proof Suppose T and T' are preference tables produced by two different executions E and E' of phase 1. Suppose that $\{x, y\}$ belongs to T but not to T', and that, during E', $\{x, y\}$ was the first such pair to be deleted. Deletion of a pair happens only when one member of the pair receives a proposal, so that it may be assumed, without loss of generality, that the deletion of $\{x, y\}$ during E' was due to some person, say u, proposing, and becoming semiengaged to x. But the presence of $\{x, y\}$ in T means that, on termination of E, u is semiengaged to someone above x in his list, say to v. It follows that $\{u, v\}$ must have been deleted before $\{x, y\}$ during E', contradicting the assumption that $\{x, y\}$ was the first such deletion. $\square$

For any problem instance, the preference table that is produced by phase 1 of the algorithm will be referred to as the *phase-1 table*. The next lemma gives some pertinent properties of the phase-1 table.

Lemma 4.2.2 *If T is the phase-1 table for some problem instance, then*
(i) $y = f_T(x)$ if and only if $x = l_T(y)$;
(ii) the pair $\{x, y\}$ is absent from T if and only if x prefers $l_T(x)$ to y or y prefers $l_T(y)$ to x.

Proof (i) From the description of the algorithm, x is semiengaged to y if and only if $l_T(y) = x$. So if $l_T(y) = x$ then $\{x, y\} \in T$, and there is no pair $\{x, z\}$ in T such that x prefers z to y, since x proposed to, and was rejected by z. Hence $f_T(x) = y$. Conversely, if $f_T(x) = y$, then $\{x, y\} \in T$, and since x has proposed to y, there is no pair $\{z, y\}$ in T such that y prefers x to z. Hence $l_T(y) = x$.

(ii) If x prefers $l_T(x)$ to y, then $\{x, y\}$ must be absent from T, by the definition of $l_T(x)$, and similarly if y prefers $l_T(y)$ to x. On the other hand, if $\{x, y\}$ was deleted during phase 1 of the algorithm, then either y received a proposal from someone he prefers to x, or x received a proposal from someone he prefers to y. In the former case, it follows that y prefers $l_T(y)$ to x, and in the latter that x prefers $l_T(x)$ to y. $\square$

The next lemma describes some conclusions relating to stable matchings that can be drawn from a phase-1 table.

Lemma 4.2.3 *Suppose that T is the phase-1 table for a roommates instance. Then*
(i) if $\{x, y\}$ does not belong to T, then $\{x, y\}$ is not a stable pair;
(ii) if some list in T is empty, then the instance has no stable matching.

Proof (i) Suppose that some stable pair is not in T, and that $\{x, y\}$ was the first such pair deleted during a particular execution of phase 1 of the algorithm. Further suppose, without loss of generality, that its deletion took place when a person z became semiengaged to x. Then x prefers z to y. Now, z can never have a stable partner better than x (because no stable pairs were previously removed from the table), so the supposed stable matching in which x and y are partners is blocked by the pair $\{x, z\}$, giving a contradiction.

(ii) This follows at once from (i), since a person who has an empty list in the phase-1 table cannot be a member of any stable pair. $\square$

In fact, it is not hard to show that, after the execution of phase 1 of the algorithm, at most one person's preference list can be empty. However, this fact will not be required, and its proof is left as an exercise for the reader.

Preference tables satisfying the two conditions of Lemma 4.2.2 turn out to have a special significance, so we introduce some terminology to describe such tables.

A preference table T is called *stable* if it satisfies the following conditions:

i. $y = f_T(x)$ if and only if $x = l_T(y)$;

ii. the pair $\{x, y\}$ is absent if and only if x prefers $l_T(x)$ to y or y prefers $l_T(y)$ to x;

iii. no person's list in T is empty.

So in particular, provided the phase-1 table contains no empty lists, it is a special case of a stable preference table. We shall use T_0 throughout this chapter to denote the phase-1 table. The concept of a stable preference table is crucial in our development of the roommates algorithm and structure. Henceforth, the term *table* will always be used as an abbreviation for stable preference table. Likewise, the term *subtable* will be reserved for a subtable that is itself a stable preference table.

Some indication of the significance of tables can be seen in the following lemma.

Lemma 4.2.4 *(i) If R is a matching embedded in a table T, then no pair that is absent from T can block R;*
(ii) If, in a table T, every list contains just one entry, then T is a stable matching;
(iii) If T, U are tables, and $f_T(x) = f_U(x)$ for all x, or equivalently $l_T(x) = l_U(x)$ for all x, then $T = U$; that is, a table is completely determined by the first (or the last) entries on each list;
(iv) Every table is a subtable of the phase-1 table.

Proof (i) This is an immediate consequence of part (ii) of the definition of a table.

(ii) This follows immediately from (i).

(iii) It follows from the first defining property of a table that $f_T(x) = f_U(x)$ for all x if and only if $l_T(x) = l_U(x)$ for all x, and it is an easy consequence of the second defining property that, if one of these conditions is satisfied, then $T = U$.

(iv) Let us call a pair that belongs to some table *semistable*. Suppose that the claim is false, and that $\{x, y\}$ is the first semistable pair deleted during a particular execution of phase 1 of the algorithm; suppose that it was deleted when a person u became semiengaged to x. Then x prefers u to y. Now, there can be no semistable pair $\{u, v\}$ such that u prefers v to x, for such a pair would have been removed before $\{x, y\}$. So, in any table T, either $x = f_T(u)$ or u prefers x to $f_T(u)$. In the former case, $u = l_T(x)$, so $\{x, y\}$ is absent, while in the latter case, the absence of $\{x, u\}$ from T implies that x prefers $l_T(x)$ to u, and therefore also to y, so that $\{x, y\}$ is again absent from T. But T was an arbitrary table, so $\{x, y\}$ is not, after all, semistable — a contradiction. $\square$

We conclude this section with some examples to illustrate the possible outcomes of the first phase of the stable roommates algorithm.

Example Consider the instance of size 4 with preference lists as given in Figure 4.3 (a particular case of the example considered earlier in Section 4.1).

1	3	2	4
2	1	3	4
3	2	1	4
4	1	2	3

Figure 4.3: An unsolvable roommates instance of size 4

Phase 1 of the algorithm could proceed as follows, where $x \rightarrow y$ means that free person x proposes to, and becomes semiengaged to, y:

- $1 \rightarrow 2$; $\{2, 4\}$ is deleted;

- $2 \rightarrow 3$; $\{3, 4\}$ is deleted;

- $3 \rightarrow 1$; $\{1, 4\}$ is deleted.

In this case, phase 1 terminates with one person, namely person 4, having an empty list, and this implies that there is no stable matching.

Example Consider the instance of size 4 with preference lists shown in Figure 4.4.

In this case, phase 1 could proceed as follows:

- $1 \rightarrow 4$; $\{4, 3\}$ is deleted;

1	4	2	3					
2	1	3	4					
3	2	4	1					
4	2	1	3					

Figure 4.4: A solvable roommates instance of size 4

- $2 \to 1$; $\{1, 3\}$ is deleted;
- $3 \to 2$; $\{2, 4\}$ is deleted;
- $4 \to 1$; $\{1, 2\}$ is deleted; note that 2, who was semiengaged to 1, becomes free at this point;
- $2 \to 3$.

Phase 1 therefore terminates with each person having a single list entry, and this implies that the matching specified by these entries, namely $\{ \{1, 4\}, \{2, 3\} \}$, is the unique stable matching.

Example Our next instance, of size 10, shown in Figure 4.5, is one that we shall pursue for illustrative purposes throughout most of this chapter.

1	8	2	9	3	6	4	5	7	10
2	4	3	8	9	5	1	10	6	7
3	5	6	8	2	1	7	10	4	9
4	10	7	9	3	1	6	2	5	8
5	7	4	10	8	2	6	3	1	9
6	2	8	7	3	4	10	1	5	9
7	2	1	8	3	5	10	4	6	9
8	10	4	2	5	6	7	1	3	9
9	6	7	2	5	10	3	4	8	1
10	3	1	6	5	2	9	8	4	7

Figure 4.5: A stable roommates instance of size 10

Phase 1 could proceed as follows:

- $1 \to 8$; $\{8, 3\}$ and $\{8, 9\}$ are deleted;
- $2 \to 4$; $\{4, 5\}$ and $\{4, 8\}$ are deleted;
- $3 \to 5$; $\{5, 1\}$ and $\{5, 9\}$ are deleted;
- $4 \to 10$; $\{10, 7\}$ is deleted;

- $5 \rightarrow 7$; $\{7, 4\}$, $\{7, 6\}$, and $\{7, 9\}$ are deleted;

- $6 \rightarrow 2$; $\{2, 7\}$ is deleted;

- $7 \rightarrow 1$; $\{1, 10\}$ is deleted;

- $8 \rightarrow 10$; $\{10, 4\}$ is deleted; notice that 4 becomes free as a result;

- $4 \rightarrow 9$; $\{9, 1\}$ is deleted;

- $9 \rightarrow 6$;

- $10 \rightarrow 3$; $\{3, 4\}$ and $\{3, 9\}$ are deleted.

So, phase 1 of the algorithm ends with the phase-1 table shown in Figure 4.6.

1	8	2	3	6	4	7		
2	4	3	8	9	5	1	10	6
3	5	6	2	1	7	10		
4	9	1	6	2				
5	7	10	8	2	6	3		
6	2	8	3	4	10	1	5	9
7	1	8	3	5				
8	10	2	5	6	7	1		
9	6	2	10	4				
10	3	6	5	2	9	8		

Figure 4.6: The phase-1 table for the roommates instance of size 10

As we have seen, the first phase of the algorithm can have one of three possible outcomes. If some list is empty in the phase-1 table, then, according to Lemma 4.2.3(ii), there is no stable matching for that instance. If every list contains just one entry, then, according to Lemma 4.2.3(i) and Lemma 4.2.4(ii), the phase-1 table constitutes the unique stable matching for that instance. In neither case is it necessary to go beyond phase 1 for a complete description of the stable matchings.

However, if the phase-1 table contains no empty lists, and two or more lists have multiple entries (there cannot be just one such list) we must embark on the second phase of the algorithm.

4.2.3   Phase 2 of the Algorithm

In the second phase of the algorithm, the preference table is further reduced until all lists contain just one entry, in which case it constitutes a stable matching, or until some list becomes empty, in which case no stable matching exists.

In the case of the stable marriage problem, the key idea in understanding the structure of the set of stable matchings is that of a rotation. This concept is also critical in roommates, not only in understanding the structure but also in the basic algorithm itself. In the roommates context, a rotation is defined relative to a table, rather than to a stable matching as in the marriage case. However, it was observed in the second and third paragraphs of Section 2.5.1 on page 87 that the rotations in the stable marriage case could be defined in terms of "reduced preference lists", so that despite the apparent difference, the two situations are really quite analogous.

Recall that $f_T(x)$, $s_T(x)$ and $l_T(x)$ represent the first, second, and last entries, respectively, in x's list in table T. For a given table T, a sequence

$$\rho = (x_0, y_0), (x_1, y_1), \ldots, (x_{r-1}, y_{r-1})$$

such that $y_i = f_T(x_i)$ and $y_{i+1} = s_T(x_i)$ for all i, $0 \leq i \leq r - 1$, where $i+1$ is taken modulo r, is called a *rotation* exposed in T. For each i, we say that x_i, y_i, and the ordered pair (x_i, y_i) are *in* the rotation ρ. The set $\{x_0, \ldots, x_{r-1}\}$ will be called the *X-set* of ρ, and the set $\{y_0, \ldots, y_{r-1}\}$ the *Y-set* of ρ. As in the stable marriage case, when discussing rotations, subscripts should be taken modulo r when appropriate.

Note that a rotation is an ordered list of pairs, but that an arbitrary ordered list of pairs is not a rotation unless there is some table in which it is exposed. As in the marriage case, the cyclic nature of a rotation implies that the choice of starting point in the sequence is arbitrary.

We state as a lemma a simple but important property of rotations.

Lemma 4.2.5 *If ρ and σ are two rotations exposed in T, then the X-sets of ρ and σ are disjoint, as are their Y-sets.*

Proof If $\rho = (x_0, y_0), (x_1, y_1), \ldots, (x_{r-1}, y_{r-1})$ is exposed in table T, then $x_{i+1} = l_T(y_{i+1}) = l_T(s_T(x_i))$. So the cyclic sequence $x_0, \ldots, x_{r-1}$, and therefore the rotation ρ, is completely determined by any one of the x_i. Since $x_i = l_T(y_i)$, ρ is also completely determined by any one of the y_i. □

Example In the phase-1 table for our example of size 10, which we reproduce in Figure 4.7, there is just one exposed rotation, namely $\rho_1 = (1, 8), (6, 2)$. So the X-set of ρ_1 is $\{1, 6\}$, and the Y-set of ρ_1 is $\{2, 8\}$. The rotation is marked in the figure by underlining the entries $f_T(x)$ and $s_T(x)$ for each x in the rotation.

Our first lemma concerning rotations is analogous to Lemma 2.5.3 of Chapter 2. By analogy with the usage in Chapter 2, we denote $l_T(s_T(x))$ by $next_T(x)$.

1	<u>8</u>	<u>2</u>	3	6	4	7			
2	4	3	8	9	5	1	10	6	
3	5	6	2	1	7	10			
4	9	1	6	2					
5	7	10	8	2	6	3			
6	<u>2</u>	<u>8</u>	3	4	10	1	5	9	
7	1	8	3	5					
8	10	2	5	6	7	1			
9	6	2	10	4					
10	3	6	5	2	9	8			

Figure 4.7: The phase-1 table with its single exposed rotation

Lemma 4.2.6 *If T is a table in which some list contains at least two entries, then there is at least one rotation exposed in T.*

Proof Because of the first defining property of a table, any person whose list in T contains just one entry appears himself on just one list, and is the only person on that list. Hence, if we denote by $\mathcal{S}(T)$ the set of people with at least two list entries in T, then every person who appears on a list of length > 1 is a member of $\mathcal{S}(T)$. It follows that, for each $x \in \mathcal{S}(T)$, $s_T(x)$ is well defined and is also a member of $\mathcal{S}(T)$, so that $y = next_T(x)$ is well defined, and y likewise is a member of $\mathcal{S}(T)$.

Let $H(T)$ be a directed graph with node set $\mathcal{S}(T)$, and for each node x, an outward edge to the node $next_T(x)$. Because every node in $H(T)$ has out-degree 1, $H(T)$ must contain at least one simple cycle. Suppose that the nodes in such a cycle are $x_0, \ldots, x_{r-1}$ in that order. Then, since $x_{i+1} = next_T(x_i)$ for $0 \leq i \leq r-1$, it follows that $f_T(x_{i+1}) = s_T(x_i)$, and therefore that $(x_0, f_T(x_0)), (x_1, f_T(x_1)), \ldots, (x_{r-1}, f_T(x_{r-1}))$ is a rotation exposed in T. □

As in the stable marriage case, the above proof gives a simple way to find a rotation exposed in T: starting from any person x in $\mathcal{S}(T)$, traverse the unique path in $H(T)$ from the node x until that node or some other node is visited twice. If ρ is the rotation generated by this traversal, we say that x *leads to* ρ in T. If x leads to ρ in T, but x is not itself in the X-set of ρ, then the path in $H(T)$ from the node x to the first node in the cycle corresponding to ρ is called a *tail* of the rotation, and x is said to *lie on* this tail. Notice that an exposed rotation can have several tails in a particular table, and can have different tails in different tables.

Example In the phase-1 table T for our instance of size 10 (see Figure 4.7), every person leads to the rotation $\rho_1 = (1, 8), (6, 2)$. The directed graph $H(T)$ in this case is as shown in Figure 4.8.

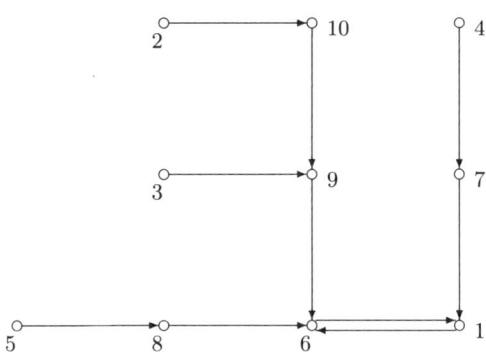

Figure 4.8: The directed graph $H(T)$

In phase 2 of the algorithm, the table is going to be progressively reduced by the elimination of rotations, this term having a meaning analogous to that introduced in Chapter 2 for the stable marriage problem. We start with the phase-1 table, which is stable, and throughout the table reduction, provided no list becomes empty, the current table will remain stable, so that Lemma 4.2.6 applies throughout, and the reduction process can continue as long as some list contains more than one entry.

If $\rho = (x_0, y_0), (x_1, y_1), \ldots, (x_{r-1}, y_{r-1})$ is a rotation exposed in the table T, then we denote by T/ρ the table obtained from T by deleting, for $0 \leq i \leq r - 1$, all pairs $\{y_i, z\}$ such that y_i prefers x_{i-1} to z. The process of replacing T by T/ρ is referred to as *eliminating* the rotation ρ. The effect of rotation elimination is summarized in the following lemma.

Lemma 4.2.7 *Let* $\rho = (x_0, y_0), (x_1, y_1), \ldots, (x_{r-1}, y_{r-1})$ *be a rotation exposed in the table* T. *Then if* T/ρ *contains no empty lists,*
(i) $f_{T/\rho}(x_i) = y_{i+1}$ *for each* i, $0 \leq i \leq r - 1$;

(ii) $l_{T/\rho}(y_i) = x_{i-1}$ *for each* i, $0 \leq i \leq r - 1$;
(iii) $f_{T/\rho}(x) = f_T(x)$ *for each* x *not in the* X-*set of* ρ, *and* $l_{T/\rho}(y) = l_T(y)$
for each y *not in the* Y-*set of* ρ.

Proof (i) The pair $\{x_i, y_i\} = \{x_i, f_T(x_i)\}$ is deleted, because y_i prefers x_{i-1} to x_i. If $\{x_i, y_{i+1}\} = \{x_i, s_T(x_i)\}$ were to be deleted, then this could only be because x_i is y_j for some j, and y_j prefers x_{j-1} to y_{i+1}, in which case all successors of y_{i+1} in x_i's list are also deleted. As a consequence, x_i's list would become empty, contrary to our assumption.

(ii) The definition of rotation elimination tells us that all successors of x_{i-1} in the list of y_i are deleted. An argument similar to that used in (i) shows that if x_{i-1} is deleted from y_i's list, then x_{i-1}'s list becomes empty, again contrary to our assumption.

(iii) The facts that, when ρ is eliminated, no person who is not in the X-set of ρ can lose his first list entry, and that no person who is not in the Y-set of ρ can lose his last list entry, are immediate consequences of the definition of rotation elimination. $\square$

We follow the terminology introduced in the stable marriage case, and say that ρ *moves* x_i *down* from y_i to y_{i+1}, and *moves* y_i *up* from x_i to x_{i-1}, though this terminology applies in the roommates case only when we know that the elimination of ρ does not produce any empty preference lists.

Example If we eliminate the rotation $\rho_1 = (6, 2), (1, 8)$ from the phase-1 table in our illustrative example (see Figure 4.6 on page 172), pairs are deleted for each person in the Y-set. Rotation ρ moves 1 down to 2 and 2 up to 1, so that the pairs deleted as a result are $\{2, 10\}$ and $\{2, 6\}$, while it moves 6 down to 8 and 8 up to 6, so that the pairs deleted as a result are $\{8, 7\}$ and $\{8, 1\}$. Figure 4.9 contains the phase-1 table with boxes marking the entries deleted on the elimination of ρ_1.

Note that, in this new table, there is again just a single exposed rotation, namely $\rho_2 = (1, 2), (10, 3), (9, 6)$, which is again marked by underlining the entries $f_T(x)$ and $s_T(x)$ for each x in the X-set of the rotation.

The next lemma gives further details of the effect of rotation elimination. It is analogous to Lemma 2.5.2 for stable marriage, though the possibility of empty lists does not arise in that case.

Lemma 4.2.8 *Let* $\rho = (x_0, y_0), (x_1, y_1), \ldots, (x_{r-1}, y_{r-1})$ *be a rotation exposed in the table* T. *Then, provided that* T/ρ *contains no empty lists, it is also a stable table, and is a subtable of* T.

Proof If T/ρ contains no empty lists, then in order to prove that T/ρ is stable, it suffices to establish

  i. $f_{T/\rho}(x) = y \iff l_{T/\rho}(y) = x$; and

1	8	2	3	6	4	7		
2	4	3	8	9	5	1	10	6
3	5	6	2	1	7	10		
4	9	1	6	2				
5	7	10	8	2	6	3		
6	2	8	3	4	10	1	5	9
7	1	8	3	5				
8	10	2	5	6	7	1		
9	6	2	10	4				
10	3	6	5	2	9	8		

Figure 4.9: Preference table on elimination of the rotation ρ_1

ii. if $\{x, y\}$ is absent from T/ρ then x prefers $l_{T/\rho}(x)$ to y, or y prefers $l_{T/\rho}(y)$ to x.

The first requirement is an immediate consequence of Lemma 4.2.7 and the fact that T is stable. The truth of (ii) follows at once from the stability of T if $\{x, y\}$ is absent from T. Otherwise, if $\{x, y\}$ is deleted on the elimination of ρ, this must be because y is y_i for some i, and y_i prefers $x_{i-1}(= l_{T/\rho}(y_i))$ to x, or x is y_i for some i, and y_i prefers x_{i-1} to y. This is sufficient to establish (ii) for all cases.

Of course, the fact that T/ρ is obtained from T by deleting pairs implies that T/ρ is a subtable of T. $\square$

We require one further lemma on subtables before we can state and prove the central theorem of this section.

Lemma 4.2.9 *Suppose that T and U are tables, and that U is a subtable of T. If $\rho = (x_0, y_0), (x_1, y_1), \ldots, (x_{r-1}, y_{r-1})$ is a rotation that is exposed in T, and if $f_U(x) \neq f_T(x)$ for at least one x that leads to ρ, then U is a subtable of T/ρ.*

Proof If x leads to ρ in T then there is a sequence $(u_0, v_0), \ldots, (u_{t-1}, v_{t-1})$ such that $x = u_0$, $v_i = f_T(u_i)$ and $u_{i+1} = next_T(u_i)$ for $i = 0, \ldots, t-1$, and $u_t = x_k$ for at least one k $(0 \leq k \leq r-1)$.

If $f_T(u_0) = v_1 \neq f_U(u_0)$, then $f_U(u_0)$ is either $v_1(= s_T(u_0))$ or someone below v_1 in u_0's list. So, by the definition of stability, $l_U(v_1)$ is either u_0 or someone above u_0 in v_1's list. But u is below u_0 in v_1's list, since $u_1 = l_T(v_1)$ and the pair $\{u_0, v_1\}$ is in T. It follows that $f_T(u_1) = v_1 \neq f_U(u_1)$. This argument may now be repeated for $u_1, u_2, \ldots, u_t = x_k, x_{k+1}, \ldots$ to show that, for every j $(0 \leq j \leq r-1)$, $f_T(x_j) \neq f_U(x_j)$ and $l_U(y_{j+1})$ is either x_j

or someone above x_j in y_{j+1}'s list. So none of the pairs deleted when ρ is eliminated from T is present in U, and as a consequence, U is a subtable of T/ρ. □

For ease of reference, we state as a corollary the special case of Lemma 4.2.9 in which x is actually in the X-set of rotation ρ.

Corollary 4.2.1 *Suppose that T and U are tables, and that U is a subtable of T. If ρ is a rotation that is exposed in T, and if $f_U(x) \neq f_T(x)$ for some x in the X-set of ρ, then U is a subtable of T/ρ.*

We also state as a corollary of Lemma 4.2.9 a result with the implication that rotation elimination generates all tables, and therefore all stable matchings.

Corollary 4.2.2 *If table U is a subtable of table T then U can be obtained from T by eliminating a sequence of rotations. In particular, every table can be obtained from the phase-1 table by eliminating an appropriate sequence of rotations.*

Proof If $T \neq U$ then, by Lemma 4.2.4(iii), $f_T(x) \neq f_U(x)$ for some x. So, if x leads to ρ, Lemma 4.2.9 implies that U is a subtable of $T_1 = T/\rho$. The argument may be repeated to produce a sequence $T_1, T_2, \ldots$ of tables of all of which U is a subtable, until, for some k, $f_{T_k}(x) = f_U(x)$ for all x. It then follows, by Lemma 4.2.4(iii), that $T_k = U$.

Since, by Lemma 4.2.4(iv) every table is a subtable of the phase-1 table T_0, the second part of the corollary follows at once. □

We can now state and prove the theorem that underlies the second phase of the roommates algorithm.

Theorem 4.2.1 *If there is a stable matching embedded in a table T, and if ρ is a rotation exposed in T, then there is a stable matching embedded in T/ρ.*

Proof Let R be a stable matching embedded in T, and suppose that $\rho = (x_0, y_0), (x_1, y_1), \ldots, (x_{r-1}, y_{r-1})$. If, for some i $(0 \leq i \leq r-1)$, x_i and y_i are not partners in R then, since an embedded stable matching is a special case of a subtable, it follows from Corollary 4.2.1 that R is embedded in T/ρ.

Otherwise, if x_i and y_i are partners in R for all i $(0 \leq i \leq r-1)$, we first show that the sets $X = \{x_0, \ldots, x_{r-1}\}$ and $Y = \{y_0, \ldots, y_{r-1}\}$ are disjoint. For if $x_i = y_j$ say, then the pairs $(x_i, y_i) = (y_j, y_i)$ and (x_j, y_j) can both be partners in R only if $x_j = y_i$. But then we deduce that $f_T(x_i) = y_i =$

$x_j = l_T(y_j) = l_T(x_i)$, with the contradictory implication that x_i's list in T contains just one entry. So $X \cap Y = \emptyset$. Now, let R_ρ be obtained from R by replacing the pair $\{x_i, y_i\}$ by $\{x_i, y_{i+1}\}$ for each $i, 0 \le i \le r-1$. It is immediate from the cyclic nature of ρ and the fact that $X \cap Y = \emptyset$ that R_ρ is a matching. Further, R_ρ is a subtable of T/ρ because $y_{i+1} = f_{T/\rho}(x_i)$ for all i, and no pair that does not contain some y_i can be deleted when ρ is eliminated. In order to complete the proof, it suffices to show that R_ρ is a stable matching.

Suppose that $\{u, v\}$ blocks R_ρ. Since R is stable, $\{u, v\}$ cannot block R. Only the $x_i \in X$ and the $y_i \in Y$, for each i, have different partners in R and R_ρ, and of these, only the x_i have poorer partners in R_ρ. Hence one of u, v, say u, must be x_i for some i. But it is known from Lemma 4.2.4(i) that no pair that is absent from T/ρ can block R_ρ, so that $\{u, v\}$ must belong to T/ρ. However, u's partner in R_ρ is first in his list in T/ρ, and since $v \in T/\rho$, u must prefer $f_{T/\rho}(u)$ to v, contradicting the assumption that $\{u, v\}$ blocks R_ρ. $\square$

This theorem, together with Corollary 4.2.2, has the following immediate corollary.

Corollary 4.2.3 *For a solvable roommates instance, every table contains at least one embedded stable matching.*

We are now in a position to describe and justify phase 2 of the roommates algorithm. Starting from the phase-1 table, a sequence of rotation eliminations takes place until some list becomes empty or a matching is obtained. In the former case we can conclude that no stable matching exists, while in the latter case the matching generated is stable. Phase 2 of the algorithm is summarized in Figure 4.10.

We know from Lemma 4.2.3(i) that every stable matching is a subtable of the phase-1 table. In addition, as long as the condition of the while loop is satisfied, Lemma 4.2.6 ensures that there is a rotation exposed in the current table, and Lemma 4.2.8 ensures that the current table is stable. Furthermore, by Corollary 4.2.3, if the given roommates instance is solvable, then there is a stable matching embedded in each successive table generated by the algorithm. It follows, therefore, that if the algorithm terminates because every list has just one entry, then the final table is itself a stable matching, whereas if termination results from a list becoming empty, there can be no stable matching for the given instance.

Note that, in the case of a solvable instance with more than one stable matching, the particular solution that is found by the algorithm depends on the particular sequence of rotations eliminated in phase 2. In fact, we shall

T := phase-1 table ;
while (some list in T has more than one entry)
                     and (no list in T is empty) do
begin
    find a rotation ρ exposed in T ;
    $T := T \,/\, \rho$ { eliminate ρ }
end ;
if some list in T is empty then
    report instance unsolvable
else
    output T, which is a stable matching

Figure 4.10: Second phase of the roommates algorithm

see later that the order in which these rotations are eliminated is immaterial, except, of course, that a rotation cannot be eliminated until it has become exposed. The relationship between the set of all stable matchings and the rotations will be explored in detail in Section 4.3.

Example After the elimination of the rotation ρ_1 from the phase-1 table for our instance of size 10, we had a table (Figure 4.9 on page 177) with another single exposed rotation $\rho_2 = (1, 2), (10, 3,), (9, 6,)$. Elimination of this rotation gives the table shown in Figure 4.11.

1	3	4	7	
2	4	3	8	9
3	5	6	2	1
4	9	1	6	2
5	7	10	8	3
6	8	3	4	10
7	1	5		
8	10	2	5	6
9	2	10	4	
10	6	5	9	8

Figure 4.11: Preference table after a further rotation elimination

There are now three further exposed rotations, $\rho_3 = (1, 3), (2, 4)$, $\rho_4 = (3, 5)$, $(10, 6)$ and $\rho_5 = (8, 10), (9, 2)$. Eliminating all three of these yields the table in

Figure 4.12.

1	4	7
2	3	8
3	6	2
4	9	1
5	7	10
6	8	3
7	1	5
8	2	6
9	10	4
10	5	9

Figure 4.12: The further reduced table

In that table there are four new exposed rotations, $\rho_6 = (1, 4)$, $(5, 7)$, $(9, 10)$, $\rho_7 = (2, 3)$, $(6, 8)$, $\rho_8 = (3, 6)$, $(8, 2)$ and $\rho_9 = (4, 9)$, $(7, 1)$, $(10, 5)$. Careful examination reveals a connection between ρ_6 and ρ_9, and between ρ_7 and ρ_8, insofar as elimination of one member of a pair causes the disappearance of the other. So, for example, elimination of ρ_6 and ρ_7 leaves a table with just one entry in each list, giving the stable matching $\{1, 7\}$, $\{2, 8\}$, $\{3, 6\}$, $\{4, 9\}$, $\{5, 10\}$.

In view of the choice of rotations available at this last stage, it is clear that this is not the only stable matching. For example, eliminating ρ_6 and ρ_8 would give a different stable matching.

Example Consider the instance of size 6 shown in Figure 4.13.

1	2	5	4	3	6
2	3	6	5	1	4
3	4	5	2	6	1
4	2	6	5	1	3
5	6	2	3	4	1
6	3	1	4	5	2

Figure 4.13: A stable roommates instance of size 6

It may be verified that the phase-1 table is as shown in Figure 4.14.

This table has a single exposed rotation, namely $\rho_1 = (1, 5)$, $(3, 4)$, as marked, and elimination of ρ_1 leads to the table shown in Figure 4.15.

Now the table has two rotations, $\rho_2 = (1, 4)$, $(4, 6)$, $(6, 1)$, and $\rho_3 = (2, 3)$, $(3, 5)$, $(5, 2)$, the elimination of either of which leaves some of the lists empty. Therefore there is no stable matching for this instance.

1	5̲	4̲	6	
2	3	5		
3	4	5̲	2	
4	6	5	1	3
5	2	3	4	1
6	1	4		

Figure 4.14: The phase-1 table for the instance of size 6

1	4	6
2	3	5
3	5	2
4	6	1
5	2	3
6	1	4

Figure 4.15: The reduced table

4.2.4 Implementation and Analysis

We now show that the fundamental roommates algorithm can be implemented so as to have $O(n^2)$ worst-case complexity for an instance involving n people, though it could be claimed that it is a linear-time algorithm, since the size of input required to specify fully such a problem instance is clearly $\Omega(n^2)$.

As observed in Section 4.2.1, the roommates algorithm bears a striking resemblance to Algorithm *minimal-differences* of Chapters 2 and 3. The purpose of Algorithm *minimal-differences* is to find all the rotations (or minimal differences) for a stable marriage instance. This is achieved by first applying the Gale-Shapley algorithm to find the man-optimal and woman-optimal matchings, and, starting from the man-optimal matching, finding and eliminating a sequence of exposed rotations until the woman-optimal matching is reached. It is not difficult to amend the implementation of that algorithm given in Figure 3.2 on page 110, which was shown to have $O(n^2)$ complexity, so as to give a $O(n^2)$ implementation of the roommates algorithm.

The implementation of phase 1 is analogous to that of the extended Gale-Shapley algorithm and can, as in that case, be accomplished in $O(n^2)$ time with appropriate choice of data structures.

Figure 4.16 contains an adaptation of that implementation of Algorithm *minimal-differences.* As in that earlier case, a stack is used to house a path traced out in the directed graph $H(T)$. When a vertex (i.e., person) x is reached that is already in the stack, a rotation has been found, and it may be recovered by popping the stack as far as x. The rotation may then be eliminated by deleting appropriate pairs from the table. Of course, in the roommates context, the algorithm must continually check for the appearance of an empty list, the sign that there is no stable matching for the instance under investigation. Each successive rotation search begins from the end of the previous tail, i.e., the top person in the stack, or, if the stack is empty, from the first person who has a list of length ≥ 2. The algorithm terminates when some list becomes empty or when every list is reduced to a single entry.

As observed for the extended Gale-Shapley algorithm of Section 1.2.4, choice of a suitable data structure for the table allows the first, second and last entry in each list, and the successor of a given entry, to be located in constant time, and also any pair to be deleted in constant time.

Since a person on the stack has a list of length ≥ 2, it is clear that the stack is empty on termination of the algorithm, so that the numbers of push and pop operations are the same. But each time a person is popped from the stack, at least one pair is deleted from the table, so the total number of push operations is $O(n^2)$. Hence the number of operations carried out in each of the inner loops is $O(n^2)$, and each is a constant time operation. It follows that the entire roommates algorithm can be implemented to run in $O(n^2)$ time.

Finally, we observe that, since the stable marriage problem is a special case of the stable roommates problem, the $\Omega(n^2)$ lower bound for finding a stable matching in the former case, proved in Section 1.5, applies also to roommates, so that the given algorithm is (asymptotically) optimal.

4.3 Structure of Roommates Matchings

4.3.1 Overview

For the stable marriage problem, the structure underlying any particular instance was shown to be a distributive lattice, and by relating the rotations to minimal differences in a ring of sets and exploiting theorems about rings of sets we were able to obtain fast algorithms for a number of associated problems.

The situation is not quite so simple in the case of the stable roommates problem. Nonetheless, we will prove a characterization theorem similar to the corresponding result for stable marriage, namely that there is a one-

find T_0 ; {using phase-1 of the algorithm}
if some list in T_0 is empty then report instance unsolvable
else if every list in T_0 has exactly 1 entry then
            output the unique stable matching T_0
      else begin
                  $T := T_0$; emptylist := false ; set up an empty stack;
                  $x :=$ lowest numbered person with at least 2 list entries in T_0 ;
                  while $(x \leq n)$ and not emptylist do
                  begin
                        if stack empty then
                              begin
                                    while $(f_T(x) = l_T(x))$ and $(x \leq n)$ do $x := x + 1$;
                                    if $x \leq n$ then push x onto stack
                              end;
                        if stack not empty then
                        begin
                              $p :=$ person on top of stack; $p := next_T(p)$;
                              while p not in stack do
                              begin
                                    push p onto stack; $p := next_T(p)$
                              end;
                              $p' :=$ top of stack; pop stack;
                              set up list ρ containing the pair $(p', f_T(p'))$;
                              while $p' \neq p$ do
                              begin
                                    $p' :=$ top of stack; pop stack;
                                    add the pair $(p', f_T(p'))$ to the head of ρ
                              end;
                              { Now execute $T := T/\rho$ }
                              for each pair (p', q') in ρ do
                              begin
                                    delete appropriate pairs from the list of q' ;
                                    if list of q' is empty then emptylist := true
                              end
                        end
                  end ;
            if emptylist then report instance unsolvable
            else output the stable matching T
      end

Figure 4.16: Implementation of the basic roommates algorithm

one correspondence between the stable matchings and certain subsets of the rotations that are closed under a natural partial order relation. It is the main purpose of the present section to describe this correspondence. In Section 4.4, this characterization of structure will be exploited to derive algorithms for various aspects of the roommates problem. However, we will see that many of these algorithms are less efficient than their stable marriage counterparts, perhaps because of the more complicated underlying structure.

Throughout the rest of this section, we restrict our attention to solvable instances of the roommates problem, and we denote by $\mathcal{R}$ the set of stable matchings for a given solvable roommates instance.

4.3.2   Singular and Dual Rotations

The essence of the roommates algorithm of Section 4.2 is that, for a solvable instance of the problem, a stable matching can be obtained from the phase-1 table by eliminating a sequence of exposed rotations until no further rotation is exposed. In order to investigate the structure underlying the set of all stable matchings, we need to establish some further properties of rotations and to introduce the concepts of singular and dual rotations. The following lemma motivates the definition of these terms.

Lemma 4.3.1 *Suppose that $\rho = (x_0, y_0), (x_1, y_1), \ldots, (x_{r-1}, y_{r-1})$ and σ are two distinct rotations exposed in the same table T. Then either ρ is exposed in T/σ, or $\sigma = (y_1, x_0), (y_2, x_1), \ldots, (y_i, x_{i-1}), \ldots, (y_0, x_{r-1})$.*

Proof   Suppose that $\sigma = (u_0, v_0), (u_1, v_1), \ldots, (u_{t-1}, v_{t-1})$. By Lemma 4.2.5, the X-sets of ρ and σ are disjoint, so that by Lemma 4.2.7(iii), none of the pairs $\{x_i, y_i\}$ $(0 \le i \le r - 1)$ is deleted when σ is eliminated. If none of the pairs $\{x_i, y_{i+1}\}$ is deleted, then ρ is exposed in T/σ. So suppose, without loss of generality, that $\{x_0, y_1\}$ is deleted when σ is eliminated. Since by Lemma 4.2.5 the Y-sets of ρ and σ are disjoint, it follows that $y_1 \ne v_k$ for any k, so $\{x_0, y_1\}$ must be deleted when σ is eliminated, because $x_0 = v_k$ for some k, and $v_k(= x_0)$ prefers u_{k-1} to y_1. But in T, x_0 prefers only y_0 to y_1, so $u_{k-1} = y_0$. Therefore $f_T(v_k) = f_T(x_0) = y_0 = u_{k-1}$, so that $l_T(u_{k-1}) = v_k = s_T(u_{k-1})$. It follows that $u_{k-1}(= y_0)$ has only two list entries in T, namely $l_T(u_{k-1}) = v_k$ and $f_T(u_{k-1}) = v_{k-1}$. But y_0 certainly has x_0 and x_{r-1} on his list in T, and since $x_0 = v_k$ we must have $x_{r-1} = v_{k-1}$.

Now, in the same way that we showed that $x_0 = v_k \implies y_0 = u_{k-1} \implies x_{r-1} = v_{k-1}$, we can show that $x_{r-1} = v_{k-1} \implies y_{r-1} = u_{k-2} \implies x_{r-2} = v_{k-2}$. Continuing in this way, we deduce that $x_{r-3} = v_{k-3}$, $y_{r-2} = u_{k-3}$, $\ldots$, proving that $\sigma = (y_1, x_0), (y_2, x_1), \ldots, (y_0, x_{r-1})$ as claimed. $\square$

A rotation $\rho = (x_0, y_0), (x_1, y_1), \ldots, (x_{r-1}, y_{r-1})$ is called *nonsingular* if $\bar{\rho} = (y_1, x_0), (y_2, x_1), \ldots, (y_i, x_{i-1}), \ldots, (y_0, x_{r-1})$ is also a rotation; otherwise ρ is called *singular*.

If $\rho = (x_0, y_0), (x_1, y_1), \ldots, (x_{r-1}, y_{r-1})$ is a nonsingular rotation, the rotation $\bar{\rho} = (y_1, x_0), (y_2, x_1), \ldots, (y_0, x_{r-1})$ is called the *dual* of ρ. Notice that the X-set and Y-set of ρ are the Y-set and X-set respectively of $\bar{\rho}$, and that the precise transformational rule that takes ρ to $\bar{\rho}$ also takes $\bar{\rho}$ to ρ, so that $\bar{\rho}$ is also nonsingular, and the dual of $\bar{\rho}$ is ρ.

Example The rotations ρ_6, ρ_9 and ρ_7, ρ_8 in our illustrative instance are clearly dual pairs of rotations. The table shown in Figure 4.12 on page 181 has both of these pairs of rotations exposed.

Recall that our main objective in this section is to prove a result analogous to the central structural result for the stable marriage problem, namely that there is a one-one correspondence between stable roommates matchings and certain closed subsets of the partially ordered set of rotations. Our first step in achieving this aim is to show that every stable roommates matching can be obtained from the phase-1 table by eliminating *all* the singular rotations and *exactly one* of each dual pair of rotations. For this purpose, we require some further lemmas on rotation elimination.

Lemma 4.3.2 *If ρ and σ are rotations exposed in a table T, and $\sigma \neq \bar{\rho}$, then $(T/\rho)/\sigma = (T/\sigma)/\rho$.*

Proof Since $\sigma \neq \bar{\rho}$ (and therefore $\rho \neq \bar{\sigma}$), it follows from Lemma 4.3.1 that σ is exposed in T/ρ and that ρ is exposed in T/σ. Hence $(T/\rho)/\sigma$ and $(T/\sigma)/\rho$ are both well-defined tables. By Lemma 4.2.7(i) and (iii), each person has the same first entry in his lists in $(T/\rho)/\sigma$ and $(T/\sigma)/\rho$, and therefore by Lemma 4.2.4(iii), it follows that $(T/\rho)/\sigma = (T/\sigma)/\rho$. $\square$

It follows from Lemma 4.3.2 that, if T is a table, and, starting from T, the sequence $\rho_1, \ldots, \rho_t$ of rotations may be eliminated to generate another table U, then the order of elimination is immaterial, subject to the constraint that a rotation may not be eliminated until it has become exposed. For this reason, we may extend our earlier notation to write, in such circumstances, $U = T/\mathcal{Z}$ where $\mathcal{Z} = \{\rho_1, \ldots, \rho_t\}$.

We saw in Corollary 4.2.2 that if table U is a subtable of table T, then U can be obtained from T by eliminating a sequence $\rho_1, \ldots, \rho_t$ of rotations. We now see that the table U is completely determined by the table T and the *set* $\mathcal{Z} = \{\rho_1, \ldots, \rho_t\}$, the order of elimination being immaterial. Furthermore, our next lemma shows that not only is U completely determined by T and $\mathcal{Z}$, but $\mathcal{Z}$ is also completely determined by T and U.

Lemma 4.3.3 *If table U is a subtable of table T, and if $U = T/\mathcal{Z} = T/\mathcal{Z}'$ then $\mathcal{Z} = \mathcal{Z}'$.*

Proof If $U \neq T$ then there is some rotation ρ_0 exposed in T, and some person x in the X-set of ρ_0 such that $f_U(x) \neq f_T(x)$. For otherwise the elimination of any rotation from T gives a table of which U is not a subtable, in contradiction of Corollary 4.2.2. By Lemmas 4.2.5 and 4.2.7(iii), the pair $\{x, f_T(x)\}$ can be deleted only by the elimination of ρ_0, so that $\rho_0 \in \mathcal{Z} \cap \mathcal{Z}'$, and by Lemma 4.2.9, U is a subtable of $T_1 = T/\rho_0$. The argument may now be repeated to derive sequences $\{\rho_i\}$ and $\{T_i\}$ such that ρ_i is exposed in T_i, $T_{i+1} = T_i/\rho_i$, $\rho_i \in \mathcal{Z} \cap \mathcal{Z}'$ and U is a subtable of T_{i+1}. So the sequence must end with $T_k = U$ for some k, and $\mathcal{Z} = \mathcal{Z}' = \{\rho_0, \ldots, \rho_{k-1}\}$. $\square$

From the special case of Lemma 4.3.3 in which $T = T_0$ and U is a stable matching, we see that each stable roommates matching is associated with a unique set of rotations, as was seen in the more specialized stable marriage problem.

Lemma 4.3.4 *If both of the rotations $\rho = (x_0, y_0), (x_1, y_1), \ldots, (x_{r-1}, y_{r-1})$ and $\bar{\rho} = (y_1, x_0), (y_2, x_1), \ldots, (y_0, x_{r-1})$ are exposed in the table T, then, for each i $(0 \leq i \leq r-1)$, the list of x_i in T contains only y_i and y_{i+1}, and the list of y_i in T contains only x_{i-1} and x_i. The elimination of ρ or $\bar{\rho}$ from T reduces the list of each x_i and each y_i to a single entry, but affects no other list.*

Proof Because ρ is exposed in T, it follows that $f_T(x_i) = y_i$, $s_T(x_i) = y_{i+1}$. Because $\bar{\rho}$ is exposed in T, it follows that $f_T(y_{i+1}) = x_i$, so that, by the definition of a stable table, $l_T(x_i) = y_{i+1}$. Hence x_i has just the two list entries y_i and y_{i+1} in T. A similar argument applies to y_i.

Elimination of ρ from T reduces the list of x_i to just y_{i+1} and the list of y_i to just x_{i-1}. Likewise, elimination of $\bar{\rho}$ from T reduces the list of y_i to just x_i and the list of x_i to just y_i. It is immediate that no other person, and therefore no other list is affected. $\square$

Lemma 4.3.5 *If rotation ρ is exposed in table T, and there is a subtable U of T in which rotation σ is exposed, then either (i) $\sigma = \rho$, (ii) $\sigma = \bar{\rho}$, or (iii) there is a subtable of T/ρ in which σ is exposed.*

Proof Let U be a maximal subtable of T in which σ is exposed, that is, such that there is no subtable U' of T in which σ is exposed, with U a proper subtable of U'. Suppose that $U = T/\mathcal{Z}$, for the set $\mathcal{Z}$ of rotations.

If $\rho \in \mathcal{Z}$, then it is immediate that U is a subtable of T/ρ, and (iii) holds. If $\bar{\rho} \in \mathcal{Z}$, then there is some subtable T' of T such that ρ and $\bar{\rho}$

are exposed in T' and U is a subtable of T'. Such a T' may be obtained from T by eliminating sufficient of the rotations in $\mathcal{Z}$ to expose $\bar{\rho}$, Lemma 4.3.1 ensuring that ρ remains exposed. By Lemma 4.3.4, elimination of $\bar{\rho}$ affects no lists other than those of its own X and Y-sets, and it follows that σ is exposed in $T/(\mathcal{Z} \setminus \{\bar{\rho}\})$, contradicting the maximality of U. Finally, if neither ρ nor $\bar{\rho}$ is in $\mathcal{Z}$, then, by Lemma 4.3.1, ρ must be exposed in U, and, if $\sigma \neq \rho, \bar{\rho}$, then σ must be exposed in U/ρ, which is a subtable of T/ρ. $\square$

We can now state and prove the main theorem of this section.

Theorem 4.3.1 *For a given solvable roommates instance, let $R = T_0/\mathcal{Z}$ be any stable matching. Then $\mathcal{Z}$ contains every singular rotation and exactly one of each dual pair of rotations.*

Proof Let σ be a rotation, and U a table in which σ is exposed. Suppose that $\mathcal{Z} = \{\rho_0, \ldots, \rho_{t-1}\}$, that ρ_0 is exposed in T_0, and that ρ_i is exposed in table $T_i = T_0/\{\rho_0, \ldots, \rho_{i-1}\}$ ($1 \leq i \leq t-1$), so that $T_t = T_0/\mathcal{Z} = R$.

Now, suppose that σ is singular, and that $\sigma \notin \mathcal{Z}$, that is $\sigma \neq \rho_i$ for all i, ($0 \leq i \leq t-1$). By Lemma 4.2.4(iv), U is a subtable of T_0. Also, $\sigma \neq \rho_0$, and since σ is singular, $\sigma \neq \bar{\rho}_0$. So it follows from Lemma 4.3.5 that there is a subtable of $T_1 = T_0/\rho_0$ in which σ is exposed. Likewise, there is a subtable of T_2, a subtable of T_3, ..., and a subtable of T_t in which σ is exposed. But this is a contradiction, since T_t is a matching and therefore contains no exposed rotations.

On the other hand, suppose that σ is nonsingular. It is clear that $\mathcal{Z}$ cannot contain both σ and $\bar{\sigma}$, since the elimination of one of these deletes certain pairs that will prevent the other becoming exposed in any subsequent table. So suppose that $\mathcal{Z}$ contains neither σ nor $\bar{\sigma}$, that is, $\sigma \neq \rho_i$, $\bar{\sigma} \neq \rho_i$ for all i, ($0 \leq i \leq t-1$). Again, since U is a subtable of T_0, and $\rho_0 \neq \sigma, \bar{\sigma}$, it follows from Lemma 4.3.5 that there is a subtable of $T_1 = T_0/\rho_0$ in which σ is exposed. Likewise, for T_2, ..., T_t, giving a contradiction as before. $\square$

Finally in this section, we establish a further lemma giving a characterization of singular and nonsingular rotations that will be useful later.

Lemma 4.3.6 *A rotation ρ is singular if and only if there is a table in which ρ is the only exposed rotation.*

Proof Suppose first that ρ is singular. There is a table T in which ρ is exposed. If there is another rotation σ exposed in T, then by Lemma 4.3.1, since σ cannot be the dual of ρ, ρ is exposed in T/σ. The same argument can now be applied to T/σ, and continued to give a sequence of nested tables, in each of which ρ exposed. The sequence can end only with a table in which ρ is the *only* exposed rotation.

Now suppose that ρ is nonsingular, and suppose that there is a table T in which ρ is the only exposed rotation. Then $T = T_0/\mathcal{Z}$ for a set $\mathcal{Z}$ of rotations that does not include $\bar{\rho}$. By repeated applications of Lemma 4.3.5, there is a subtable U of T in which $\bar{\rho}$ is exposed. By Corollary 4.2.2, U can be obtained from T by a sequence of rotation eliminations, but that sequence cannot include ρ. Hence ρ cannot, after all, be the only rotation exposed in the table T. $\square$

4.3.3 The Roommates Rotation Poset

Theorem 4.3.1 describes a mapping from the set $\mathcal{R}$ of stable roommates matchings to the sets of rotations that contain every singular rotation and exactly one of each dual pair. Further, by Lemma 4.3.3, this mapping is one-one. But it is not onto, since not every such set of rotations represents a stable matching; a rotation cannot be eliminated until it has become exposed. This situation parallels that of the stable marriage problem: in that case, every stable matching M is uniquely determined by the set of rotations on any M_0-chain from M_0 to M in $\mathcal{M}$, and each such chain contains exactly the same set of rotations. However, only *certain* sets of rotations, the closed sets in $\Pi(\mathcal{M})$, correspond to stable matchings — see Theorem 2.5.7.

It is our main goal now to generalize this result, establishing a one-one correspondence between the stable roommates matchings and certain closed sets of rotations in a partial order defined on the rotations. This partial order is based on the predecessor relation for rotations.

A rotation π is a *predecessor* of a rotation ρ, written $\pi \prec \rho$, if, whenever T is a table in which ρ is exposed and $T = T_0/\mathcal{Z}$, π belongs to $\mathcal{Z}$. Informally, π is a predecessor of ρ if π must be eliminated for ρ to become exposed. Equivalently, consider the set of all sequences of possible rotation eliminations that lead to a stable matching. Then $\pi \prec \rho$ if and only if π appears before ρ on every sequence that contains ρ. This definition generalizes that given in Section 2.5.4 for the predecessor relation in $\Pi(\mathcal{M})$.

It may easily be verified that the reflexive closure $\preceq$ of the predecessor relation is a partial order on the set of rotations for a given problem instance, and this set under the $\preceq$ relation will be referred to as the *roommates rotation poset*, denoted by $\Pi(\mathcal{R})$.

The following lemma describes how the predecessor relation relates to singular and dual pairs of rotations.

Lemma 4.3.7 *If ρ, σ are nonsingular rotations and π is a singular rotation, then* *(i)* $\rho \not\prec \bar{\rho}$;

(ii) $\rho \prec \sigma \Longleftrightarrow \bar{\sigma} \prec \bar{\rho}$;

(iii) $\tau \prec \pi \Longrightarrow \tau$ *is singular; i.e., a predecessor of a singular rotation is also singular.*

Proof (i) If $\rho = (x_0, y_0), (x_1, y_1), \ldots, (x_{r-1}, y_{r-1})$, the elimination of ρ deletes all the pairs $\{x_i, y_i\}$. But these pairs must be present in order for $\bar{\rho}$ to become exposed.

(ii) We need prove the implication in one direction only, since the other will follow by duality. Suppose that $\rho \prec \sigma$, and that $\bar{\sigma} \not\prec \bar{\rho}$, i.e., there is a $T = T_0/\mathcal{Z}$ with $\bar{\rho} \in \mathcal{Z}, \bar{\sigma} \notin \mathcal{Z}$. Since $\bar{\rho} \in \mathcal{Z}$ it follows that $\rho \notin \mathcal{Z}$, and therefore that $\sigma \notin \mathcal{Z}$. Now, there is some table in which σ is exposed, for otherwise σ would not be a rotation. Since $\sigma \notin \mathcal{Z}$ and $\bar{\sigma} \notin \mathcal{Z}$, repeated application of Lemma 4.3.5 implies that there is a subtable U of T in which σ is exposed. But then, by Corollary 4.2.2, U can be obtained from T by eliminating a set of rotations, and this set cannot contain ρ. So σ is exposed in a table $U = T_0/\mathcal{Z}'$, where the set $\mathcal{Z}'$ does not contain ρ, contradicting the assumption that ρ is a predecessor of σ.

(iii) Suppose that τ is nonsingular, so that $\bar{\tau}$ is also a rotation. So there exists a table T in which $\bar{\tau}$ is exposed, and $T = T_0/\mathcal{Z}$ for some set $\mathcal{Z}$ of rotations that does not include τ. By Corollary 4.2.3, any table for a solvable roommates instance contains at least one embedded stable matching, so this must be true, in particular, of the table $T/\bar{\tau}$. But a stable matching embedded in $T/\bar{\tau}$ can be obtained from $T/\bar{\tau}$, and therefore from T_0, by eliminating a set of rotations that does not include τ and therefore cannot include π. But the existence of such a stable matching would contradict Theorem 4.3.2, so we conclude that τ must be singular. $\square$

The next Lemma allows us to concentrate our attention on a table that is, in general, somewhat smaller than the phase-1 table.

Lemma 4.3.8 *If $\mathcal{Z}_0$ denotes the set of all singular rotations, then $\mathcal{Z}_0$ is closed, and every stable matching is embedded in the table $T_0/\mathcal{Z}_0$.*

Proof If $\rho \in \mathcal{Z}_0$, and $\pi \prec \rho$, then, by Lemma 4.3.7(iii), π is singular, and so $\pi \in \mathcal{Z}_0$ also. Hence $\mathcal{Z}_0$ is closed. Since every stable matching is obtained by eliminating a set of rotations that includes all the singular rotations, and since the order of rotation elimination, subject to the precedence relation, is immaterial, it follows that every stable matching is embedded in $T_0/\mathcal{Z}_0$. $\square$

We shall refer to the table $T_0' = T_0/\mathcal{Z}_0$ of Lemma 4.3.8 as the *reduced phase-1 table*, and the set of all *nonsingular* rotations, under the $\preceq$ relation, will be called the *reduced rotation poset*, denoted $\Pi'(\mathcal{R})$. A subset of the reduced rotation poset that contains exactly one of each dual pair will be called *complete*.

Finally, we can state and prove the main theorem that gives us the precise one-one correspondence between stable roommates matchings and particular closed subsets of $\Pi(\mathcal{R})$.

Theorem 4.3.2 *For a solvable roommates instance, there is a one-one correspondence between the stable matchings and the complete closed subsets of the reduced rotation poset.*

Proof By Theorem 4.3.1, every stable matching can be obtained from T_0' by eliminating the rotations in a particular complete subset $\mathcal{Z}$ of $\Pi'(\mathcal{R})$. The subset $\mathcal{Z}$ is closed because, by the definition of $\Pi'(\mathcal{R})$, every subset that can be eliminated must be closed. On the other hand, if $\mathcal{Z}$ is a complete closed subset of $\Pi'(\mathcal{R})$, then $\mathcal{Z}$ can be eliminated from T_0', and since the problem instance is solvable, Lemma 4.2.8 implies that $T_0'/\mathcal{Z}$ is a table. Further, no list in this table can have more than one entry; otherwise, by Lemma 4.2.6, there would be an exposed rotation ρ such that neither ρ nor $\bar{\rho}$ is in $\mathcal{Z}$. Hence, by Lemma 4.2.4(ii), the table is, in fact, a stable matching. $\square$

Example For the example instance that we first introduced on page 171, we saw on page 173 that the phase-1 table contains just a single rotation ρ_1. So, by Lemma 4.3.6, ρ_1 must be singular. After the elimination of ρ_1, there is again just one exposed rotation ρ_2 (see page 176), so, for the same reason, ρ_2 must be singular. However, for each of the rotations $\rho_3, \ldots, \rho_7$ described on page 180, it is possible to start from a table in which the rotation is exposed and eliminate a sequence of other exposed rotations until the dual is exposed. So each is nonsingular. Hence the reduced phase-1 table is obtained from the phase-1 table itself by the elimination of just ρ_1 and ρ_2, and is exactly the table that appears in Figure 4.11 on page 180.

The nonsingular rotations are

$$
\begin{aligned}
\rho_3 &= (1,3), (2,4) & \bar{\rho}_3 &= (4,1), (3,2) \\
\rho_4 &= (3,5), (10,6) & \bar{\rho}_4 &= (6,3), (5,10) \\
\rho_5 &= (8,10), (9,2) & \bar{\rho}_5 &= (2,8), (10,9) \\
\rho_6 &= (4,9), (7,1), (10,5) & \bar{\rho}_6 &= (9,10), (1,4), (5,7) \\
\rho_7 &= (3,6), (8,2) & \bar{\rho}_7 &= (2,3), (6,8).
\end{aligned}
$$

Rotation ρ_6 does not become exposed until ρ_4 is eliminated, so $\rho_4 \prec \rho_6$. Rotation ρ_7 requires the elimination of both ρ_4 and ρ_5, so $\rho_4 \prec \rho_7, \rho_5 \prec \rho_7$. Further, $\bar{\rho}_3$ requires the elimination of ρ_6 and ρ_7, and $\bar{\rho}_6$ the elimination of ρ_5. These observations, together with Lemma 4.3.7, give us the structure for the reduced rotation poset shown in Figure 4.17.

There are seven complete closed sets of rotations, namely

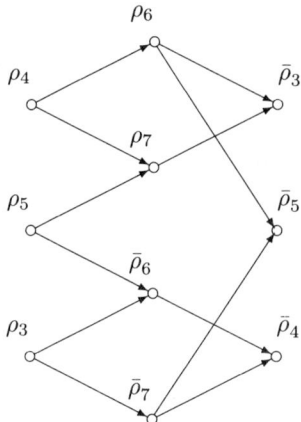

Figure 4.17: A representation of the reduced rotation poset

$$\mathcal{Z}_1 = \{\bar{\rho}_3, \rho_4, \rho_5, \rho_6, \rho_7\}$$
$$\mathcal{Z}_2 = \{\rho_3, \bar{\rho}_4, \rho_5, \bar{\rho}_6, \bar{\rho}_7\}$$
$$\mathcal{Z}_3 = \{\rho_3, \rho_4, \bar{\rho}_5, \rho_6, \bar{\rho}_7\}$$
$$\mathcal{Z}_4 = \{\rho_3, \rho_4, \rho_5, \rho_6, \rho_7\}$$
$$\mathcal{Z}_5 = \{\rho_3, \rho_4, \rho_5, \rho_6, \bar{\rho}_7\}$$
$$\mathcal{Z}_6 = \{\rho_3, \rho_4, \rho_5, \bar{\rho}_6, \rho_7\}$$
$$\mathcal{Z}_7 = \{\rho_3, \rho_4, \rho_5, \bar{\rho}_6, \bar{\rho}_7\}$$

Hence the seven stable matchings are given by $T_0' / \mathcal{Z}_i$, $(i = 1, \ldots, 7)$, where T_0' denotes the reduced phase-1 table. These matchings are as shown in Figure 4.18.

4.3.4   Alternative Representations

Roommates Matchings as Maximal Independent Sets

An alternative representation of the stable roommates matchings, that is of some interest, is in terms of the maximal independent sets in an undirected graph. (An *independent set* in a graph is a set of nodes no two of which form an edge, and an independent set is *maximal* if it is not contained in any larger independent set.)

Given a solvable roommates instance, let G be a graph, the nodes of which are the nonsingular rotations, with $\{\rho, \sigma\}$ forming an edge if and

$$R_1 = T_0'/\mathcal{Z}_1 = \{\{1,3\},\{2,4\},\{5,7\},\{6,8\},\{9,10\}\}$$
$$R_2 = T_0'/\mathcal{Z}_2 = \{\{1,7\},\{2,8\},\{3,5\},\{4,9\},\{6,10\}\}$$
$$R_3 = T_0'/\mathcal{Z}_3 = \{\{1,4\},\{2,9\},\{3,6\},\{5,7\},\{8,10\}\}$$
$$R_4 = T_0'/\mathcal{Z}_4 = \{\{1,4\},\{2,3\},\{5,7\},\{6,8\},\{9,10\}\}$$
$$R_5 = T_0'/\mathcal{Z}_5 = \{\{1,4\},\{2,8\},\{3,6\},\{5,7\},\{9,10\}\}$$
$$R_6 = T_0'/\mathcal{Z}_6 = \{\{1,7\},\{2,3\},\{4,9\},\{5,10\},\{6,8\}\}$$
$$R_7 = T_0'/\mathcal{Z}_7 = \{\{1,7\},\{2,8\},\{3,6\},\{4,9\},\{5,10\}\}$$

Figure 4.18: The seven stable matchings

only if $\bar{\rho} \preceq \sigma$ (or equivalently, in view of Lemma 4.3.7(ii), $\bar{\sigma} \preceq \rho$). So, in particular, each dual pair of rotations $\{\rho, \bar{\rho}\}$ forms an edge in G.

Theorem 4.3.3 *There is a one-one correspondence between the maximal independent sets in G and the stable matchings for the underlying roommates instance.*

Proof By Theorem 4.3.2, the result will follow if we show that there is a one-one correspondence between the maximal independent sets in G and the complete closed subsets of the reduced rotation poset.

Let ρ, σ be two distinct nonsingular rotations in a complete closed subset $\mathcal{S}$ of the rotation poset, so that $\bar{\rho} \notin \mathcal{S}$, $\bar{\sigma} \notin \mathcal{S}$. Then $\{\rho, \sigma\}$ cannot be an edge in G, for $\bar{\rho} \neq \sigma$, and if $\bar{\rho} \prec \sigma$, then, since $\bar{\rho} \notin \mathcal{S}$, $\mathcal{S}$ would not be closed. Hence the rotations in $\mathcal{S}$ form an independent set in G; the set is maximal because, for any $\pi \notin \mathcal{S}$, $\bar{\pi}$ is in $\mathcal{S}$, and $\{\pi, \bar{\pi}\}$ is an edge in G, because $\bar{\pi} \preceq \pi$.

On the other hand, let $\mathcal{U}$ be a maximal independent set of nodes in G. We have to show that, as a set of rotations, $\mathcal{U}$ is closed in $\Pi(\mathcal{R})$ and it contains exactly one of each dual pair.

If $\rho \in \mathcal{U}$, $\sigma \notin \mathcal{U}$ and $\sigma \prec \rho$ then, since $\mathcal{U}$ is maximal, there must be an edge $\{\sigma, \pi\}$ in G for some node π in $\mathcal{U}$, so that $\bar{\pi} \preceq \sigma$. But then, since $\sigma \prec \rho$, we have $\bar{\pi} \prec \rho$, which implies that $\{\pi, \rho\}$ is an edge, and contradicts the independence of $\mathcal{U}$. Hence $\mathcal{U}$ is closed.

Finally, if $\rho \notin \mathcal{U}$ and $\bar{\rho} \notin \mathcal{U}$, then, since $\mathcal{U}$ is maximal, there must be edges $\{\rho, \sigma\}$ and $\{\bar{\rho}, \pi\}$ in G, where $\sigma \in \mathcal{U}$, $\pi \in \mathcal{U}$. But then $\bar{\rho} \preceq \sigma$ and $\rho \preceq \pi$, contradicting the fact, just proved, that $\mathcal{U}$ must be closed under $\preceq$. $\square$

Example Figure 4.19 shows the graph G for our roommates instance of size 10. It contains 10 nodes, one for each nonsingular rotation, and it may be verified directly that the maximal independent sets are precisely the sets $\mathcal{Z}_1, \ldots, \mathcal{Z}_7$ listed on page 192, and therefore correspond to the seven stable matchings.

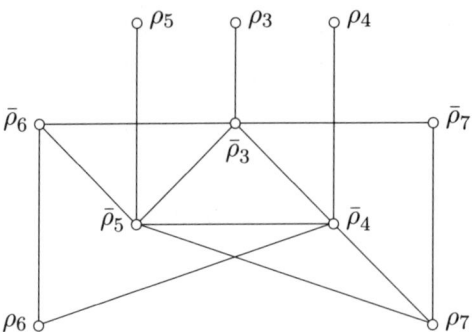

Figure 4.19: The graph representation of the reduced rotation poset

Stable Roommates as 2-SAT

Yet another possible representation of the stable roommates matchings is in terms of the satisfying assignments for an instance of *2-SAT*, the problem of determining whether a boolean expression is satisfiable, where the expression is in conjunctive normal form with exactly two literals in each clause.

Given a stable roommates instance, with reduced rotation poset $\Pi_0(\mathcal{R})$, suppose that an instance $E = E(\Pi_0(\mathcal{R}))$ of 2-SAT is constructed as follows: each nonsingular rotation ρ and its dual $\bar{\rho}$ form a pair of complementary literals (i.e., ρ and $\sim \rho$); the clauses in E are of the form $(\rho \vee \sim \sigma)$ for each pair ρ and σ such that $\rho \prec \sigma$ in $\Pi_0(\mathcal{R})$.

Theorem 4.3.4 *The stable matchings in $\mathcal{R}$ are in one-one correspondence with the satisfying assignments for $E(\Pi_0(\mathcal{R}))$.*

Proof If $\mathcal{Z}$ is a complete closed subset of $\Pi_0(\mathcal{R})$, then we may assign the literals representing the rotations in $\mathcal{Z}$ to be simultaneously true, since there are no complementary pairs among them. This is a satisfying assignment for E since every clause in E is of the form $(\rho \vee \sim \sigma)$ with $\rho \prec \sigma$ in $\Pi_0(\mathcal{R})$, and if ρ is false (i.e., not in $\mathcal{Z}$) then σ must be false also (since $\mathcal{Z}$ is closed), and $\sim \sigma$ is therefore true.

On the other hand, the true literals in a satisfying assignment for E

certainly yield a complete set $\mathcal{Z}$ of nonsingular rotations (i.e., one of each dual pair); further, the set must be closed, since if σ is true (i.e., σ is in $\mathcal{Z}$), and $\rho \prec \sigma$ in $\Pi_0(\mathcal{R})$, then ρ must be in $\mathcal{Z}$ also to ensure the truth of the clause $(\rho \vee \sim \sigma)$. $\square$

Note that $E(\Pi_0(\mathcal{R}))$ has $O(n^2)$ variables and clauses, and can certainly be constructed in $O(n^2)$ time from the reduced rotation poset. Note also, that the 2-SAT reduction does not depend on the reduced rotation poset, and in fact it is not hard to see that an analogous reduction holds if the instance of 2-SAT is constructed using only the precedences in the Hasse diagram of $\Pi_0(\mathcal{R})$, or indeed in any poset whose transitive closure is $\Pi_0(\mathcal{R})$.

4.3.5 Semilattice Structure in the Roommates Problem

The lattice structure, under the dominance relation, of the set of stable matchings in the stable marriage problem does not carry over in any simple way to the roommates problem. However, in this section we will show that at least the roommates matchings do exhibit a semilattice structure under a relation that generalizes dominance. (A *semilattice* is a weaker structure than a lattice — it has just a single operation, meet or join, and is closed under this operation.)

Medians

We first define what is meant by a person's *median choice* relative to three stable matchings. Let R_1, R_2 and R_3 be roommates matchings, and let x be any person. If x has the same partner y in two or more of the three matchings, then x's median choice relative to these matchings is y; otherwise, if x's partners in the matchings are v, y, and z, and x prefers v to y and y to z, then x's median choice is y.

To establish the structure, we first prove a result that is of interest in its own right, namely that if we have any three stable matchings R_1, R_2, and R_3 for a roommates instance, then assigning each person to his median choice relative to these three matchings gives a stable matching. This medians result is proved with the aid of a lemma that is analogous to Theorem 1.3.1 in the stable marriage case.

Lemma 4.3.9 *If R and R' are stable roommates matchings, and if x and y are partners in R but not in R', then one of x, y prefers R to R' and the other prefers R' to R.*

Proof Let $\mathcal{S}$ be the set of people who prefer R to R', and $\mathcal{S}'$ the set who prefer R' to R. In R, any member of $\mathcal{S}$ is partnered by a member of $\mathcal{S}'$, for if two members of $\mathcal{S}$ are partners in R, then these two will block R'. So $|\mathcal{S}| \leq |\mathcal{S}'|$. But, similarly, in R', any member of $\mathcal{S}'$ is partnered by a member of $\mathcal{S}$, for if two members of $\mathcal{S}'$ are partners in R', then these two will block R. So $|\mathcal{S}'| \leq |\mathcal{S}|$. It follows that $|\mathcal{S}| = |\mathcal{S}'|$, and in R, any member of $\mathcal{S}'$ is partnered by a member of $\mathcal{S}$. This establishes the stated conclusion. $\square$

Theorem 4.3.5 *If R_1, R_2, and R_3 are three distinct stable roommates matchings, then mapping each person to his median choice relative to R_1, R_2, R_3 gives a stable matching.*

Proof We first prove that this mapping is a matching. Suppose that x's median choice is y. If x and y are partners in at least two of R_1, R_2, R_3, then it is immediate that y's median choice is x. Otherwise, suppose x prefers R_1 to R_2 to R_3, so that x and y are partners in R_2. By Lemma 4.3.9, y prefers R_3 to R_2 to R_1, so again y's median choice is x.

Next we prove stability. Suppose that $\{x, y\}$ is a blocking pair for the median matching. Then x strictly prefers y to his partners in at least two of R_1, R_2, R_3, and y prefers x to his partners in at least two of R_1, R_2, R_3. So $\{x, y\}$ must block at least one of R_1, R_2, R_3, giving a contradiction, since each of these is stable. $\square$

Example Consider our instance of size 10 with full preference lists as given in Figure 4.5 on page 171. Among the seven stable matchings, which are listed in Figure 4.18 on page 193, are

$$R_1 = \{\{1,3\}, \{2,4\}, \{5,7\}, \{6,8\}, \{9,10\}\}$$
$$R_2 = \{\{1,7\}, \{2,8\}, \{3,5\}, \{4,9\}, \{6,10\}\}$$
$$R_3 = \{\{1,4\}, \{2,9\}, \{3,6\}, \{5,7\}, \{8,10\}\}.$$

It is easy to verify that the median of R_1, R_2 and R_3 is the stable matching

$$R_5 = \{\{1,4\}, \{2,8\}, \{3,6\}, \{5,7\}, \{9,10\}\}.$$

As a final observation on medians, it is interesting to note that this result generalizes the closure under meet and join of the stable matchings in the stable marriage problem. For in stable marriage, the median of M_0, M_i and M_j is $M_i \wedge M_j$, and the median of M_z, M_i and M_j is $M_i \vee M_j$ (where, as usual, M_0 is the man-optimal and M_z the woman-optimal stable matching).

Semilattice Structure

For a given stable roommates instance, and a given stable matching R, define $P(R)$ to be the set of ordered pairs (x, y) such that $\{x, y\} \in R$ or x prefers y to his partner in R.

Relative to a *fixed* stable matching R_0, define $P_0(R) = P(R) \oplus P(R_0)$, where $\oplus$ denotes symmetric difference.

Theorem 4.3.6 *The sets $P_0(R)$, taken over all stable matchings R, are closed under intersection, and so can be regarded as a meet-semilattice in which $P_0(R_0)$ is the minimal element.*

Proof By definition, $P_0(R) = P(R) \oplus P(R_0)$ is the set of ordered pairs (x, y) such that y lies strictly between x's partners in R and R_0 in x's preference list. For stable matchings R and R', let $\bar{R}$ denote the median matching of R_0, R and R', and let x be a fixed person.

If $p_R(x) = p_{R_0}(x)$, or $p_{R'}(x) = p_{R_0}(x)$, then there are no pairs (x, y) in $P_0(R) \cap P_0(R')$, nor are there any in $P_0(\bar{R})$, since $p_{\bar{R}}(x) = p_{R_0}(x)$.

If $p_R(x) = p_{R'}(x) \neq p_{R_0}(x)$, then the pairs (x, y) in $P_0(R) \cap P_0(R')$ are those in $P_0(R)$, and are precisely those in $P_0(\bar{R})$, since $p_{\bar{R}}(x) = p_R(x)$ in this case.

If no two of $p_R(x)$, $p_{R'}(x)$, $p_{R_0}(x)$ are equal, then
(a) if $p_{\bar{R}}(x) = p_{R_0}(x)$, there are no pairs (x, y) in $P_0(R) \cap P_0(R')$, and none in $P_0(\bar{R})$;
(b) if $p_{\bar{R}}(x) = p_R(x)$, the pairs (x, y) in $P_0(R) \cap P_0(R')$ are those in $P_0(R)$, and these are precisely the pairs in $P_0(\bar{R})$;
(c) if $p_{\bar{R}}(x) = p_{R'}(x)$, the pairs (x, y) in $P_0(R) \cap P_0(R')$ are those in $P_0(R')$, and these are precisely the pairs in $P_0(\bar{R})$.

So, in all cases, we have shown that the pairs (x, y) in $P_0(R) \cap P_0(R')$ are precisely those in $P_0(\bar{R})$, and this is true for all x. So $P_0(R) \cap P_0(R') = P_0(\bar{R})$, and the sets are closed under intersection as claimed.

It is immediate that $P_0(R_0)$ is the minimal element, since it contains no pairs and is therefore the empty set. □

Example For our instance of size 10, with 7 stable matchings $R_1, \ldots, R_7$ (see page 193), let R_4 be the fixed matching, and let $P_i = P(R_i) \oplus P(R_4)$. The intersection table for the sets is shown in Figure 4.20. Hence the semilattice structure is as shown in Figure 4.21.

This semilattice structure is of interest precisely because it generalizes the lattice structure of the stable marriage case. If we view a stable marriage instance as a special case of roommates (Lemma 4.1.1 on page 163), and if we take $R_0 = M_0$, the man-optimal stable matching, then the semilattice relation specializes to the dominance relation.

4.3.6 Specializing Roommates Structure to Marriage

We observed in Section 4.1 that the stable marriage problem is a special case of the stable roommates problem, so the question arises as to how the structural results established in this section specialize to the marriage case.

	P_2	P_3	P_4	P_5	P_6	P_7
P_1	P_4	P_4	P_4	P_4	P_4	P_4
P_2		P_5	P_4	P_5	P_6	P_7
P_3			P_4	P_5	P_4	P_5
P_4				P_4	P_4	P_4
P_5					P_4	P_5
P_6						P_6

Figure 4.20: Intersection table for the sets P_i

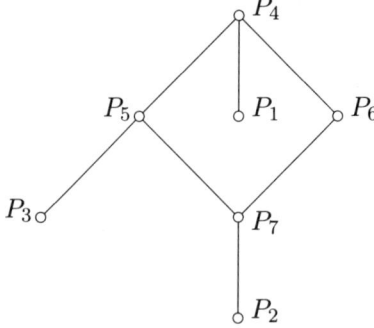

Figure 4.21: The semilattice structure

Recall that a stable marriage instance can be transformed to a stable roommates instance by appending to the end of each person's list all the other members of the same sex in arbitrary order. The stable matchings for the derived roommates instance are precisely the stable matchings for the original marriage instance. As far as structure is concerned, we state without proof the following properties of any roommates instance derived from a marriage instance:

    i. There are no singular rotations.

    ii. For any rotation ρ, all the people in the X-set are of one sex and all the people in the Y-set are of the opposite sex; so we can refer to the sex of a rotation as male or female depending on the sex associated with, say, its X-set.

    iii. No male rotation is a predecessor of a female rotation and vice versa, so the rotation poset Π consists of two disjoint subposets comprising the male and female rotations respectively.

    iv. $\mathcal{Z}$ is a closed set of male rotations if and only if $\Pi \setminus \mathcal{Z}^d$ is a closed set of female rotations, where $\mathcal{Z}^d$ is the set of duals of rotations in $\mathcal{Z}$; hence the union of $\mathcal{Z}$ and $\Pi \setminus \mathcal{Z}^d$ is closed, and since this union contains exactly one of each dual pair of rotations, it represents a stable matching. The converse is also true. Hence there is a one-one correspondence between the stable matchings and the closed subsets of the male rotations, or, indeed, of the female rotations. (Of course, when considered as a marriage instance, only the male rotations are recognized as rotations in any case.)

These facts, in particular the absence of singular rotations and the natural partition of the dual pairs, give some insight into why marriage structure is simpler than that of roommates. In the next section, we will see that this more complex roommates structure appears to make the solution of certain algorithmic problems associated with roommates somewhat harder than the corresponding problems in stable marriage.

4.4 Exploiting the Structure

In this section, we exploit the algorithmic and structural results of Sections 4.2 and 4.3 in order to obtain efficient algorithms to build the roommates rotation poset and to solve a range of problems associated with stable roommates. The problems in question are meaningful only for *solvable* roommates instances, so we restrict our attention to these throughout.

4.4.1   Constructing the Roommates Rotation Poset

In sections 3.3.1 and 3.3.3 we saw how, for a given stable marriage instance, all the rotations and a representation of the rotation poset could be found in $O(n^2)$ time. In view of the somewhat analogous characterization result that we have obtained for the stable roommates problem, we might hope for an algorithm of similar complexity to find the roommates rotations and to build a representation of the roommates rotation poset. However, the roommates case seems to be more difficult to handle. In contrast to the stable marriage case, carrying out a single complete sequence of rotation eliminations is not sufficient to identify all the rotations. By Theorem 4.3.1, such a process merely generates all the singular rotations and one of each dual pair but does not distinguish between them, so that we cannot infer the duals. It is this need to identify the singular rotations that apparently makes the exploitation of roommates structure more difficult than the exploitation of stable marriage structure.

Suppose that a particular rotation ρ is found by an application of the basic roommates algorithm. The singularity or otherwise of ρ can be established by reapplying the algorithm but without eliminating ρ. If $\bar{\rho}$ is a rotation, then there must be a table T in which $\bar{\rho}$ is exposed and, by Corollary 4.2.3, the table $T/\bar{\rho}$ has at least one embedded stable matching. There is therefore at least one stable matching whose corresponding set of rotations contains $\bar{\rho}$ rather than ρ. So applying the algorithm without eliminating ρ will lead to a stable matching if and only if ρ is nonsingular.

Now, the total number of rotations in a stable marriage instance cannot exceed $n(n-1)/2$, since, in deriving a stable matching from T_0, every singular rotation and one of each pair of dual rotations is eliminated and each elimination deletes at least two pairs from the preference lists. Each of the $O(n^2)$ rotations can be checked for singularity in $O(n^2)$ time by a further application of the basic roommates algorithm, so that this "brute force" approach will identify all the singular rotations and all the dual pairs in $O(n^4)$ time. However, by using a more subtle approach to establish the status of each rotation, it is possible to reduce this complexity to $O(n^3 \log n)$.

For any particular person x, and a particular execution E of the basic roommates algorithm, consider the distinct persons who appear at the head of x's list during phase 2; suppose these are $y_1, \ldots, y_m$ in turn, so that $y_1 = f_{T_0}(x)$, and y_m is x's partner in the stable matching found by E.

For each i $(1 \le i \le m-1)$, the pair (x, y_i) is in a rotation — say (x, y_i) is in rotation ρ_i $(1 \le i \le m-1)$. Further, if $1 \le j < i \le m-1$, then the rotation ρ_j is clearly a predecessor of rotation ρ_i. So, by Lemma 4.3.7(iii), if (x, y_i) belongs to a singular rotation, then so does (x, y_j) for all $j < i$. Hence there exists a *cutoff point* $k = k(x)$ $(1 \leq k \leq m - 1)$ such that (x, y_i) is in a singular rotation for $1 \leq i < k$ and in a nonsingular rotation for $k \leq i < m$. If we were to determine the cutoff point for each x, then we would know the singular rotations.

For a particular x, the cutoff point may be found by binary search among the rotations in the sequence $\rho_1, \ldots, \rho_{m-1}$. For each rotation, we determine in $O(n^2)$ time whether it is singular or nonsingular by the method above. Since $m \leq n - 1$, the search is among at most $n - 2$ items, and the cutoff point for each person can be found in $O(n^2 \log n)$ time, with the consequent determination of the singular and nonsingular rotations in $O(n^3 \log n)$ time.

We summarize our findings as a theorem.

Theorem 4.4.1 *For roommates instances of size n, every rotation can be found and identified as singular or nonsingular in $O(n^3 \log n)$ time.*

Once all of the rotations have been identified, the construction of a (sparse) representation of the roommates rotation poset can be carried out in a manner quite analogous to the construction of $G(\mathcal{M})$ for the stable marriage case.

The concepts of type 1 and type 2 predecessors can be defined in an exactly similar way, and the rotation digraph $G(\mathcal{R})$ has a node for each rotation and a directed edge from ρ to σ if and only if ρ is a type 1 or a type 2 predecessor of σ. The fact that the transitive closure of $G(\mathcal{R})$ is precisely the rotation poset $\Pi(\mathcal{R})$ follows exactly as in the stable marriage case. Of course, in roommates it is the reduced rotation poset that is of interest for most purposes, so we would normally choose to discard all singular rotations and build only the reduced rotation digraph $G'(\mathcal{R})$ using the nonsingular rotations.

The construction of $G(\mathcal{R})$ (or $G'(\mathcal{R})$), once again, is analogous to the construction of $G(\mathcal{M})$ in the stable marriage case and, as described in Section 3.3.3, can be achieved in $O(n^2)$ time once we have found the rotations.

A Coarser but Faster Construction

Although the algorithm that we have described for constructing a representation of the (reduced) rotation poset is no better that $O(n^3 \log n)$ in the worst case, we can construct in $O(n^2)$ time a representation of an alternative, larger poset with an exactly analogous property. This larger poset, which we shall call the *extended rotation poset*, contains an element representing the syntactic dual of every rotation, nonsingular or singular, and is built without knowledge of which rotations are, in fact, singular. Here, the *syntactic dual* of the sequence $(x_0, y_0), (x_1, y_1), \ldots, (x_{r-1}, y_{r-1})$ is the sequence

$(y_1, x_0), (y_2, x_1), \ldots, (y_0, x_{r-1})$; clearly the latter sequence is a rotation if and only if the former is a nonsingular rotation.

It turns out that a sparse representation of the extended rotation poset can be built, as was the case for the reduced rotation poset, by processing the preference lists in a manner similar to that described in Section 3.3.3 for the stable marriage case. However, construction of the former, as in the marriage case, takes only $O(n^2)$ time, since there is no need to identify the singular rotations. A single application of the basic roommates algorithm will generate all singular rotations, and one of each pair of dual rotations, and we simply take all of these, together with their syntactic duals, as the elements of the poset. If we knew which rotations were singular, then removing those and their syntactic duals yields the familiar reduced rotation poset.

Furthermore, and crucially, it is not difficult to prove that every singular rotation precedes its syntactic dual in the extended rotation poset, so that every "complete" closed subset of the extended rotation poset contains all of the singular rotations (where *complete* here means containing exactly one of each pair of syntactic duals).

Hence, we have the analogous result to Theorem 4.3.2, namely that there is a one-one correspondence between the stable matchings and the complete closed subsets of the extended rotation poset. In general, this representation of the stable matchings will be coarser and less precise than the reduced rotation poset because it includes the singular rotations and their syntactic duals, but, as we have indicated, it can be built in $O(n^2)$ time, whereas the best bound for the latter is $O(n^3 \log n)$ time.

Finally, we observe that the transformations described in Section 4.3.4 can be applied to this coarser representation, and thereby, in particular, an instance of stable roommates can be reduced in $O(n^2)$ time to an instance of 2-SAT. However, it remains to be seen whether this faster transformation can be effectively used to speed up any of the algorithmic methods described in subsequent sections. Another reflection of the coarseness of the extended poset is the fact that variables corresponding to singular rotations are fixed in the resulting instance of 2-SAT whereas the 2-SAT expression derived from the reduced rotation poset has no fixed (or even equivalent) variables.

4.4.2   Finding the Stable Pairs

In the stable marriage case, we saw that the stable pairs are precisely those pairs that are in a rotation, together with the pairs in the woman-optimal matching. Hence all stable pairs can be found by applying Algorithm *minimal-differences*, and this can be implemented to run in $O(n^2)$ time.

As we shall see, the roommates situation is somewhat analogous, but nevertheless, because of the difficulty of identifying the singular rotations, the best available algorithm for finding all stable pairs in roommates has the same $O(n^3 \log n)$ complexity that we saw in Section 4.4.1.

As in stable marriage, a pair $\{x, y\}$ is said to be *fixed* in a solvable roommates instance if x and y are partners in all stable matchings. We can now state the lemma that characterizes the stable pairs.

Lemma 4.4.1 *In a solvable roommates instance,*
(i) $\{x, y\}$ *is a fixed pair if and only if* x's *list in the reduced phase-1 table contains only* y *and* y's *contains only* x;
(ii) otherwise, $\{x, y\}$ *is a stable pair if and only if the pair* (x, y), *or the pair* (y, x), *is in a nonsingular rotation.*

Proof (i) If x and y are the only entries in each other's lists in the reduced phase-1 table, then it is clear that $\{x, y\}$ is a fixed pair, since all stable pairs are contained in that table.

On the other hand, suppose that u and v are the first and last entries in x's list in the reduced phase-1 table, with $u \neq v$, so that x is first in v's list in that table. Since the reduced phase-1 table is obtained by eliminating all the singular rotations, every subtable of it that is not itself a matching contains at least two rotations, by Lemma 4.3.6. If we start from the reduced phase-1 table and eliminate a sequence of rotations, always choosing a rotation other than the one that x leads to, then the pair $\{x, u\}$ is never deleted, and we obtain a stable matching containing $\{x, u\}$. But if, instead, we always choose a rotation other than the one that v leads to, the pair $\{v, x\}$ is never deleted, and we obtain a stable matching containing $\{v, x\}$. So x cannot be in a fixed pair.

(ii) If (x, y) is in a nonsingular rotation ρ, then there is a table T in which ρ is exposed. Starting from T and eliminating rotations, the pair $\{x, y\}$ can be deleted only by the elimination of ρ. But because ρ is nonsingular, it is never the only exposed rotation, by Lemma 4.3.6, so that a stable matching can be derived from T without eliminating ρ, and x and y are bound to be partners in this stable matching. On the other hand, suppose that x and y are partners in the stable matching $R = T_0/\{\rho_0, \ldots, \rho_{t-1}\}$, and that the rotations may be eliminated in the given order. If y is the only entry in x's list in $T_0/\{\rho_0, \ldots, \rho_s\}$ but not in $T_0/\{\rho_0, \ldots, \rho_{s-1}\}$, then (x, y) or (y, x) must be in $\bar{\rho}_s$. $\square$

It follows from Lemma 4.4.1 that once we have identified the singular and nonsingular rotations, we can easily find the stable pairs. It suffices to

eliminate the singular rotations, starting from the phase-1 table, so as to
identify the fixed pairs, and this can clearly be achieved in $O(n^2)$ time. We
summarize our findings as a theorem.

Theorem 4.4.2 *The stable pairs for a roommates instance of size n can be
found in $O(n^3 \log n)$ time.*

4.4.3 Minimum Regret Stable Matchings

In seeking a "minimum regret" stable matching we are, loosely speaking,
trying to make the least happy person as happy as possible, where a person's
happiness is measured by the position of his roommate in his preference list.

Relative to a fixed stable matching R in a given roommates instance, the
regret of a person x is the position in x's original list occupied by x's R-
partner. The *regret* of a matching is the maximum regret of any person
relative to that matching. A *minimum regret* stable matching is a stable
matching for which the regret is as small as possible.

The concept of regret can be extended to any stable preference table T.
The *regret* of a person x *relative to T* is the position in x's original list
occupied by $l_T(x)$, his last list entry in T.

A minimum regret matching may be found by an adaptation of the basic
roommates algorithm in which the rotation to be eliminated at each stage of
phase 2 is chosen according to an appropriate criterion, as we now explain.

Relative to a given stable preference table T, let x be a person with
maximum regret, and let $y = l_T(x)$. If, in applying the algorithm to T, the
rotation that y leads to is never eliminated, then the pair $\{y, x\}$ will not
be deleted, and x and y will be partners in the stable matching generated.
Hence, of all the stable matchings embedded in T, this matching will have
maximum regret.

Therefore, in our search for a minimum regret stable matching, we should
successively eliminate from the current table T the rotation that $l_T(x)$ leads
to for the person x whose regret in T is as large as possible. Recall that when
several rotations are exposed, the basic roommates algorithm can choose
arbitrarily which rotation to eliminate, so that choosing according to the
above criterion will certainly lead to a stable matching, if one exists.

It turns out that we can incorporate this criterion into the basic roommates algorithm at essentially no extra cost, as follows. The sequence of
rotation eliminations in phase 2 is enclosed within a loop that successively
examines the last entry in each (original) list, then the second last entry,
and so on. Whenever an entry is reached that is actually the last entry
in that list in the *current* table, then that entry becomes the target for

removal. Of course, if the list in question has just that single entry, then it cannot be removed, and the entry in question determines the regret of the minimum regret stable matching; any particular minimum regret stable matching can then be found by eliminating an arbitrary sequence of exposed rotations from that point. Otherwise, if the list in question has ≥ 2 entries, and if the entry in question is $\{x, l_T(x)\}$, then we repeatedly eliminate the rotation that $l_T(x)$ leads to (using a stack, as in Section 4.2.4) until the entry $\{x, l_T(x)\}$ is itself deleted, i.e, until the stack becomes empty. The backward scan through the original lists then continues in search of the next most pressing entry to eliminate, until a complete set of rotations has been eliminated. The stable matching so derived must have the minimum regret property.

In terms of the implementation of the roommates algorithm described in Figure 4.16, the only difference is that whenever the stack is empty, the next person to be pushed onto it is determined by the ongoing backward scan of all the preference lists rather than by the simpler ongoing scan in search of a list of length ≥ 2. However, the total cost of the backward scan is $O(n^2)$, so that the overall complexity of this amended roommates algorithm remains $O(n^2)$.

Hence we have the following theorem.

Theorem 4.4.3 *For a stable roommates instance of size n, the minimum regret stable matching can be found in $O(n^2)$ time.*

4.4.4   Finding All the Stable Matchings

We will describe an algorithm for all stable matchings that is expressed as a recursive procedure with the current table T as a parameter. The purpose of the procedure is to generate, exactly once, each stable matching that is embedded in T, so that if it is called initially with T equal to the reduced phase-1 table, it will generate every stable matching exactly once.

When the procedure is called with a parameter, table T, that is itself a matching, it simply outputs T. When T is not itself a matching, then, by Lemma 4.2.6, it contains an exposed rotation ρ. In order to find all stable matchings that are embedded in T and that correspond to complete closed sets that contain ρ, the procedure calls itself with T/ρ as parameter. The only other stable matchings embedded in T correspond to complete closed sets that contain $\bar{\rho}$ rather than ρ. In order to generate these, any uneliminated predecessors of $\bar{\rho}$ must be eliminated to give the maximal table T' that is a subtable of T and in which $\bar{\rho}$ is exposed; then a recursive call is made with parameter $T'/\bar{\rho}$. Hence, the algorithm is guaranteed to generate every stable matching exactly once.

An outline of the algorithm appears in Figure 4.22.

---

procedure Enumerate (T : Tables) ;
{ Finds all the stable matchings embedded in the table T }
begin
    if T is a matching then
        output T
    else
        begin
            ρ := a rotation exposed in T ;
            Enumerate (T/ρ) ;
            T' := maximal subtable of T in which $\bar{\rho}$ is exposed ;
            Enumerate ($T'/\bar{\rho}$)
        end
end ;

Figure 4.22: Procedure to enumerate all stable roommates matchings

The structure of the recursive calls of the procedure can be viewed as a binary tree in which each internal node has two children, and represents a call of the procedure in which T is not itself a matching, while each leaf node represents a stable matching. It is well known that the number of leaf nodes, and hence the number of stable matchings, is one greater than the number of internal nodes. So, if we can show that the number of operations carried out during each call of the procedure is $O(n^2)$, then the generation of all stable matchings can be achieved in $O(n^3 \log n + n^2 |\mathcal{R}|)$ time. Here, the first term arises from the algorithm that builds the rotation poset and the second term from the work done at each of the $|\mathcal{R}| - 1$ internal nodes.

To see that the time required by each call of the procedure is $O(n^2)$, we first observe that an exposed rotation can be found in $O(n)$ time by following a path in the digraph $H(T)$ (see page 174), and an exposed rotation can be eliminated in $O(m) = O(n^2)$ time, where m is the number of pairs thereby deleted from the table.

It remains to consider the generation of the table T' from the table T. Suppose that $\rho = (x_0, y_0), (x_1, y_1), \ldots, (x_{r-1}, y_{r-1})$. In order that the dual rotation $\bar{\rho} = (y_1, x_0), (y_2, x_1), \ldots, (y_0, x_{r-1})$ should become exposed, pairs of the following two kinds must be deleted from T.

(a) $\{y_i, z\}$ such that y_i prefers z to x_{i-1};

(b) $\{y_i, z\}$ such that y_i prefers x_{i-1} to z and z to x_i.
We must identify the rotations that have to be eliminated in order to delete these pairs.

To deal with pairs of type (a), suppose that $f(y_i) \neq x_{i-1}$. Then the pair $\{y_i, f(y_i)\}$ cannot be deleted until the rotation that y_i leads to has been eliminated. So, as in the implementation of the basic roommates algorithm in Section 4.2.4, we use such a y_i to initialize the stack, and continue with rotation identification and elimination until the stack is empty, at which point the pair $\{y_i, f(y_i)\}$ has been deleted. This can be repeated as often as necessary for as many of the y_i as necessary until $f(y_i) = x_{i-1}$ for all i.

For pairs of type (b), we observe that such a pair $\{y_i, z\}$ can only be deleted during or after the elimination of the rotation containing the pair $(l(z), f(l(z))$. So, we embark on the same process, this time using $l(z)$ to initialize the stack and then continuing until no such pairs $\{y_i, z\}$ remain. The resulting table is the required T', and its derivation from T has been achieved essentially by a partial execution of the basic roommates algorithm, and so occupies $O(n^2)$ time.

In summary, we have the following theorem.

Theorem 4.4.4 *For a solvable roommates instance of size n, all stable matchings can be found in $O(n^3 \log n + n^2 |\mathcal{R}|)$ time, where $\mathcal{R}$ is the set of stable matchings.*

4.5 Variations and Extensions

4.5.1 Sets of Odd Cardinality

Suppose that each of an odd number of persons ranks all of the others strictly in order of preference. Given a (partial) matching R, i.e., a set of disjoint pairs, two persons x, y are said to *block R* if

    i. x is either unmatched in R or prefers y to his partner in R, and

    ii. y is either unmatched in R or prefers x to his partner in R.

A matching R is stable if there are no blocking pairs. Clearly, in this case, at least one person is left unmatched in any matching, stable or otherwise.

Phase 1 of the roommates algorithm may be applied in this setting as before, and, as observed in Section 4.2.2, at most one preference list can become empty during this phase of the algorithm. In an odd cardinality instance, if phase 1 leaves all preference lists nonempty then there can be no stable matching. For any person x is first in the phase-1 list of some other person, say y, and if x were to be left unmatched, as someone must be, then the pair $\{x, y\}$ would inevitably block the matching.

If one person's list does become empty, then by Lemma 4.2.3(i), which still applies, that person cannot be matched in any stable matching. However, if there is a stable matching, by the same argument as in the previous paragraph, there can be no other unmatched person. Whether or not such a matching exists can be determined by application of phase 2 of the algorithm, as in the even cardinality case.

The following theorem summarizes the situation in the odd cardinality case.

Theorem 4.5.1 *In a solvable stable roommates instance of odd cardinality, all stable matchings exclude the same one person, and this person is the one person whose list becomes empty in phase 1 of the algorithm.*

4.5.2   Unacceptable Partners

In Section 1.4.2, we considered how the stable marriage problem was affected by allowing unacceptable partners, and in this section we derive similar results for the stable roommates problem.

Suppose that any person may class one or more of the others as an unacceptable partner; in other words, he would prefer to remain unmatched rather than be matched with such a person. In this context, it is natural to define a blocking pair for a matching as a pair $\{x, y\}$ each of whom is acceptable to the other and is either unmatched or prefers the other to his partner in the matching. As usual, a matching, which may be partial in this case, is stable if and only if there are no blocking pairs.

If phase 1 of the stable roommates algorithm is applied in this setting, then one or more of the preference lists may become empty, though this does not necessarily imply that there is no stable matching. (Of course, if the lists of x and y both become empty, and x and y are acceptable to each other, then there can indeed be no stable matching.) However, it is certainly the case that any person with an empty list at this stage cannot be matched in any stable matching, whereas by an argument analogous to that used in Section 4.5.1, any person with a nonempty list after phase 1 must be matched in every stable matching. Once again, the existence or nonexistence of a stable matching can be determined by application of phase 2 of the algorithm.

The situation is summarized in the following theorem.

Theorem 4.5.2 *For a solvable stable roommates instance involving unacceptable partners, the set of persons is partitioned into two subsets, those that*

are matched in every stable matching and those that are matched in none.
The former subset comprises precisely those persons who have a nonempty
list after phase 1 of the algorithm.

4.5.3   Allowing Indifference

Suppose that indifference is allowed in a stable roommates instance, so that
any person may have one or more ties in his preference list. For the notion
of stability that is most natural in this context, we say that persons x and
y block a matching if each *strictly* prefers the other to his partner in the
matching. In the stable marriage case, we saw in Section 1.4.3 that breaking
ties arbitrarily and applying the Gale-Shapley algorithm to the resulting
strictly ordered preference lists is sufficient to obtain a matching that is
stable in this sense.

However, in the case of stable roommates, the situation is quite different.
Certainly, ties can be broken arbitrarily and the basic stable roommates
algorithm applied to the resulting no-tie instance. If a stable matching is
found, then it is also stable for the original instance, but if no stable matching
exists for the derived instance, no conclusion can be reached regarding the
original instance; it may be that if the ties were to be broken in a different
way, a stable matching would be found by this means. One way of resolving
the issue with certainty would be to apply the roommates algorithm to a
sequence of no-tie instances derived by breaking ties in all possible ways,
but there may well be exponentially many ways of breaking the ties, so that
such an algorithm would not have polynomial-time worst-case complexity.

In fact, perhaps rather surprisingly, it turns out that the stable roommates problem with ties, as described, is NP-complete. Hence, unless P
= NP, there cannot exist an algorithm that is guaranteed to determine, in
polynomial-time, whether a given instance admits a stable matching.

Henceforth, we use the abbreviation RWT to stand for the stable roommates problem with ties.

Membership of RWT in the class NP is easy to establish. We observed in
Section 4.1 that the $O(n^2)$ stability checking algorithm that was introduced
in Section 1.1.2 for stable marriage could easily be adapted to apply to
roommates, and it is a trivial matter to take account of ties in the preference
lists. So every solvable instance of RWT has a "certificate" that may be
checked in polynomial-time.

To establish NP-completeness, it suffices to describe a polynomial-time
transformation from some known NP-complete problem to RWT. The NP-
complete problem that we choose is one that is commonly used in establish-

ing NP-completeness results, namely 3-SAT, i.e., the problem of determining whether a boolean expression in conjunctive normal form, with at most three literals per clause, is satisfiable. In fact, we use as our starting point for the transformation a restricted version of 3-SAT in which each literal appears at most twice. We first show that this problem, which we refer to as restricted-3-SAT (R-3-SAT), is itself NP-complete by describing a polynomial-time transformation from 3-SAT to R-3-SAT.

Lemma 4.5.1 *R-3-SAT is NP-complete.*

Proof Membership in NP is immediate. Given an arbitrary instance E of 3-SAT, we construct an instance of R-3-SAT as follows. Suppose that variable x, either as literal x or literal $\bar{x}$, appears in m clauses. Introduce $m-1$ new variables $x_1, \ldots, x_{m-1}$, together with m clauses $(x \vee \bar{x}_1)$, $(x_i \vee \bar{x}_{i+1})$ for $1 \leq i \leq m - 2$, and $(x_{m-1} \vee \bar{x})$. Also, for $1 \leq i \leq m - 1$, replace the $(i + 1)$th occurrence of the variable x by x_i. This process is repeated for each variable x, and if the original instance contains n variables, and a total of k occurrences of variables in clauses, then $k - n$ new variables and k new clauses are introduced. So, it should be clear that the transformation can be carried out in polynomial-time and that the derived boolean expression is an instance E' of R-3-SAT.

We claim that E' is satisfiable if and only if E is satisfiable. Given a satisfying assignment for E, then if we give $x_1, \ldots, x_{m-1}$ the same truth value as x, for each x, we find that all the clauses in E' are true, so that we have a satisfying assignment for E'. On the other hand, in any satisfying assignment for E', the new clauses ensure that $x, x_1, \ldots, x_{m-1}$ all have the same truth value, so that a satisfying assignment for E is induced in an obvious way. $\square$

Lemma 4.5.1 allows us to use R-3-SAT as the starting point in proving the NP-completeness of RWT.

Theorem 4.5.3 *The stable roommates problem with ties (RWT) is NP-complete.*

Proof We have already observed that the problem is in NP, so the description of a polynomial-time transformation from R-3-SAT will complete the proof. So, given an arbitrary instance of R-3-SAT — a boolean expression E in conjunctive normal form with at most 3 literals per clause and no literal occurring more than twice — we describe how to construct, in polynomial-time, an instance of RWT that is solvable if and only if E is satisfiable.

Suppose that E contains n variables and c clauses. We may assume that every clause in E contains ≥ 2 literals, since the literal in a single-literal clause must be true in any satisfying assignment. So the total number of occurrences of literals is $\geq 2c$. But this number is at most $4n$, since each variable can appear at most 4 times. Hence $2n - c \geq 0$.

The derived instance of RWT is of size $8n + 2c$. Representing each clause C_j there are 3 persons denoted u_j, v_j and w_j $(j = 1, \ldots, c)$, and for each variable x_i there are 6 persons denoted p_{ik}, q_{ik} and r_{ik} $(i = 1, \ldots, n;\ k = 1, 2)$. Finally, there are a further $2n - c$ persons $g_1, \ldots, g_{2n-c}$ referred to as the "garbage collectors".

The preference lists for the derived RWT instance are shown in Figure 4.23, where i runs from 1 to n, j from 1 to c, k from 1 to 2, and l from 1 to $2n - c$.

u_j	$f_1(C_j)$	$f_2(C_j)$	$f_3(C_j)$	v_j	w_j	$\ldots$
v_j	w_j	u_j	$\ldots$			
w_j	u_j	v_j	$\ldots$			
p_{ik}	$(q_{ik}$	$r_{ik})$	$\ldots$			
q_{ik}	p_{ik}	$r_{ik'}$	$u(q_{ik})$	all g's, in any order	$\ldots$	
r_{ik}	p_{ik}	$q_{ik'}$	$u(r_{ik})$	all g's, in any order	$\ldots$	
g_l	all q's and r's in any order	$\ldots$				

Figure 4.23: The preference lists for the derived RWT instance

In Figure 4.23,

- $(q_{ik}\ r_{ik})$ means q_{ik} and r_{ik} are tied;

- $k' = 3 - k$, i.e. $k' = 1$ if $k = 2$ and $k' = 2$ if $k = 1$;

- $\ldots$ at the end of a list means all other persons in arbitrary order;

- $f_m(C_j) = q_{ik}$ or r_{ik} according as the mth literal in C_j is x_i or $\bar{x}_i$ and this is the kth occurrence of this literal in E; if there are fewer than m literals in C_j this entry is simply missing;

- $u(q_{ik})$ is u_j for the unique value of j such that the kth occurrence of the literal x_i is in C_j; this entry is simply missing if x_i does not appear in as many as k clauses;

- $u(r_{ik})$ is u_j for the unique value of j such that the kth occurrence of the literal $\bar{x}_i$ is in C_j; this entry is simply missing if $\bar{x}_i$ does not appear in as many as k clauses.

Given a stable matching for the RWT instance, we can demonstrate the existence of a satisfying truth assignment for the original instance of R-3-SAT as follows. In the stable matching,

(i) for each $i = 1, \ldots, n$ and $k = 1, 2$, p_{ik} must be matched with q_{ik} or r_{ik}, for otherwise $\{p_{ik}, q_{ik}\}$ or $\{p_{ik}, r_{ik}\}$ would block the matching;

(ii) for each $j = 1, \ldots, c$, u_j must be matched with one of $f_1(C_j)$, $f_2(C_j)$ or $f_3(C_j)$, and v_j must be matched with w_j, for otherwise there is no stable configuration involving u_j, v_j and w_j;

(iii) if q_{ik} is matched with a u, then neither r_{ik} nor $r_{ik'}$ can be, the former because of (i) and the latter because $\{q_{ik}, r_{ik'}\}$ would block the matching;

(iv) in view of (iii), each variable x_i can be assigned true if some u is matched with q_{ik} or $q_{ik'}$ and false if some u is matched with r_{ik} or $r_{ik'}$. Further, this (possibly partial) truth assignment satisfies E, since, for each j, u_j is matched with a person that arises from a literal in C_j that is assigned true.

On the other hand, given a satisfying truth assignment for the expression E, we can demonstrate the existence of a stable matching for the derived RWT instance as follows.

(1) For each $i = 1, \ldots, n$, if x_i is true, then match p_{ik} with r_{ik}, $k = 1, 2$, else match p_{ik} with q_{ik}. So no blocking pair can contain a p_{ik}; nor can it contain a q_{ik} for which x_i is false, or an r_{ik} for which x_i is true.

(2) For each $j = 1, \ldots, c$, select the first true literal in C_j, match u_j with the corresponding person $f(C_j)$, and match v_j with w_j. Now, any person whom u_j prefers to his partner is either a q_{ik} for which x_i is false or an r_{ik} for which x_i is true, and since, by (1), neither of these can be in a blocking pair, the same is true of u_j, for all j.

(3) If q_{ik} is so far unmatched, then x_i is true but either $u(q_{ik})$ does not exist or x_i is not the first true literal in the unique clause determined by $u(q_{ik})$. Likewise, if r_{ik} is so far unmatched, then x_i is false but either $u(r_{ik})$ does not exist or $\bar{x}_i$ is not the first true literal in the unique clause determined by $u(r_{ik})$. Let us call these q's and r's the *leftovers*. Provided each leftover is matched with a garbage collector, then no pair involving a q or an r and a non garbage collector can block the matching. For q_{ik} prefers only p_{ik} (excluded by (1)), $u(q_{ik})$ (excluded by (2)) and $r_{ik'}$ to the garbage collectors, and again by (1), either q_{ik} or $r_{ik'}$ is matched with his first choice. A similar observation applies to r_{ik}.

(4) The number of leftovers is $2n - c$, since, of the $4n$ q's and r's, exactly c are matched with u's and $2n$ with p's. Hence, in view of the possible blocking pairs excluded by (3), a stable matching can be completed by pairing the leftovers and garbage collectors according to a stable matching in the stable *marriage* instance induced on these two equal-sized sets by the original preference lists. Of course, we are assured of the existence of such a stable

matching, so the stable roommates matching derived from the satisfying assignment for E is now complete. $\square$

Note that, in the instances of RWT involved in the proof of Theorem 4.5.3, no preference list contains more than one tied pair. It is remarkable that the introduction of such a relatively small number of ties into the preferences has such a dramatic effect on the complexity of the problem.

4.6   Notes and References

The roommates problem was introduced by Gale and Shapley [22] who used Example 4.1 to show the existence of unsolvable instances. Knuth [59] included the roommates problem as one of his twelve unsolved problems associated with stable marriage, asking whether a polynomial-time algorithm could be found or whether determining the solvability of roommates instances might be NP-complete.

Knuth's question was answered by Irving [46], with the publication of the stable roommates algorithm of Section 4.2. Also in [46] is a full implementation (in Pascal) of this algorithm, though the implementation differs somewhat from that given in Section 4.2.4. A similar solution method for the roommates problem, arising out of a more general problem involving network stability and circuit value problems, was recently given by Subramanian [115]. Subramanian's method has the same worst case running time as Irving's, but it is more flexible in its execution. In fact, Irving's method can be viewed as an optimization of Subramanian's method, obtained by adding more implementation detail. It is possible that the added flexibility in Subramanian's method will have some future use, particularly in parallel computation. A generalization of Subramanian's circuit model to fixed point problems of restricted functions was developed by Feder [15] who gave a polynomial time algorithm to find fixed points of these function. When specialized to the roommate problem, the fixed point approach gives a very different, but less efficient, method for finding a stable matching.

The structural and algorithmic results of Sections 4.3 and 4.4 were derived by Gusfield [32, 33] and, independently, by Irving [47]. The medians theorem of Section 4.3.5 is due to Feder [14], though the proof given here is new. The connection between roommates and 2-SAT was first obtained by Feder [15], although the expression described at the end of Section 4.3.3 is different than the one given in [15]. The use of medians to establish the semilattice structure of the roommates matchings is new.

Feder [15] first showed that a 2-SAT expression for stable roommates can be built in $O(n^2)$ time, and suggested [14] the idea of the extended rotation poset discussed in Section 4.4.1. It is not yet clear if the method in [15] gives the same 2-SAT expression as that discussed in Section 4.4.1. However, it is claimed in [15] that the expression obtained there does allow faster identification of stable pairs, and faster enumeration of stable matchings. Details are not yet available to evaluate these claims.

As was observed in Chapter 3 for the stable marriage case, the complexity of the various algorithms can be expressed in terms of m, the total number of entries in the preference lists. It is straightforward to verify that the basic roommates algorithm is linear in m, that the rotation poset and the stable pairs can be found in $O(m^2)$ or $O(nm \log n)$ time, that the minimum-regret stable matching can be found in $O(m)$ time, that the 2-SAT expression obtained from the reduced (or extended) rotation poset can be constructed in $O(m)$ time, and that all the stable matchings can be enumerated in $O(m)$ time per matching, after $O(m^2)$ preprocessing time.

The NP-completeness of the roommates problem with ties was first proved by Ronn [94]. A neater proof, on which the material of Section 4.5.3 is based, appears in [93].

A three-dimensional version of the stable roommates problem has been shown to be NP-complete by Ng and Hirschberg [79], and an alternative proof was recently obtained by Subramanian [115]. Some other aspects of the stable roommates problem are explored in [74] and [29].

Appendix

Open Problems

In the first book devoted to Stable Marriage [59], Don Knuth concluded with a set of twelve open problems that provided a considerable stimulus to subsequent workers in the field. We now do likewise, in the hope of encouraging others to enjoy the challenge and fascination of the subject.

We begin by observing that, of Knuth's original list of twelve problems, the first four were concerned with detailed aspects of the analysis of the Gale-Shapley algorithm and, as far as we know, remain open. However, these problems are quite different in flavor from those that we have considered in this book, so we choose to omit them from our list. We do, however, include at the beginning of our list one of Knuth's counting problems that remains open, as we believe that a better understanding of the underlying structure may offer some hope of progress with this. As observed earlier, the other counting problem raised by Knuth has recently been solved by Pittel [84], who used probabilistic arguments to show that the average number of stable matchings, taken over all instances of size n, is asymptotic to $e^{-1}n \ln n$.

Six of Knuth's problems relate to structure and the existence of efficient algorithms, and only one of these — problem 2 in our list below — remains completely unsolved. The *Notes and References* sections of the earlier chapters refer to the solutions that have been found to three of the other problems, namely, the characterization of the set of stable matchings, the $\Omega(n^2)$ lower bound on finding a stable matching, and the efficient algorithm for stable roommates. A further problem — that of extending the stable marriage problem to 3 sets of objects ("men, women, and dogs") — has recently been studied by Ng and Hirschberg [79], who proved that determining whether a stable matching exists in such a situation is NP-complete.

The last of these six problems, that of determining whether there is a relationship between the stable marriage problem and the classical assignment problem (also known as the weighted bipartite matching problem) has been solved in three ways. First, Theorem 3.8.7 shows how to represent all stable matchings as the minimum s-t cuts in a graph, and it is well known [64] how to reduce the minimum cuts problem in a general graph to a weighted bipartite matching problem. Similarly, it is mentioned in [121] that the linear inequalities shown in Section 3.7.2 specify the dual of a network flow problem, and hence specify a minimum cut problem. Note that these two reductions are polynomial-time reductions and that they preserve all the stable matchings. Finally, Subramanian [115] has given a different, fast reduction of the stable marriage problem to the assignment problem, such that the solution of the assignment problem specifies the man-optimal stable matching, but information about all other stable matchings is lost.

The other problems on our list arise directly and naturally from the structural and algorithmic results that form the core of the book, and give some indication that the stable marriage problem and its extensions will continue to be an active area of research for some time to come.

1   Maximum Number of Stable Matchings

In Section 1.3.2, we showed that the maximum number of stable matchings for a stable marriage instance of size n grows exponentially with n. However, the problem of determining the instance(s) of size n with the largest possible number of stable matchings and of finding this largest possible number remains open.

Using the composition method of Lemma 1.3.3, we generated problem instances of size $n = 2^k$, for each positive integer k, and it can be shown that the number x_n of stable matchings for the instance of size n so generated satisfies

$$x_n = 3x_{n/2}^2 - 2x_{n/4}^4$$

for $n \geq 4$, with $x_1 = 1$ and $x_2 = 2$. This leads to the table of values given on page 25, with $x_n > 2^{n-1}$ for $n \geq 4$. Knuth [58] has shown that the solution x_n of this recurrence satisfies

$$x_n > 2.28^n/(1 + \sqrt{3}).$$

We conjecture that, at least when n is a power of 2, this family of instances realizes the maximum possible number of stable matchings. The structural results established in Chapter 2 may offer some hope of progress with this conjecture.

2   The "Divorce" Digraph

For a given stable marriage instance of size n, the divorce digraph is defined as follows: the digraph has $n!$ vertices, one for each matching; there is a directed edge from matching M to matching M' if and only if (m, w) is a blocking pair for M, and M' differs from M only insofar as the pairs $(m, p_M(m))$ and $(p_M(w), w)$ are replaced by (m, w) and $(p_M(w), p_M(m))$. Hence the stable matchings correspond exactly to the sinks in the digraph.

The question arises as to whether the divorce digraph has any useful structure, and in particular, whether there is a path from every vertex to a sink — in other words, whether any matching can be transformed to a stable matching by a sequence of partner interchanges arising from blocking pairs. It is known [59], that the digraph can have cycles, so not all paths lead to a sink.

3 Parallel Algorithms for Stable Matchings

No mention has been made in the text of parallel algorithms for the stable marriage problem, although such algorithms have appeared in the literature — see [41, 87, 119].

In a sense, the Gale-Shapley algorithm lends itself in an obvious way to parallelization since, in general, several men may propose simultaneously. However, after the first round of proposals in which *all* the members of the favored sex may propose, it may happen that only one person has been rejected, and at each subsequent step, there may be just one free person who is ready to make a further proposal. An example instance of this kind is presented in detail in [119]. So, such direct attempts at parallelizing the Gale-Shapley algorithm will lead to no significant improvement, in the worst case, over the sequential algorithm. Indeed, no parallel algorithm is known for the stable marriage problem with better than $O(n^2)$ worst-case complexity. However, it has recently been shown in [118] that the parallel stable marriage algorithm in [119] has an average $O(\log \log n)$ running time, on a CREW PRAM using $O(n)$ processors.

It might be conjectured that the problem of finding a stable matching for an instance of the stable marriage problem is not in the class NC. Ronn [94] examined the stable marriage problem with ties in the preference lists and showed that certain questions about the behavior of a variation of the Gale-Shapley algorithm on this input are log-space complete for P. However, these results do not seem applicable to the original problem, which remains open.

Other preliminary progress on the parallel question has been noted by Mayr and Subramanian [68], who showed how to encode the stable room-mates problem as a problem concerning a restricted class of circuits, and also showed that, with respect to the class NC, the stable roommates problem and other matching problems are equivalent to a number of circuit value problems on these restricted circuits; unfortunately, the complexity of these circuit value problems is unknown, but Mayr and Subramanian conjecture that these problems are part of a distinct class that are neither log-space complete for P, nor are in NC. Feder [15] recently claimed that given the circuit encoding a roommates instance, the problem of deciding whether the instance is solvable has the same parallel complexity as the problem of explicitly finding a stable roommate matching. That is, the decision and the search problems are reducible to each other by NC^1 reductions.

There are matching problems that might be more easily parallelized than the basic stability problem. For example, even if it is not possible to find the first stable matching fast in parallel, perhaps, after sufficient preprocessing, the stable matchings could be enumerated in parallel, with small parallel time per matching.

4 Batch Stability Testing

We know that $\Omega(n^2)$ time is needed to check whether a single pair is stable, and yet $O(n^2)$ time suffices to determine the stability of every pair in a stable marriage instance. Checking whether a single matching is stable also requires $\Omega(n^2)$ time. Can the stability of every matching in a set of matchings be tested significantly faster than by checking each of the matchings from scratch? Along these lines, can the results of Section 3.4.2 be improved so that the time for testing the stability of matchings improves after some "reasonable" ($O(n^4)$ time, say) preprocessing?

4.1 Heuristics

A different approach might be to find a heuristic that runs fast on average. As mentioned earlier, Pittel [84] has shown that the expected number of stable matchings for a stable marriage instance of size n is asymptotic to $e^{-1}n \ln n$, and this number is very small in comparison with $n!$, the number of distinct matchings. So one might seek very simple tests that will catch most unstable matchings. For example, Theorem 1.3.1 (see page 18) says that if (m, w) is a pair in some stable matching M, but not in stable matching M', then one member of the pair is strictly better off, and the other is strictly worse off in M' as compared to M. Hence if, for a fixed problem instance, we needed to check many matchings for stability, we might first enumerate several (fairly different) stable matchings $M_1, \ldots, M_q$; then when a matching M is proposed, we check to see whether the pair (M, M_i) satisfies Theorem

1.3.1 for each i ($1 \leq i \leq q$). If it does not, then we know that M is unstable; otherwise we check for stability with a $O(n^2)$ method. One source of stable matchings that might be used is the continuum of stable matchings obtained from parametric optimization (Section 3.6.3). What can be proved, or even empirically demonstrated about this or other heuristic methods?

5   Structure of Stable Marriage with Ties

When all preferences are strict, the stable matchings form a distributive lattice and a ring of sets, and the structural results of Chapter 2 follow from these facts. As observed in Section 1.4, these results hold for incomplete preference lists but do not seem to hold for preference lists that are not strict. It is an open question to characterize or compactly represent the set of stable matchings when ties are permitted.

A related open problem is to reduce the problem with ties to linear programming in a way similar to the reduction of the no-tie case described in Section 3.7.

6   Sex-Equal Matching

The egalitarian stable marriage problem represents each person equally in the objective function. However it is still possible for one sex to fare much better than the other in an egalitarian stable matching. We might therefore define a *sex-equal* stable matching as one with the property that the sum of the male scores is as close as possible to the sum of the female scores. Is there an efficient algorithm for this problem?

7   Lying and Egalitarian Matchings

The most interesting theorems discussed in Section 1.7 were about lying when the Gale-Shapley algorithm is used. We have shown that there are practical alternatives to the use of this algorithm, and so issues of lying are open when other stable matchings are to be obtained. For example, what kind of lying is advantageous for an individual or coalition when an egalitarian stable matching is to be obtained?

8   Solvable Roommates Instances

We have seen in Chapter 4 that an instance of stable roommates may or may not admit a stable matching. So the natural question arises as to what proportion of instances of size n do admit a stable matching; in other words, what is the probability p_n that an arbitrary roommates instance of size n is solvable?

Since the number of instances of size n is so large, exhaustive search is scarcely a feasible option, except to reveal that $p_2 = 1$ (trivially) and $p_4 = 0.963$ ($= 1248/1296$).

Figure 1 displays the results of simulations carried out for values of n up to 200, in each case based on 10000 randomly generated problem instances. The evidence might lead to conjectures such as

- p_n is a strictly decreasing function of n;

- $lim_{n \to \infty} p_n = 0$;

but no proofs of these conjectures, nor of any bounds on the value of p_n are in sight.

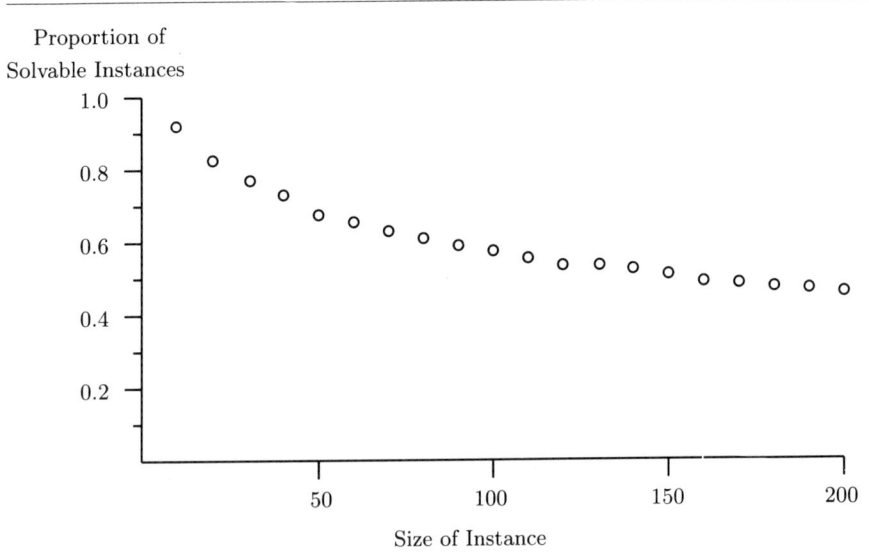

Figure 1: The proportion of roommates instances that are solvable

9 Roommates to Marriage

We have seen that the stable marriage problem is reducible in polynomial time to the roommates problem. Is there a polynomial time reduction of a solvable roommates instance to an instance of the stable marriage problem, so that the stable matchings in the marriage instance define the stable matchings in the roommates instance, or can it be proven that no such reduction is possible? Such a reduction, for example, might involve turning each person into two persons, one male and one female (splitting one's personality into its animus and anima), whose preference lists are related in some way to that person's original roommates preference list.

10 Succinct Certificates

We saw in Section 1.5 that it requires $\Omega(n^2)$ time to check whether a matching is stable. However, once instability is established, there is a very succinct certificate of instability, namely a blocking pair. Is there a succinct certificate $(o(n^2)$ size) of stability?

In the roommates case, if the problem is unsolvable, is there a succinct certificate of that fact? In small examples short cycles of "inconsistent preferences", that demonstrate that the instance is unsolvable, can easily be found. Is there always such a succinct certificate?

10.1 Characterizing Roommate Solvability

Related to the question of succinct certificates for the roommates problem, we would like a "natural" characterization of the solvable or unsolvable instances. Such a characterization might be in terms of forbidden preference patterns, and would be of interest even if it were not the basis for efficient algorithms. An analogy here is Kuratowski's theorem for planar graphs. It is not the basis of fast algorithms to test planarity, and yet it is a concise, insightful characterization of planar graphs.

10.2 Lower Bounds for Roommate Solvability

Do the lower bound arguments in Section 1.5 have any bearing on the question of whether the solvability of an instance of the roommates problem can be determined in $o(n^2)$ time?

11   Algorithmic Improvements

We believe that the following problems can be solved more efficiently. We should note that Tomás Feder [15] has claimed new results for each of these problems, but written details and proofs were not available at the time this book went to press, and we were not able to fully evaluate these claims.

- Egalitarian stable marriage

  We conjecture that this problem can be solved in $O(n^2)$ time (or in $O(m)$ time if the preference lists are sparse and contain a total of m entries). Recall that all steps in this algorithm ran in $O(n^2)$ time except the $O(n^4)$ time network flow computation. However, the flow computation runs in $O(n^4)$ time using even the Ford-Fulkerson algorithm, suggesting that improvements may be obtained using more sophisticated network flow algorithms. A speed up in the optimal stable marriage problem would also speed up the parametric version of the problem. By Theorem 3.6.7 the number of breakpoints is bounded by $O(n^{4/3})$, so all the breakpoints could then be found by the Eisner-Severance method in time $O(n^2 n^{4/3})$, significantly faster than the present $O(n^4 \log n)$ method. Feder [15] has claimed a $O(n^{2.5} \log n)$ method for the egalitarian stable marriage problem.

- Finding roommates rotations

  We conjecture that all the rotations in the roommates problem can be found in $O(n^2)$ time ($O(m)$ for the sparse case). The bottleneck to obtaining this result using the methods of Chapter 4 is the need to distinguish singular from nonsingular rotations. The main tool we used for this is the fact that a rotation is singular if and only if it is the only exposed rotation in some stable table, and we do not have a useful structural characterization of which rotations are singular. We conjecture that such a characterization exists and that it will lead to a $O(n^2)$ algorithm for finding all the rotations.

  Any improvement in finding the rotations will also improve the time to find all the stable pairs, due to Lemma 4.4.1. The converse is also true, for a rotation $\rho = (x_0, y_0), (x_1, y_1), \ldots, (x_{r-1}, y_{r-1})$ is singular if and only if no $\{x_i, y_i\}$ is a stable pair. Feder [15] has claimed a $O(m)$ time method for finding all the stable pairs, and hence such a method would resolve the rotation problem as well.

- Roommates enumeration

  The matchings in the stable marriage problem can be enumerated in $O(n)$ time per matching, but the result presented for the roommates problem is $O(n^2)$ per matching. Hence we would like a faster method for roommates enumeration, or an explanation of why the two problems differ. For this problem, Feder [15] has claimed such a $O(n)$ time result, equaling the result for stable marriage.

12 Optimal Roommates

We pose the problem of whether the optimal roommates problem can be solved in polynomial time. For a roommates matching R we define the *value* of R, denoted $v(R)$, to be

$$v(R) = \sum_{\{i,j\} \in R} (r(i,j) + r(j,i))$$

where $r(i,j)$ is the position of person j in the list of person i. Then the *optimal roommates problem* is to find, for a given problem instance, a stable matching R that minimizes $v(R)$. The optimal stable roommates problem can be generalized by introducing weights into the preference lists. Then $r(i,j)$ indicates the level of dislike that i feels for j, and the definition of preference is inherited from these values: person i prefers j to k if and only if $r(i,j) < r(i,k)$.

Feder [15] has claimed that the unweighted problem is NP-complete, and that a factor of two approximation for it can be found in $O(n^2)$ time, but details of the reduction and approximation were not available before this book went to press. Instead, we sketch a polynomial time ($O(n^4)$) factor of two approximation, obtained earlier, for the weighted problem.

First, there is a general factor of two approximation to the problem of finding a minimum weight set of variables satisfying a 2-SAT expression [39]. This problem is known to be NP-complete [27]. We omit the details of this general approximation method, but direct the reader to [39]. Below we apply this approximation to the optimal (weighted) roommates problem.

For every person p we define $b(p)$ as the best stable partner p can have. Given Lemma 4.4.1, the $b(p)$ values can be found in $O(n^3 \log n)$ time. For a rotation $\rho = (x_0, y_0), (x_1, y_1), \ldots, (x_{r-1}, y_{r-1})$, define $c(\rho)$ to be

$$c(\rho) = \sum_{i=0}^{r-1} [r(x_i, y_{i+1}) - r(x_i, y_i)]$$

and define B to be

$$B = \sum_p r(p, b(p)).$$

Then, for any complete closed subset S of $\Pi(\mathcal{R})$, and its corresponding stable matching R,

$$v(R) = B + \sum_{\rho \in S} c(\rho).$$

Now since B is a known constant, the problem of finding the optimal roommates solution (in either the weighted or unweighted version) reduces to finding a minimum weight complete closed subset of $\Pi(\mathcal{R})$.

Theorem 1 *The minimum weight complete closed subset problem in $\Pi(\mathcal{R})$ reduces to a weighted 2-SAT problem.*

Proof Given $\Pi(\mathcal{R})$ (or more specifically $G(\mathcal{R})$), we create a 2-SAT formula F that is somewhat different from the formula discussed in Section 4.3.4. Each variable x_ρ in F corresponds to a rotation ρ in $\Pi(\mathcal{R})$, and in any satisfying assignment for F, the variables set to "true" specify a complete closed subset of $\Pi(\mathcal{R})$, and conversely. For each directed edge (ρ, ρ') in $G(\mathcal{R})$, we create the clause $(x_\rho \vee \neg x_{\rho'})$ in F. These clauses ensure that the variables of the expression that are set to "true" specify a closed subset of $\Pi(\mathcal{R})$. Further, for every dual pair of rotations $(\rho, \bar{\rho})$ we create the clauses $(x_\rho \vee x_{\bar{\rho}})$ and $(\neg x_\rho \vee \neg x_{\bar{\rho}})$. These clauses ensure that for every dual pair of rotations, exactly one of the associated variables is set to "true" in F. Hence any satisfying assignment for F specifies a complete closed subset of $\Pi(\mathcal{R})$, and the converse also holds. Now if we assign to each variable x_ρ the weight $c(\rho)$, it is immediate that the minimum weight satisfying assignment for F specifies a minimum weight complete closed subset of $\Pi(\mathcal{R})$. $\square$

Since in the above reduction there is a one-one correspondence between rotations and variables, and each variable has the same weight as its corresponding rotation, the following conclusion is immediate.

Theorem 2 *An approximation within a factor of two to the minimum weight satisfying assignment for F specifies an approximation within a factor of two to the minimum weight complete closed subset of $\Pi(\mathcal{R})$, and hence an approximation within a factor of two to the (weighted) optimal stable roommates problem.*

Note that the 2-SAT expression F has $O(n^2)$ variables and clauses. The total time for the approximation (starting from the preference lists) is $O(n^4)$. Note also that if T is the weight of the optimal roommates matching, and

H is the weight of the roommates matching obtained from the 2-SAT approximation, then $H/T \leq 2H/(B+H)$. Both B and H are determined by the heuristic, and hence for any given problem instance the guarantee $2H/(B+H)$ of the approximation can be determined more precisely than indicated in Theorem 2. Such tighter bounds are often useful in complex optimization methods, such as branch and bound, that seek more exact solutions. Finally, note that we can modify the method to ensure that $H/T < 2$, by the fact that B is greater than zero unless the assignment of each person to the first person on his preference list is a stable matching. That case is easily checked, and if it is a stable matching, then it is surely optimal; if it is not a stable matching then $B > 0$ and so $2H/(B+H) < 2$.

12.1 Linear Programming for Roommates

Related to the optimal roommates problem, we pose the question of whether there is an efficiently obtainable linear programming formulation of the roommates problem, similar to that for the marriage problem. Such reductions would probably be ruled out if the optimal roommates problem is NP-complete, but even if this is the case, it is still conceivable that a linear program, whose extreme points specify the stable roommates matchings, could be efficiently obtained. The linear program would not necessarily be usable to solve the optimal roommates problem, for the correct linear objective function may still be difficult to obtain.

Note that in this problem we seek a linear program that preserves *all* the stable matchings. In contrast, it is already known that the *decision* problem of whether there is a stable roommates matching, can be efficiently reduced to linear programming, for linear programming is log-space complete for P [27].

Bibliography

[1] L. Allison. Stable marriage by coroutines. *Information Processing Letters*, 16:61–65, 1983.

[2] G. Birkhoff. *Lattice Theory*. American Mathematical Society, Providence, R.I., 1967.

[3] R. Bixby, W.H. Cunningham, and D. Topkis. The partial order of a polymatroid extreme point. *Mathematics of Operations Research*, 10:367–378, 1985.

[4] C. Blair. Every finite distributive lattice is a set of stable matchings. *Journal of Combinatorial Theory (A)*, 37:353–356, 1984.

[5] C. Blair. The lattice structure of the set of stable matchings with multiple partners. *Mathematics of Operations Research*, 13:619–628, 1988.

[6] J. Bulnes and J. Valdes. Notes on the complexity of the stable marriage problem. 1972. unpublished manuscript, Stanford University.

[7] V.P Crawford and E.M. Knoer. Job matching with heterogeneous firms and workers. *Econometrica*, 49:437–450, 1981.

[8] W.H. Cunningham. Optimal attack and reinforcement of a network. *Journal of the A.C.M.*, 32:549–561, 1985.

[9] G. Demange and D. Gale. The strategy structure of two-sided matching markets. *Econometrica*, 53:873–888, 1985.

[10] G. Demange, D. Gale, and M. Sotomayor. A further note on the stable matching problem. *Discrete Applied Mathematics*, 16:217–222, 1987.

[11] L.E. Dubins and D. Freedman. Machiavelli and the Gale-Shapley algorithm. *American Mathematical Monthly*, 88:485–494, 1981.

[12] A. Dulmage and N. Mendelsohn. A structure theory of bipartite graphs of finite exterior dimension. *Transactions of the Royal Society of Canada*, 53:1–14, 1959.

[13] M. Eisner and D. Severance. Mathematical techniques for efficient record segmentation in large shared databases. *Journal of the A.C.M.*, 23:619–635, 1976.

[14] T. Feder. Personal Communication.

[15] T. Feder. A new fixed point approach for stable networks and stable marriages. Extended Abstract. To appear in the Twenty-First Annual Symposium on Theory of Computing, 1989.

[16] L.R. Ford and D. R. Fulkerson. *Flows in Networks*. Princeton University Press, Princeton, New Jersey, 1962.

[17] N.D. Francis and D.I. Fleming. Optimum allocation of places to students in a national university system. *BIT*, 25:307–317, 1985.

[18] S. Fujishige. Lexicographically optimal base of a polymatroid with respect to a weight vector. *Mathematics of Operations Research*, 5:186–196, 1980.

[19] S. Fujishige. Principal structures of submodular systems. *Discrete Applied Math*, 2:77–79, 1980.

[20] H. Gabow and H. Westerman. Forests, frames and games: algorithms for matroid sums and applications. In *Proceedings of the 20th ACM Symposium on the Theory of Computing*, pages 407–421, 1988.

[21] D. Gale. Equilibrium in a discrete exchange economy with money. *International Journal of Game Theory*, 13:61–64, 1984.

[22] D. Gale and L.S. Shapley. College admissions and the stability of marriage. *American Mathematical Monthly*, 69:9–15, 1962.

[23] D. Gale and M. Sotomayor. Ms. Machiavelli and the stable matching problem. *American Mathematical Monthly*, 92:261–268, 1985.

[24] D. Gale and M. Sotomayor. Some remarks on the stable matching problem. *Discrete Applied Mathematics*, 11:223–232, 1985.

[25] G. Gallo, M. Grigoriadis, and R.E. Tarjan. A fast parametric network flow algorithm. *SIAM Journal on Computing*, 18:30–55, 1989.

[26] P. Gardenfors. Match making: assignments based on bilateral preferences. *Behavioural Science*, 20:166–173, 1975.

[27] M.R. Garey and D.S. Johnson. *Computers and Intractability*. Freeman, San Francisco, CA, 1979.

[28] A. Goldberg and R.E. Tarjan. A new approach to the maximum flow problem. In *Proceedings of the 18th ACM Symposium on the Theory of Computing*, pages 136–146, 1986.

[29] D. Granot. A note on the room-mates problem and a related revenue allocation problem. *Management Science*, 30:633–643, 1984.

[30] G. Grätzer. *Lattice Theory*. Freeman, San Francisco, 1971.

[31] D. Gusfield. Computing the strength of a network in $O(n^3)$ time. Technical Report CSE-87-2, University of California, Davis, 1987.

[32] D. Gusfield. The structure of the stable room-mate problem. Technical Report DCS/TR 482, Yale University, 1986.

[33] D. Gusfield. The structure of the stable roommate problem: efficient representation and enumeration of all stable assignments. *SIAM Journal on Computing*, 17:742–769, 1988.

[34] D. Gusfield. Three fast algorithms for four problems in stable marriage. Technical Report DCS/TR 407, Yale University, 1985.

[35] D. Gusfield. Three fast algorithms for four problems in stable marriage. *SIAM Journal on Computing*, 16:111–128, 1987.

[36] D. Gusfield and R.W. Irving. Parametric stable marriage. Technical Report CSE-88-2, University of California, Davis, 1988.

[37] D. Gusfield and R.W. Irving. The parametric stable marriage problem. *Information Processing Letters*, 30:255-259, 1989.

[38] D. Gusfield, R.W. Irving, P Leather, and M. Saks. Every finite distributive lattice is a set of stable matchings for a small stable marriage instance. *J. Combinatorial Theory (A)*, 44:304–309, 1987.

[39] D. Gusfield and L. Pitt. A bounded approximation for the minimum cost 2-SAT problem. Technical Report CSE-89-4, March 1989, University of California, Davis, 1989.

[40] G.H. Hardy and E.M. Wright. *An Introduction to the Theory of Numbers*. Oxford University Press, fifth edition, 1979.

[41] M.E.C. Hull. A parallel view of stable marriages. *Information Processing Letters*, 18:63–66, 1984.

[42] J.S. Hwang. The algebra of stable marriages. *Intern. J. Computer Math.*, 20:227–243, 1986.

[43] M. Iri. Applications of matroid theory. In *Mathematical Programming, the State of the Art*, pages 159–201, Springer-Verlag, 1983.

[44] M. Iri. Structural theory for the combinatorial systems characterized by submodular functions. In *Progress in Combinatorial Optimization*, pages 197–219, Academic Press, 1984.

[45] M. Iri and S. Fujishige. Use of matroid theory in operations research, circuits and systems theory. *International Journal on Systems Science*, 12:27–54, 1981.

[46] R.W. Irving. An efficient algorithm for the stable room-mates problem. *Journal of Algorithms*, 6:577–595, 1985.

[47] R.W. Irving. On the stable room-mates problem. Technical Report CSC/86/R5, University of Glasgow, 1986.

[48] R.W. Irving and P. Leather. The complexity of counting stable marriages. *SIAM Journal on Computing*, 15:655–667, 1986.

[49] R.W. Irving, P. Leather, and D. Gusfield. An efficient algorithm for the "optimal" stable marriage. *Journal of the A.C.M.*, 34:532–543, 1987.

[50] S.Y. Itoga. A generalization of the stable marriage problem. *Journal of the Operational Reseach Society*, 32:1069–1074, 1981.

[51] S.Y. Itoga. A probabilistic version of the stable marriage problem. *BIT*, 23:161–169, 1983.

[52] S.Y. Itoga. The upper bound for the stable marriage problem. *Journal of the Operational Reseach Society*, 29:811–814, 1978.

[53] P.C. Jones. A polynomial time market mechanism. *Journal of Information and Optimization Sciences*, 4:193–203, 1983.

[54] A.S. Kelso Jr. and V.P. Crawford. Job matching, coalition formation and gross substitutes. *Econometrica*, 50:1483–1504, 1982.

[55] M. Kaneko. The central assignment game and the assignment markets. *Journal of Mathematical Economics*, 10:205–232, 1982.

[56] M. Kaneko. On the core and competitive equilibria of a market with indivisible goods. *Naval Research Logistics Quarterly*, 23:321–337, 1976.

[57] D. Kapur and M.S. Krishnamoorthy. Worst-case choice for the stable marriage problem. *Information Processing Letters*, 21:27–30, 1985.

[58] D.E. Knuth. 1988. Personal Communication.

[59] D.E. Knuth. *Mariages Stables*. Les Presses de l'Université de Montréal, Montreal, 1976.

[60] D.E. Knuth, R. Motwani, and B. Pittel. Stable husbands. Technical Report STAN-CS-88-1241, Stanford University, 1988.

[61] J.F. Korsh and L.J. Garrett. *Data Structures, Algorithms and Program Style using C*. PWS-Kent, Boston, 1988.

[62] R.T. Kuo and S.S. Tseng. Effect of machination on the fairness of assigning colleges to students. manuscript, 1989.

[63] R.T. Kuo and S.S. Tseng. The reciprocal stable matching problem and its properties. manuscript, 1989.

[64] E. Lawler. *Combinatorial Optimization: Networks and Matroids.* Holt, Rhinehart and Winston, 1976.

[65] C.L. Liu. *Introduction to Combinatorial Mathematics.* McGraw-Hill, New York, NY., 1968.

[66] L. Lovász. Submodular functions and convexity. In *Mathematical Programming, the State of the Art*, pages 235–257, Springer-Verlag, 1983.

[67] L. Lovász and M. Plummer. *Matching Theory.* North-Holland, Amsterdam, 1986.

[68] E.W. Mayr and Subramanian. The complexity of circuit value problems and network stability problems. To appear in the Fourth Annual Conference on Structure in Complexity Theory, 1989.

[69] D. McVitie and L.B. Wilson. The application of the stable marriage assignment to university admissions. *Operational Research Quarterly*, 21:425–433, 1970.

[70] D. McVitie and L.B. Wilson. Stable marriage assignment for unequal sets. *BIT*, 10:295–309, 1970.

[71] D. McVitie and L.B. Wilson. The stable marriage problem. *Communications of the A.C.M.*, 14:486–490, 1971.

[72] D. McVitie and L.B. Wilson. Three procedures for the stable marriage problem. *Communications of the A.C.M.*, 14:491–492, 1971.

[73] N. Megiddo. Optimal flows in networks with multiple sources and sinks. *Mathematical Programming*, 97–107, 1974.

[74] A. Mehrez, Y. Yuan, and A. Gafni. Stable solutions vs. multiplicative utility solutions for the assignment problem. *Operations Research Letters*, 7:131–139, 1988.

[75] S. Menju. The stable marriage assignment and related problems. Technical Report C-83, Tokyo Institute of Technology, 1987.

[76] S. Mongell and A.E. Roth. Sorority rush as a two-sided matching mechanism. manuscript, University of Pittsburgh, 1988.

[77] C.L. Monma and D.M. Topkis. Minimum cuts and equivalent combinatorial structures. Unpublished manuscript, Bell Laboratories, 1982.

[78] M. Nakamura. Boolean sublattices connected with minimization problems on matroids. *Math. Programming*, 22:117–120, 1982.

[79] C. Ng and D.S. Hirschberg. Complexity of the stable marriage and stable roommate problems in three dimensions. 1988. manuscript.

[80] C. Ng and D.S. Hirschberg. Lower bounds for the stable marriage problem and its variants. 1988. To appear in SIAM Journal on Computing.

[81] J. Picard. Maximum closure of a graph and applications to combinatorial problems. *Management Science*, 22:1268–1272, 1976.

[82] J. Picard and M. Queyranne. On the structure of all minimum cuts in a network and applications. *Math. Programming Study*, 13:8–16, 1980.

[83] J. Picard and M. Queyranne. Selected applications of minimum cuts in networks. *INFOR — Canadian Journal of Operations Research and Information Processing*, 20:394–422, 1982.

[84] B. Pittel. The average number of stable matchings. Technical Report STAN-CS-88-1234, Stanford University, 1988.

[85] G. Polyá, R.E. Tarjan, and D.R. Woods. *Notes on Introductory Combinatorics*. Birkhauser-Verlag, 1983.

[86] J.S. Provan and M.O. Ball. The complexity of counting cuts and of computing the probability that a graph is connected. *SIAM Journal on Computing*, 12:777–788, 1983.

[87] M.J. Quinn. A note on two parallel algorithms to solve the stable marriage problem. *BIT*, 25:473–476, 1985.

[88] T. Quint. An algorithm to find the core point for a two-sided matching model. Technical Report CAM 88-03, UCLA, Department of Mathematics, 1988.

[89] T. Quint. The core of an m-sided assignment game. manuscript, 1988.

[90] T. Quint. A proof of the non-emptiness of the core of two sided matching markets. Technical Report CAM 87-29, UCLA, Department of Mathematics, 1987.

[91] M. Quinzii. Core and competitive equilibria with indivisibilities. *International Journal of Game Theory*, 13:41–60, 1984.

[92] S.C. Rochford. Symmetrically pairwise-bargained allocations in an assignment market. *Journal of Economic Theory*, 34:262–281, 1984.

[93] E. Ronn. NP-complete stable matching problems. to appear in Journal of Algorithms.

[94] E. Ronn. *On the complexity of stable matchings with and without ties*. PhD thesis, Yale University, 1986.

[95] A.E. Roth. The college admissions problem is not equivalent to the marriage problem. *Journal of Economic Theory*, 36:277–288, 1985.

[96] A.E. Roth. Common and conflicting interests in two-sided matching markets. *European Economic Review*, 27:75–96, 1985.

[97] A.E. Roth. Conflict and coincidence of interest in job matching: some new results and open questions. *Mathematics of Operations Research*, 10:379–389, 1985.

[98] A.E. Roth. The economics of matching: stability and incentives. *Mathematics of Operations Research*, 7:617–628, 1982.

[99] A.E. Roth. The evolution of the labor market for medical interns and residents: a case study in game theory. *Journal of Political Economy*, 92:991–1016, 1984.

[100] A.E. Roth. Incentive compatability in a market with indivisible goods. *Economics Letters*, 9:127–132, 1982.

[101] A.E. Roth. Misrepresentation and stability in the marriage problem. *Journal of Economic Theory*, 34:383–387, 1984.

[102] A.E. Roth. On the allocation of residents to rural hospitals: a general property of two-sided matching markets. *Econometrica*, 54:425–427, 1986.

[103] A.E. Roth. Stability and polarization of interests in job matching. *Econometrica*, 52:47–57, 1984.

[104] A.E. Roth. Two sided matching with incomplete information about others' preferences. To appear in Games and Economic Behavior.

[105] A.E. Roth and A. Postlewaite. Weak versus strong domination in a market with indivisible goods. *Journal of Mathematical Economics*, 4:131–137, 1977.

[106] A.E. Roth and M. Sotomayor. The college admissions problem revisited. To appear in Econometrica.

[107] A.E. Roth and M. Sotomayor. Interior points in the core of two-sided matching markets. *Journal of Economic Theory*, 45:85–101, 1988.

[108] A.E. Roth and M. Sotomayor. *Two sided matching: a study in game-theoretic modelling and analysis.* Book to be published by Cambridge University Press, Econometrics Series.

[109] R. Sedgewick. *Algorithms.* Addison-Wesley, second edition, 1988.

[110] L.S. Shapley and H. Scarf. On cores and indivisibility. *Journal of Mathematical Economics*, 1:23–38, 1974.

[111] L.S. Shapley and M. Shubik. The assignment game I: the core. *International Journal of Game Theory*, 1:111–130, 1972.

[112] M. Shubik. *A Game Theoretic Approach to Political Economy.* MIT Press, Cambridge, MASS, 1984.

[113] M. Shubik. *Game Theory in the Social Sciences: Concepts and Solutions.* MIT Press, Cambridge, MA, 1982.

[114] D. Sleator and R.E. Tarjan. A data structure for dynamic trees. *Journal of Computer and System Science*, 26:362–391, 1983.

[115] A. Subramanian. A new approach to stable matching problems. manuscript, 1989.

[116] R.E. Tarjan. *Data Structures and Algorithms*. SIAM, Philadelphia, PA, 1983.

[117] D. Topkis. Activity selection games and the minimum-cut problem. *Networks*, 13:93–105, 1983.

[118] S.S. Tseng. The average performance of a parallel stable marriage algorithm. To appear in BIT.

[119] S.S. Tseng and R.C.T. Lee. A parallel algorithm to solve the stable marriage problem. *BIT*, 24:308–316, 1984.

[120] J.H. Vande Vate. Fractional matroid matchings. manuscript, November 1988.

[121] J.H. Vande Vate. Linear programming brings marital bliss. To appear in Operations Research Letters.

[122] J.H. Vande Vate. Structural properties of matroid matchings. manuscript, 1988.

[123] E. Veklerov. On decomposability of the stable marriage problem. To appear in BIT.

[124] L.B. Wilson. An analysis of the stable marriage assignment algorithm. *BIT*, 12:569–575, 1972.

[125] N. Wirth. *Algorithms + Data Structures = Programs*. Prentice-Hall, Englewood Cliffs, NJ, 1976.

[126] R.O. Woods. A note on incentives in the college admissions market. 1984. unpublished manuscript, Stanford University.

Index to First Use of Major Notation

Notation that is only used within a few pages of its definition might not be listed.

Index

The MIT Press, with Peter Denning, general consulting editor, and Brian Randall, European consulting editor, publishes computer science books in the following series:

ACM Doctoral Dissertation Award and Distinguished Dissertation Series

Artificial Intelligence, Patrick Henry Winston and J. Michael Brady founding editors; J. Michael Brady, Daniel G. Bobrow, and Randall Davis, current editors

Charles Babbage Institute Reprint Series for the History of Computing, Martin Campbell-Kelly, editor

Computer Systems, Herb Schwetman, editor

Exploring with Logo, E. Paul Goldenberg, editor

Foundations of Computing, Michael Garey and Albert Meyer, editors

History of Computing, I. Bernard Cohen and William Aspray, editors

Information Systems, Michael Lesk, editor

Logic Programming, Ehud Shapiro, editor; Fernando Pereira, Koichi Furukawa, and D. H. D. Warren, associate editors

The MIT Electrical Engineering and Computer Science Series

Research Monographs in Parallel and Distributed Processing, Christopher Jesshope and David Klappholz, editors

Scientific Computation, Dennis Gannon, editor

Technical Communication, Edward Barrett, editor